Macmillan Business Masters

Cost and Management Accounting

Macmillan Business Masters

Business Accounting Jill Hussey and Roger Hussey
Company Accounts Roger Oldcorn
Cost and Management Accounting Jill Hussey and Roger Hussey
Economics S. F. Goodman
Financial Management Geoffrey Knott
Management Roger Oldcorn
Marketing Geoff Lancaster and Paul Reynolds
Marketing Research Christopher West
Operations Management Howard Barnett
Personnel Management Margaret Attwood and Stuart Dimmock

Cost and Management Accounting

Second Edition

Jill Hussey and Roger Hussey

MACMILLAN
Business

First edition 1989
Reprinted seven times
Second edition 1999

Published by
MACMILLAN PRESS LTD
Houndmills, Basingstoke, Hampshire RG21 6XS
and London
Companies and representatives
throughout the world

ISBN 0–333–69407–4

A catalogue record for this book is available from the British Library.

This book is printed on paper suitable for recycling and made from fully managed and sustained forest sources

10	9	8	7	6	5	4	3	2	1
08	07	06	05	04	03	02	01	00	99

Copy-edited and typeset by Povey–Edmondson
Tavistock and Rochdale, England

Printed and bound in Great Britain by
Creative Print & Design (Wales), Ebbw Vale

Contents

List of Figures		ix
Preface		x
Acknowledgements		xi

1 Cost and Management Accounting in Context — **1**
  1.1 Introduction — 1
  1.2 Purpose of cost and management accounting — 1
  1.3 Definition of terms — 3
  1.4 Control, planning and decision-making — 4
  1.5 Costing methods — 5
  1.6 Principles and techniques — 6
  1.7 The role of financial accounting — 7
     Practice questions — 9

2 Cost Classification — **10**
  2.1 Introduction — 10
  2.2 What is cost? — 10
  2.3 Cost units and cost centres — 11
  2.4 Types of cost — 11
  2.5 Elements of cost — 14
  2.6 Coding systems — 15
     Practice questions — 15

3 Costing for Materials — **17**
  3.1 Introduction — 17
  3.2 Overview of the materials control system — 17
  3.3 Purchase and receipt of materials — 19
  3.4 Storage of materials — 19
  3.5 Stocktaking — 20
  3.6 Stores control — 21
  3.7 Pricing issues of materials and stock — 22
  3.8 Comparing pricing methods — 24
     Practice questions — 27

4 Costing for Labour — **29**
  4.1 Introduction — 29
  4.2 Methods of employee remuneration — 29
  4.3 Recording and costing labour — 32
  4.4 Wages office procedure — 33
     Practice questions — 34

5 Integrated and Interlocking Accounts — **35**
  5.1 Introduction — 35
  5.2 Integrated accounts — 35

5.3	Interlocking accounts	41
5.4	Reconciliation of the financial and cost ledgers	46
	Practice questions	47
6	**Allocation and Apportionment of Overheads**	**50**
6.1	Introduction	50
6.2	Sharing overheads	50
6.3	Classifying and collecting overheads	51
6.4	Cost allocation and apportionment	52
6.5	Overhead analysis	52
6.6	Service cost centres	55
	Practice questions	60
7	**Overhead Absorption**	**61**
7.1	Introduction	61
7.2	Bases of absorption	61
7.3	Applying absorption rates	64
7.4	Predetermined overhead absorption rates	66
7.5	Underabsorption or overabsorption	67
7.6	Non-production overheads	69
	Practice questions	69
8	**Job and Batch Costing**	**72**
8.1	Introduction	72
8.2	Job costing procedures	73
8.3	Collecting job costs	73
8.4	Job cost cards or job cost sheets	74
8.5	Costing a job or batch	74
	Practice questions	77
9	**Contract Costing**	**79**
9.1	Introduction	79
9.2	Main features	79
9.3	Contract costing procedures	80
9.4	Completed contracts	81
9.5	Incomplete contracts	82
	Practice questions	84
10	**Continuous-Operation Costing**	**87**
10.1	Introduction	87
10.2	Output costing	87
10.3	Service costing	88
	Practice question	90
11	**Process Costing**	**91**
11.1	Introduction	91
11.2	Main features	91
11.3	Cost elements	93
11.4	Valuation of work-in-progress	96
11.5	Waste	98
	Practice questions	101

12 By-product Costing and Joint Product Costing   **104**
    12.1 Introduction   104
    12.2 By-products   104
    12.3 Joint products   105
    12.4 Physical units basis of apportionment   106
    12.5 Sales value basis of apportionment   107
          Practice questions   108

13 Marginal Costing   **111**
    13.1 Introduction   111
    13.2 Purpose of marginal costing   111
    13.3 Definition of terms   113
    13.4 Cost behaviour   114
    13.5 Contribution   116
    13.6 Marginal cost statements   117
          Practice questions   118

14 Marginal Costing and Decision-Making   **120**
    14.1 Introduction   120
    14.2 Limiting factors   120
    14.3 Ranking of products   121
    14.4 Ceasing an activity   122
    14.5 Accepting a special order   124
    14.6 Making or buying a product   124
          Practice questions   125

15 Break-even Analysis   **129**
    15.1 Introduction   129
    15.2 Constructing a break-even chart   129
    15.3 Using formulae   133
    15.4 Limitations of break-even analysis   134
    15.5 Alternative break-even charts   135
          Practice questions   137

16 Absorption Costing and Marginal Costing Compared **140**
    16.1 Introduction   140
    16.2 Main features of the techniques   140
    16.3 Main arguments for using each technique   141
    16.4 Valuation of stock using the two techniques   142
          Practice question   144

17 Budgetary Control   **145**
    17.1 Introduction   145
    17.2 Purpose of budgetary control   146
    17.3 The budgetary control process   147
    17.4 Interrelationship of budgets   149
    17.5 Main requirements of an effective budgetary control
          system   150
    17.6 Advantages and disadvantages of budgetary control 151
          Practice questions   152

18   Budgets   **154**
   18.1   Introduction   154
   18.2   Variance analysis   154
   18.3   Cash budgets   155
   18.4   Production budgets   157
   18.5   Fixed and flexible budgets   159
      Practice questions   160

19   Standard Costing – Materials and Labour   **163**
   19.1   Introduction   163
   19.2   Setting standards   163
   19.3   Variance analysis   164
   19.4   Direct materials variances   165
   19.5   Direct labour variances   168
   19.6   Advantages and disadvantages of standard costing   170
      Practice questions   171

20   Standard Costing – Overhead Variances and Sales Variances   **173**
   20.1   Introduction   173
   20.2   Fixed overhead variances   173
   20.3   Variable overhead variances   175
   20.4   Fixed and variable overhead variances compared 177
   20.5   Sales margin variances   178
      Practice questions   180

21   Capital Investment Appraisal   **184**
   21.1   Introduction   184
   21.2   Purpose of capital investment appraisal   184
   21.3   Payback period method   185
   21.4   Accounting rate of return   188
   21.5   Discounted cash flow   189
   21.6   Net present value and internal rate of return compared   192
      Practice questions   192

22   Developments in Management Accounting   **193**
   22.1   Introduction   193
   22.2   Activity-based costing   193
   22.3   Advantages and disadvantages of activity-based costing   196
   22.4   Throughput accounting   197
      Practice questions   200

Appendix A Present Value Tables   202
Appendix B Glossary   204
Appendix C Outline Answers to Practice Questions   209
Index   235

List of Figures

1.1	Costing methods	5
1.2	Costing principles and techniques	7
2.1	Elements of cost	14
3.1	Overview of the materials control system	18
4.1	Typical labour recording and costing system	33
5.1	Information flows in an integrated cost accounting system	36
5.2	Information flows in an interlocking cost accounting system	43
8.1	Job cost card	75
11.1	The build-up of costs	92
12.1	Processing of joint products	106
13.1	Cost behaviour	114
13.2	Identifying fixed and variable costs	115
15.1	Break-even chart – plotting fixed costs	130
15.2	Break-even chart – plotting the total cost line	131
15.3	Break-even chart – plotting the revenue line	131
15.4	Break-even chart – reading off the profit	132
15.5	Possible fixed cost behaviour	135
15.6	Contribution break-even chart	136
15.7	Profit chart	136
17.1	Interrelationship of budgets	149
19.1	Direct materials variances	166
19.2	Direct labour variances	169
20.1	Fixed overhead variances	174
20.2	Variable overhead variances	176
20.3	Comparison of overhead calculations	178
20.4	Sales margin variances	179

Preface

The purpose of cost and management accounting is to provide financial information to managers that will help them to plan the progress of the organisation, control the activities and see the financial implications of any decisions they may take. If cost and management accounting does not make a useful contribution to the management of the organisation, it is of no value and should not be undertaken. Although providing detailed accounting information incurs costs in the collection and analysis of data, experience shows that, if properly applied, the techniques and methods of cost and management accounting make a significant contribution to effective management.

Cost and Management Accounting has been written for students who have no prior knowledge of accounting. Although those who are studying financial accounting at the same time may find some of the concepts and approaches familiar, such knowledge is not a prerequisite. The book can be used on professional courses in accounting and other courses in universities and other institutions of higher and further education where management accounting forms part of the syllabus.

In this book we have set out to introduce students to the methods and techniques of management accounting by writing in a clear, accessible style, avoiding technical jargon and by using simple examples. The early chapters lay the foundation for the later ones which introduce the various methods and techniques of cost and management accounting.

The second edition of the book is divided into 22 chapters in a logical teaching sequence, and is ideal for a one-year course. In addition, the text has been updated and we have added a number of interactive features. The aim of the Self-Check Questions is to highlight the key points and allow students to test their comprehension of what has just been read. The other Activities are intended to serve as the basis of discussion and explanation. At the end of each chapter there are a number of Practice Questions which have mainly been taken from the examination papers of the professional accounting bodies. Outline answers to these questions are given in Appendix C.

JILL HUSSEY
ROGER HUSSEY

Acknowledgements

The authors and publishers acknowledge with thanks permission from the following to reproduce copyright examination papers. CIMA, for November 1995, May and November 1996 and November 1997 Stage 1 papers, and for May and November 1995–1997 Stage 2 papers. ACCA, for June 1995, June and December 1996 and June 1997 Module B papers.

The authors and publishers are also grateful to the Chartered Institute of Management Accountants for their permission to use definitions from *Management Accounting Official Terminology* (revised 1996), to Chapman & Hall Ltd for tables from Samuels and Wilkes, *Management of Company Finance*, 4th edn (1986, p. 626) and to Letts Educational for the reproduction of net present value tables from M. Bendrey, R. Hussey and C. West, *Accounting and Finance in Business* (4th edn 1996).

Every effort has been made to trace all the copyright-holders, but if any have been inadvertently overlooked the publishers will be pleased to make the necessary arrangement at the first opportunity.

1 Cost and Management Accounting in Context

1.1 Introduction

This chapter explains why the techniques and methods of *cost and management accounting* are important tools in many organisations. In practice, the phrase *management accounting* is often used to cover both cost and management accounting. Whether the activity is producing game shows for television, manufacturing computers, running a hospital ward or taking tourists on holiday, the organisation's managers require financial information to help them do their job efficiently and effectively. Cost and management accounting contribute to good management by providing financial information that assists managers in controlling activities, making plans and deciding between alternative courses of action. There are no legal requirements for businesses and other forms of organisation to have a cost and management accounting system, but experience shows that such a system plays a valuable part in the efficient running of any establishment.

In this chapter we introduce the different aspects of cost and management accounting and define some of the main terms used. We review the main methods and techniques that are examined more fully in subsequent chapters and explain the differences between financial and cost and management accounting.

1.2 Purpose of Cost and Management Accounting

Information is required to run any type of organisation successfully. A considerable proportion of this information will be financial. The *purpose* of cost and management accounting is to provide financial information to managers that will help them to plan the activities, control the activities for which they are responsible and see the financial implications of any decisions they may take. If cost and management accounting does not make a useful contribution to the management of the organisation, it is of no value and should not be undertaken. Providing detailed cost and management accounting information incurs costs in the collection and analysis of data, but experience shows that if properly applied, the techniques and methods of cost and management accounting make a significant contribution to effective management.

1

Activity

A colleague claims that cost and management accounting is of value only in a manufacturing company. Identify other sectors and organisations where it would be useful, and give some illustrations of how it would be of value.

Although we have not progressed very far in this book, you should be able to answer this question by drawing on your own experience. If you have ever tried to organise a social event to which people are expected to contribute, you will know that the first question you need to ask yourself is 'How much is it going to cost?' Organising a surfing trip to the coast, for example, will necessitate finding out the cost of transport, food and hire of equipment. If you contemplate running a small business, such as a news agency, you will need to know the costs of renting premises, the goods you purchase, advertising, telephone, and wages if you employ staff.

Whether the activity is of a leisure activity, such as organising a fishing trip or a party, a community activity, such as providing services for the elderly, or part of industry, such as manufacturing cars or pizzas, those responsible for the activity will require financial information. Although these activities are very different in nature, there are a number of similarities in respect of the types and detail of the financial information required. The most important information relates to the individual costs. So, in our examples, the cost of hiring the boat for a fishing trip will be required, the cost of wages and travel in providing home visitors for the elderly, the cost of the materials for making cars or ingredients for making pizzas. With large service and manufacturing organisations there are costs associated with premises, machinery, equipment, advertising, employee benefits, etc. With all activities it is essential to know what the costs are to determine whether the activity can be afforded or whether alternatives should be sought; in profit organisations, the costs are required to help establish selling prices.

Because cost and management accounting has been shown to be essential to the efficient running of an organisation, it has become widely used in both the public and the private sectors of industry, in both service and manufacturing organisations. Traditionally, costing information was mostly used in the manufacturing industry and provided fairly basic data on the costs that had been incurred in the manufacturing processes. As the economy became more complex and competitive, and with the growth of the service sector and the need for more rigorous information for running public services, so the demand for more sophisticated financial information has grown. From being a record of past events, techniques have been developed that allow managers to examine the financial consequences of alternative courses of action and to predict the financial consequences of future changes.

Self-check question

What is the purpose of cost and management accounting?

1.3 Definition of terms

The twin topics of *cost accounting* and *management accounting* can be studied separately, but because the two subjects are closely integrated there is an advantage in taking a collective view. Cost accounting can be considered to be a part of management accounting. It is concerned with the collection and ordering of data to show the actual costs of operations, departments or products. Management accounting is broader in nature than cost accounting, and is part of the function of management.

With cost accounting in its simplest form, data may be collected only on past events. The costs actually incurred by the organisation in carrying on its activities will be identified and recorded. The costing system may provide such information as the cost of making one unit of production, the cost of running a particular department and the cost of scrap material. In more advanced costing systems, planned costs will be decided before any activity takes place. The subsequent costs incurred can be compared with the planned costs, the differences identified and the reasons for these differences examined. Such planned costs are known as *budgets* and *standard costs*.

Management accounting encompasses the methods and procedures of cost accounting, with the purpose of providing information to managers so that policies can be formulated, activities planned and controlled, decisions on alternative courses of action taken, assets safeguarded, and the activities of the enterprise reported to interested parties.

In theory and in practice, the division between cost accounting and management accounting is blurred. In general, cost accounting concentrates on the simpler techniques and the systems and procedures for collecting and analysing data. Management accounting adopts a more advanced approach, with a greater involvement in the process of the management of all the activities of the organisation. Because cost and management accounting systems and procedures within an organisation must be designed to meet the needs of the managers of that particular establishment, there are a range of systems in use. But at the foundation of all systems is the requirement for cost and management accounting to assist managers by providing relevant and timely information.

Self-check question

What are the main differences between cost accounting and management accounting?

1.4 Control, Planning and Decision-Making

The activities of managers can be divided into three main functions to which cost and management accounting makes a contribution. The first is concerned with the *control* of the organisation, both on a day-to-day basis and longer-term. The second function is concerned with *planning* for the future and setting policies to ensure the success of the enterprise. Third, managers are concerned with looking at alternative courses of action open to them and *deciding* which is the preferred course.

Most organisations have a number of control systems to ensure that progress is made towards achieving set objectives. In many businesses there is a quality control department to safeguard the fitness of the product or service. In manufacturing companies there is some form of production control to monitor and coordinate the production processes. Cost and management accounting provides the fundamental financial control system that is essential for the efficient working of the organisation. For control to be maintained, detailed information is required on such matters as the various costs of products and processes, the monitoring of labour efficiency and the identification of sources and purposes of all expenditures.

Some form of control can be maintained by comparing present results with what has happened in the past. Unfortunately, as the business environment is subject to rapid change, such a retrospective comparison may prove of little value. The organisation may be currently operating in an economic climate very different from that of even a few months ago. More rigorous control can be achieved by comparing actual results with planned results. Without plans and policies an organisation has no sense of direction or purpose. Cost and management accounting allows plans and policies to be formulated in financial terms and provides managers with information on targets and standards which the organisation intends to achieve.

Much management time is taken up with making decisions on the organisation's present and future activities. In establishing plans, managers have to decide which of the various courses of action they should take. Cost and management accounting supplies information on the financial implications of the various courses of action, thus helping managers to select the most appropriate one. It is at this more complex level of decision-making that the emphasis falls on the techniques and principles associated with management accounting, rather than the simpler methods of cost accounting.

Self-check question

How does cost and management accounting contribute to the other functions of management?

1.5 **Costing Methods**

Cost and management accounting establishes systems and procedures for collecting, analysing, summarising and presenting information to management. The methods adopted are determined by the nature of the organisation's activities. *Costing methods* can be classified into two main groups which are determined by the nature of the activities as shown in Figure 1.1.

Specific-order costing is used where the activity results in units, or products, which are normally different from each other. The work produced consists of separate contracts or batches which can be easily identified. For example a jobbing printer will carry out a unique job for each customer. On a larger scale, the construction of a bridge over a river will be the result of a specific order to do so. Specific-order costing can be broken down into three particular methods. Although they have much in common, each has its own specific requirements depending upon the nature of the industry:

- *Job costing* is used when customers specify their requirements and the job, normally small in size and of short duration. Although it may move through various operations, every job remains identifiable.
- *Contract costing* is used when customers specify their requirements and the job, normally large in size and of long duration, is carried out on one site. This method is used widely in the construction industry.
- *Batch costing* is used when a quantity of identical articles is processed as one batch. The batch is treated as one job and all the costs charged to it. The total costs for the batch are then divided by the number of good units in the batch to give an average cost per unit. Spoilt or scrap units are not included in the calculations.

Fig. 1.1 Costing methods

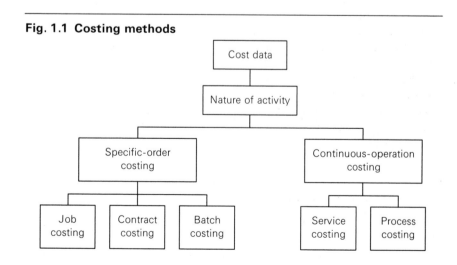

Continuous-operation costing is used where the units are normally identical, or are capable of being made so by conversion. It is used when the goods or services result from a sequence of continuous operations or processes to which costs are charged before being averaged over the units produced during the period. Many manufacturing processes are of this nature. Continuous-operation costing can be divided into two particular methods:

- *Service costing* is used when specific functions or services are costed – for example, canteens or personnel departments. The method may be used to ascertain the cost of a service provided internally, or a service provided for external customers.
- *Process costing* is used where goods or services result from a series of continuous processes or operations. At each stage of the process costs are charged before being averaged over the units produced during the period.

Self-check question

What are the different costing methods used in organisations?

1.6 Principles and Techniques

The *costing principles* and *techniques* applied are determined by the purposes for which it is required and the form in which it is required by management. Figure 1.2 illustrates the six main techniques:

- *Absorption costing* is where both fixed costs and variable costs are charged to the cost units to give a total cost per unit. By using various techniques, described in Chapter 16, cost units are charged with what is regarded as a fair share of the organisation's overheads. The difference between the selling price and the total cost of a unit is the profit per unit.
- *Activity-based costing* is a relatively new technique which is popular in organisations which have advanced manufacturing technology. It attempts to identify the most realistic way for charging overheads to those activities which cause the costs to be incurred.
- *Budgetary control* establishes plans in monetary terms which relate managers' responsibilities to policies. A comparison of budgeted with actual results leads either to managerial action to achieve the original policy, or to a revision of the policy.

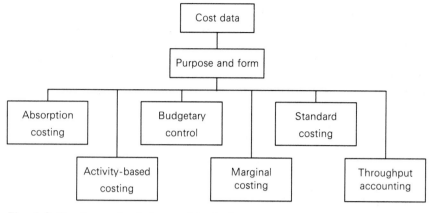

Fig. 1.2 Costing principles and techniques

- *Marginal costing* is where the variable costs only are charged to cost units. The difference between the selling price and variable costs of a unit is known as the *contribution*. The fixed costs for a particular period are charged in full against the total contribution for that period to arrive at a figure of profit for the business.
- *Standard costing* establishes predetermined standards for costs and revenues. By comparing the actual results with the standards, variances can be calculated and used by management to monitor progress and maintain control.
- *Throughput accounting* focuses on the fact that a number of organisation are constrained in the level of activity they can achieve by the presence of bottlenecks in the operations process. Managers strive to increase profitability by increasing throughput and reducing the cost of holding inventories and operational expenditure. Throughput accounting uses a similar approach to marginal costing.

Self-check question

What is meant by absorption costing, marginal costing and budgetary control?

1.7 **The role of financial accounting**

Financial accounting is concerned with classifying and recording in monetary terms the transactions conducted by an organisation. The main purpose of this is so that an account can be given to those who have authority for the organisation, whether that is the government, the committee of a tennis club, the partners in a firm of solicitors or the shareholders of a limited company.

The form that the financial account of the transactions takes depends on the nature of the organisation and to whom it is reporting. Possibly the most familiar is the report and accounts of limited companies when they are reporting to shareholders. The accounts of major firms such as Marks & Spencer, J Sainsbury, ICI and Cadbury–Schweppes are good examples. The financial reports and accounts of companies are intended to give a true and fair view of the financial progress of the company over a period of time in the form of a profit statement and the financial position as at one particular date in the form of a balance sheet.

Financial accounting is thus mainly concerned with reporting to external parties, although the information may also be used inside the organisation for management purposes. Normally, however, it is not suitable for internal purposes as there will be insufficient detail, the financial accounts will be drawn up for the organisation as a whole, often on an annual basis, and the manner in which the financial accounts are drawn up is usually specified by legislation or other regulations. For example, the accounts of limited companies are controlled by the amended *Companies Act 1985* and accounting standards issued by the *Accounting Standards Board* (ASB).

Most organisations produce both financial accounts and management accounts. Although the financial accountant and management accountant may classify and use information in different ways and for different purposes, the same base of raw data is used. In organisations where there is some form of cost accounting system in addition to the financial accounting system there is a strong relationship between the two. Both systems may be integrated into a single accounting system or there may be an interlocking system where cost accounts are maintained separately and reconciled periodically with the financial accounts (see Chapter 5).

Activity

From the following list, identify which activities are mainly concerned with financial accounting and which are concerned with cost and management accounting:

a Drawing up a balance sheet at the year-end.
b Calculating the cost of scrap on one of the production lines in a factory.
c Keeping the cash book for the local rugby club.
d Deciding which of two possible products is the most profitable.
e Ensuring that PAYE records are properly maintained.
f Calculating the energy costs used at the local hospital.
g Deciding the selling price for tickets for a rock concert.
h Ensuring that payments made by a company are shown in the bank statement.

Financial accounting is **a, c, e** and **h**; the rest are management accounting. Although some of the transactions may have been unfamiliar to you, you should have been able to distinguish between them based on their underlying purpose. In this book, financial accounting and the regulations surrounding it are not discussed further. The focus is cost and management accounting used for control, planning and decision-making. In Chapter 2 we take a closer look at some of the terms used.

Practice questions

1 A friend, who is an engineer, owns a small factory and has relied on the annual financial accounts to run the business. You have suggested that he employs a management accountant, but your friend is uncertain how this will be of benefit. Write a letter to your friend describing the management activities to which the person appointed could make a contribution.

2 Describe the main costing methods an organisation can use.

3 Compare the activities of a management accountant with those of a financial accountant.

4 Explain how cost and management accounting can assist management.

2 Cost Classification

2.1 Introduction

In order to run a business successfully, managers need to know the *cost* of making the products, supplying the services and conducting other activities. This information is required in some detail so that the cost of materials, wages and other items can be identified separately. The cost of an item can be very hard to determine and it is made more difficult by our differing perspectives, which vary according to whether we are buying or selling. There are also problems concerned with the meaning attached to the term *cost*, which can be used as a verb, a noun or an adjective.

In this chapter we look at the detailed elements of a company: the individual products and services and the various departments. We begin by clarifying what we mean by the term *cost*, before going on to describe *cost units* and *cost centres*. We then examine the various ways in which cost can be classified and the reasons for using them in organisations, before going on to describe the *elements of cost*.

2.2 What is Cost?

The *cost* of an item can be very hard to determine. A large part of this book is concerned with how we decide what is meant by cost. The main difficulty is that our views of cost are influenced by our differing perspectives. For example, if you buy a personal computer from a local retailer you might consider the cost to be what you paid for it. The retailer, however, may have a different opinion. Not only will the cost be what he paid the manufacturer for the computer, but he may wish to include a share of the costs of running his shop: the rent, lighting and salaries, etc. He must be certain that his selling price is sufficiently high to cover these costs, to ensure that he makes a profit.

You may have bought a pack of 10 disks for your computer for £10. A friend wishes to buy one from you one Sunday for some urgent work she is doing. The original cost to you was £1 per disk, but you know that if you replace that single disk the following Monday, it will cost you £1.25. What will you decide is the cost, if you agree to sell to your friend?

Because the term *cost* can be used in these ways with various interpretations, we normally try to make the meaning clearer. The word used as a verb means to calculate the cost of a specified thing or activity; used as a noun, it means the amount of actual or notional expenditure incurred on, or attributable to, a specified thing or activity. However the word is used it must be in context and defined by specific terms or a classification.

2.3 Cost Units and Cost Centres

Most organisations exist to provide an identifiable service or product. This output can be measured by devising some form of *cost unit*. This can be formally defined as a quantitative unit of product or service in relation to which costs are ascertained. What the precise unit of quantity is depends on the type of industry and cost units vary accordingly. In a brick works the cost unit may be 1,000 bricks and costs are identified which refer to that unit. In a service industry the cost unit may be of a somewhat more abstract nature. A hospital, for example, may use patient-bed-occupied as a cost unit and record all the costs relevant to that unit. A distribution company may regard a cost unit as a tonne-mile, so that the costs associated with moving one tonne of goods over one mile can be recorded.

As well as attributing costs to cost units, they can also be attributed to a *cost centre*. Any specific part of an organisation to which costs can be attributed may be designated a cost centre. It can be geographical (such as a department) or an item of equipment (such as a fork-lift truck). Even a person, such as a consultant or a salesperson, can be a cost centre.

Self-check question

What is meant by a cost unit and a cost centre?

2.4 Types of Cost

Costs can be described in a variety of way depending on the purposes for which the information is intended. These different *types* help us to understand better what is meant by the word *cost*.

Direct and indirect costs

A *direct cost* can be identified with a specific product or saleable service. Direct costs comprise direct materials used in the product, direct wages paid to the production workers for working on the product, direct expenses incurred on the product such as subcontract work, royalties or special tools. An *indirect cost* is one which cannot be identified with any one particular product, but has to be shared over a number of products because it is common to or jointly incurred by them. Examples are rates, supervisors' salaries, consumable materials.

Some costs may be theoretically direct, in so far as it is possible to identify them with a product, but management find it more convenient to treat the costs as indirect. For example, some material costs may be insignificant and the value gained in identifying them with particular products may be outweighed by the inconvenience in attempting to do so. Whether a cost is direct or indirect will depend on the analysis made at the time – in other words, what is being costed. For example, if a department is being costed, the supervisor's salary of that department is regarded as a direct cost. If one of the cost units passing through that department is being costed, the salary is regarded as an indirect cost. It is the focus of the analysis which determines the classification.

Self-check question

What is the difference between direct and indirect costs?

Fixed and variable costs

Fixed costs are those costs which, in total, tend to remain the same irrespective of changes in the level of activity (which may be production levels). *Variable costs* are those costs which, in total, tend to change in direct proportion to changes in the level of activity. It can be seen from this explanation that direct costs will always be variable costs.

Activity

Are the following statements true or false?

a Variable costs are constant per unit of output.
b Variable costs vary per unit of output as production volume changes.
c Variable costs are constant in total when production volume changes.
d Variable costs vary, in total, from period to period when production is constant.

The only true answer is **a**; all the others are false. As defined above, variable costs change in total in direct proportion with changes in the level of activity. Therefore they must be constant per unit of output. For example, if the cost of materials is £2 per unit of output, the total cost of materials for 20 units of output is £40. There are some complications to this simple example and we will look more closely at fixed and variable costs in Chapter 13.

Classification by Nature

It is essential for management to know the *nature* of the costs incurred. The basic classifications are *materials*, *labour* and *expenses*. These broad categories can be further subdivided. For example, materials may be broken down into raw materials, maintenance materials, etc. depending on the type of organisation and the information needs of managers.

Classification by function

Costs frequently relate to specific *functions*, such as the production function and the selling function. It is normally advantageous to classify them as follows:

- *Production costs* are costs incurred from receipt of the raw materials to completion of the finished product.
- *Selling costs* are costs incurred in creating demand for products and securing orders.
- *Distribution costs* are costs incurred from receipt of the finished goods from the production department to delivery to the customer.
- *Administration costs* are costs incurred in managing the organisation, but not specific to any of the other functions.

Product and period costs

Product costs are those costs which are identified with goods purchased or produced for resale. *Period costs* are those not identified with a particular product but with a period of time. In retailing or wholesaling organisations the costs of goods purchased are regarded as product costs and all other costs – e.g. administration, selling and distribution – are regarded as period costs. In a manufacturing organisation all the costs associated with manufacture are regarded as product costs and all non-manufacturing costs are regarded as period costs.

Sunk costs

Sunk costs are those costs that have been incurred in acquiring resources and where the total will not be affected by choosing between alternative courses of action. For decision-making purposes such costs are irrelevant as they cannot be changed by any further decision. For example, if you have some old equipment recorded in your accounts at a value of £1,000 that cost will have to be charged irrespective of what action you decide to take.

Relevant costs

Relevant costs are future costs that will be changed by the decisions made. For example, if a restaurant is deciding whether to serve only French wines or only Spanish wines the costs of maintaining the cellar are the same whichever alternative is chosen and are therefore irrelevant to the decision.

2.5 **Elements of Cost**

The total cost of a product is built up from a number of *elements of cost*. This classification is essential in understanding later topics and you should commit it to memory. Figure 2.1 refers to a manufacturing company.

Self-check question

What are the elements of cost?

Fig. 2.1 Elements of cost

		£	£
	Direct materials	x	
Add	Direct labour	x	
Add	Direct expenses	x	
	Prime cost		x
Add	Production overheads		x
	Production cost		x
Add	Administration overheads		x
Add	Sales overheads		x
Add	Distribution overheads		x
	Total cost		x

Notes

1 *Direct materials* may be charged to the cost unit by a materials requisition or stores issue note. The direct materials become part of the finished goods.
2 *Direct labour* converts the direct materials into the finished goods. The time spent on cost units may be calculated from time sheets, job cards or computerised records.
3 *Direct expenses* are not always present, but may be such items as subcontract work, or special tools or equipment bought for a particular job.
4 *Production overheads* are indirect costs that arise from the provision of the production resources. Examples of production overheads include factory rent and rates, factory insurance and canteen costs.
5 *Administration overheads* are indirect costs that arise from the provision of the administrative function.
6 *Sales overheads* are those indirect costs arising from the selling of the cost unit – for example, advertising and salespersons' salaries.
7 *Distribution overheads* are indirect costs that arise from the activity of getting the cost unit to the customer, such as packing and transport costs.

2.6 **Coding Systems**

Codes are used so that items can be properly recorded, collated and analysed. To use descriptions only of the items would lead to ambiguities and difficulties in recording and processing the information. Although the appropriate classification of costs will have been determined by the company, the items need to be logically coded. For example, 5 cm brass plates may be coded as 05677 and no other class of item should be coded the same.

The coding system should match the nature of the production process, the data processing and collection procedures and the purposes for which the information is required. The organisation will determine its own coding system, but the following characteristics are normally present:

- The codes will either be all numerical or all alphabetical, with the former preferred.
- The codes will be brief, have a logical structure and be of the same length – for example, 5 digits long.
- There will be no ambiguities in the codes and the system must be such that all items can be assigned a code.
- The code must be capable of expansion so that new items can be accommodated.
- The control of the coding system will be centralised to avoid the proliferation and duplication of codes.

Self-check question

What are the characteristics of a good coding system?

Practice questions

1 In decision-making, costs which need to be considred are said to be RELEVANT COSTS. Which of the following are characteristics associated with relevant costs?

(i) future costs
(ii) unavoidable costs
(iii) common costs
(iv) differential costs

A (ii) and (iii) only.
B (i) and (ii) only.
C (ii), (iii) and (iv) only.
D (i) and (iv) only.
E (i), (ii), (iii) and (iv).

CIMA, Stage 2, November 1997

2 A direct cost is a cost which

A   is incurred as a direct consequence of a decision.
B   can be economically identified with the item being costed.
C   cannot be economically identified with the item being costed.
D   is immediately controllable.
E   is the responsibility of the Board of Directors.

CIMA, Stage 2, November 1997

3 Your company regularly uses material X and currently has in stock 500 kgs for which it paid £1,500 two weeks ago. If this were to be sold as raw material, it could be sold today for £2.00 per kg. You are aware that the material can be bought on the open market for £3.25 per kg, but it must be purchased in quantities of 1,000 kgs.

   You have been asked to determine the relevant cost of 600 kgs of material X to be used in a job for a customer. The relevant cost of the 600 kgs is

   A £1,200.   **B** £1,325.   **C** £1,825.   **D** £1,950.   **E** £3,250.

CIMA, Stage 2, May 1997

3 Costing for Materials

3.1 Introduction

In many organisations *materials* can be a substantial part of the total costs of their operations. This can be items such as the raw materials used by a manufacturer, finished part units which are put together in an assembly organisation, the goods which are traded by wholesalers and retailers, the drugs and medical supplies held by a hospital or the many supplies required to keep an army going. Management needs to establish procedures to ensure that:

- the correct quantities of materials are ordered at the right price and the right time;
- the correct materials are delivered;
- adequate arrangements exist to store materials until they are required;
- materials are issued from stores only with proper authorisation, and records are maintained of materials issued or returned;
- a consistent and realistic system is operated to charge production or the appropriate department with the cost of materials used and to give a satisfactory valuation of materials in store.

In this chapter we consider various stages of the procedures to ensure that the above activities are conducted efficiently. We begin with an overview of the entire system before looking at its component parts. From a costing and management accounting viewpoint, the main aim is to ensure that materials issued to departments and the production process are correctly charged out, and that an appropriate value is placed on the materials held in store.

3.2 Overview of the Materials Control System

The purchase of materials, their receipt from the supplier, the correct charging to departments and holding materials in stores will involve various departments within the organisation. It must be remembered that even a small organisation will have a number of different types of materials, and the system must be able to differentiate between these. To ensure control of the activities and the proper recording of the transactions an effective system of documentation must be maintained. In smaller organisations this may be done on using a *manual system*, but it is more normal for a *computerised system* to be in operation. Although organisations devise systems and procedures most suitable for their own business, there are some standard terms for documents used.

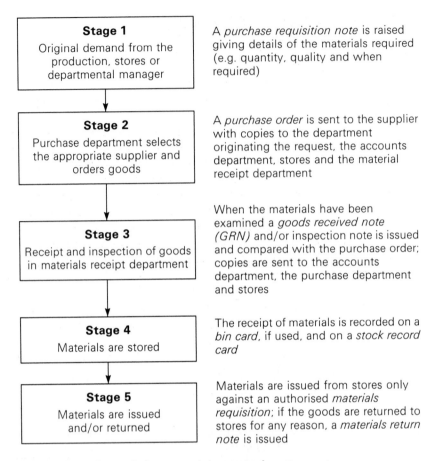

Fig. 3.1 Overview of the materials control system

Figure 3.1 gives an overview of the various stages, together with the names and purposes of the documents most commonly in use. The illustration assumes that a computerised system is not in operation. However, this does not detract from the general principles of the process and the need to maintain accurate records and controls.

Self-check question

What are the main stages in a materials control system?

3.3 **Purchase and Receipt of Materials**

Purchasing materials is a highly specialised activity and includes responsibility for price, quality and time of delivery of materials. Ineffective purchasing has a direct effect on profitability; the purchase of the wrong quantity or quality of materials or late delivery can lead to delays in production.

The first stage in the process of materials acquisition is that the purchasing department is informed that materials are required. This contact may come through the production department which raises a *purchase requisition note* specifying the quantity, quality and delivery date for materials. In some organisations a schedule of materials requirements, specifying delivery dates and production needs over a period, is prepared and used by the purchasing department to raise *purchase orders* at the appropriate time. By using a purchase order a legal contract is entered into by the business and its supplier. It is therefore imperative that only properly authorised managers issue purchase orders.

Depending on the size of the company, materials may be received directly into store or there may be a special materials receipt department. In either case the materials should be examined to ensure that they comply in quality and quantity with the purchase order. A *goods received note (GRN)* is then made out and copies sent to the appropriate departments; the goods are taken into store and the GRN is signed.

Self-check question

What are the main documents used in the purchase and receipt of materials?

3.4 **Storage of Materials**

Materials must be kept safe and secure, and in a position where they can be handled conveniently and issued to production or the requesting department. Materials are issued only on presentation of a properly authorised material requisition, showing the type and quantity of materials and the job or cost centre for which they are required. Stores pass the materials requisition note to the department responsible for maintaining the stock records and it is then passed to the cost department for pricing and charging to the relevant job or department. If materials are returned to the store for any reason, a *materials return note* is completed and processed in the same way as the material requisition.

Stock issues and receipts must be recorded accurately. In some organisations, *bin cards* are attached to where the actual materials in question are stored. The card shows only the physical movement of materials with receipts being entered from the GRNs and issues from the materials requisition notes. The card also shows the balance of materials in stock.

Because of the practical difficulty in ensuring that stores staff keep bin cards up to date and the growth of integrated stock records and inventory procedures, which are often computer-based, the use of bin cards is declining.

Self-check question

What is the purpose of a bin card?

3.5 Stocktaking

Although adequate records may be maintained, for proper control it is essential that a physical examination and count of items in store is taken at intervals. This is known as *stocktaking*. With a periodic stocktake, the physical quantities of materials of all types is taken at a given date. This exercise, normally an annual event, requires a substantial amount of work and organisation. Sufficient numbers of staff must be available who are fully instructed and the stocktake may have to take place at a weekend so as not to disrupt production.

As a periodic stocktake is such a large undertaking, many organisations use an alternative system. Staff are employed who carry out continuous stocktaking throughout the year. Some items of stock are checked every day so that all stock is checked at least once in a year. Fast-moving and valuable items are checked a number of times throughout the year.

Activity

What are the advantages of continuous stocktaking?

Continuous stocktaking offers many advantages in addition to the absence of the need to halt production as with the annual stocktake. Trained staff without time constraints can be used, thus improving the quality of the work. The regular monitoring ensures that all staff adhere to systems and procedures and any irregularities can be quickly spotted and rectified. This improved control will aid the efficiency of production and the profitability of the enterprise.

Some companies operate a *perpetual inventory system*, whereby the physical balance is calculated after each receipt and issue of stock. A *record card* is maintained for each item of stock showing the balance after every transaction. In this system there is continuous stocktaking to ensure that the actual quantities of stock agree with the records and differences are corrected immediately. The advantage of perpetual inventory is that the stock levels at any time are known without having to conduct a physical stocktake. This information improves managerial control and decision-making.

Self-check question

What is meant by perpetual inventory?

3.6 Stores Control

The cost of storing materials is very high and it is important that overstocking is avoided, as this would be a drain on the company's profits. However, it is essential that understocking does not take place because a shortage of materials could mean a stoppage in production and a delay in meeting orders. To avoid the difficulties of overstocking and understocking, *stores control* is maintained by establishing predetermined levels for each item of stock. There will be a maximum level based on the storage space available, the rate of usage and wastage, the possibility of deterioration and the cost of storing above normal levels of stock. The minimum level can be considered as a buffer stock or free stock which is not committed to any particular activity. This is not normally used, but allows priority replenishment if stock falls to this level. The *re-order level* is the level at which a purchase requisition is made out to ensure that new supplies are received just before the minimum level is reached. The *re-order quantity* is the amount to be re-ordered in normal circumstances.

Issues Goods

Activity

A wholesaler has 8,450 units outstanding for Part X100 on existing customers' orders; there are 3,925 units in stock and the calculated free stock is 5,525 units. How may units does the wholesaler have on order with his supplier?

a 9,450
b 10,050
c 13,975
d 17,900.

This is a fairly simple calculation which can be laid out as follows:

Outstanding order Part X100		8,450
Free stock required	5,525	
Units held in stock	3,925	1,600
Total on order		10,050

Even in the best organised and controlled stores losses may be revealed when stocktaking is carried out. Some of these losses are unavoidable or the result of human error. Investigations should be conducted to find the cause of the loss and any weaknesses in the system should be rectified. The losses must be valued and written off from the stores records with the authority of the manager responsible.

To overcome the costs and problems associated with maintaining large stock levels, large organisations often come to an agreement with their suppliers that deliveries will be made which coincide with production requirements. Instead of holding stock, the manufacturer will inform the supplier when, where and what quantities of materials they require delivered to fit in with the manufacturing process.

3.7 Pricing Issues of Materials and Stock

Establishing a *price* at which to issue materials from store is far more complex than it appears. The materials in store normally consist of several receipts at various dates and these may have been made at a number of different purchase prices. It is often impractical, if not impossible, to identify each issue of materials with its corresponding delivery. It is therefore necessary to determine a method of pricing that is most appropriate for a particular company. All methods need a proper stock recording system, and five methods are commonly in use.

First in, first out

First in, first out (FIFO) uses the price of the first delivery of materials to the company for all issues of materials from stores until that particular consignment is exhausted. The next batch delivered is then used for the issue price. It therefore reflects good stocktaking practice to issue the oldest stock first. As this method is based on actual prices, no fictitious profits or losses arise. Materials remaining in store at the end of a period are be valued at the latest delivery price and are therefore closest to up-to-date market values. This method is acceptable to the Inland Revenue and is in accordance with *Statement of Standard Accounting Practice 9, Stock Valuation,* but it requires considerable record keeping and does have some drawbacks.

Activity

Are the following statements true or false?

Using FIFO for pricing stock issues means that when prices are rising product costs are:

a overstated and profits understated   **c** understated and profits understated
b kept in line with price changes   **d** understated and profits overstated.

Only **d** is true. When prices of materials are rising, product costs are understated and profits overstated; when prices are falling, product costs are overstated and profits are understated. A major problem of using FIFO is that the issue price of materials may not reflect current market values. This means that product costs can lag behind current market values and different jobs may have different material costs, even when issues are made on the same day, thus making comparisons difficult. Fluctuating material prices have an impact on product costs and profit.

Last in, first out

Last in, first out (LIFO) uses the price of the last delivery of materials to the company for all issues of stores until that particular consignment is exhausted. The previous batch delivered is then used for the issue or 'last in' price until that has been exhausted or a new delivery received.

As this method is based on actual cost, no fictitious profits or losses arise. The value of issue is close to current market prices and the valuation of stock is usually very conservative. The basis of charging issues may mean that a number of batches in store are only partly charged to production where a subsequent batch has been received. As with FIFO, this system is administratively clumsy and comparison between the cost of different jobs is difficult. This method is not normally acceptable to the Inland Revenue and is not recommended by *Statement of Standard Accounting Practice 9, Stock Valuation*.

Replacement price method

This method uses the *replacement price* on the day of issue to value materials issued from stores. This means that production is charged at current prices. As this method does not use actual cost prices, fictitious profits or losses may arise and cost comparison between jobs is difficult. It is difficult to keep up to date with replacement prices and this method is not acceptable to the Inland Revenue.

Average price method

A *simple average price* can be calculated by adding all the different prices and dividing by the number of prices. This method is very crude and should be used only where the value of issues is low. A more sophisticated approach is to calculate the weighted average price by multiplying the prices by the quantities and then dividing by the quantities. The *weighted average price* is calculated only after receipt of a delivery of materials and not after each issue.

The weighted average method is somewhat simpler to operate than FIFO or LIFO and being based on actual costs no fictitious profits or losses arise.

This method is acceptable to the Inland Revenue and is recommended by *Statement of Standard Accounting Practice 9, Stock Valuation.* It smooths out price fluctuations and cost comparisons between jobs are simpler. However, the issue price of materials is often fictitious in so far as it is not an actual buying in price and issues may not necessarily be made at current economic values.

Standard price method

The *standard price method* uses a predetermined (standard) price for all issues and returns of materials. This method is simple to apply and as price fluctuations are eliminated the cost of different jobs can be compared. The setting of standards establishes a measure of control over purchasing operations. As it is not an actual cost, profits or losses may arise. The greatest difficulty with this method is in determining the standard price to be adopted.

3.8 Comparing Pricing Methods

The above methods can be explained and compared by using the example of a stores department which has a record of the following receipts and issues of materials:

> 1 January received   1,000 kg of materials at £2.00 per kg
> 2 January received   1,000 kg of materials at £2.20 per kg
> 3 January issued   500 kg to production

From the information given, the cost of 500 kg of materials issued to production on 3 January can be calculated using FIFO, LIFO and average price methods.

> FIFO: 500 kg @ £2.00 per kg = £1,000
> LIFO: 500 kg @ £2.20 per kg = £1,100
> Average price: 500 kg @ £2.10 per kg = £1,050

The cost of materials used in production varies according to the method used. All these methods are correct and other methods which organisations use may also be acceptable. However, each method has advantages and disadvantages.

Activity

Calculate the value of the remaining 1,500 kg of materials in stock using the three methods, FIFO, LIFO and average price.

The answer is as follows:

FIFO

Receipts		**£**
1 January	1,000 kg at £2.00 per kg	2,000
2 January	1,000 kg at £2.20 per kg	2,200
Total stock	2,000 kg	4,200
Issues		
3 January	500 kg at £2.00	1,000
Value of remaining stock	(1,500 kg)	3,200

LIFO

Receipts		**£**
1 January	1,000 kg at £2.00 per kg	2,000
2 January	1,000 kg at £2.20 per kg	2,200
Total stock	2,000 kg	4,200
Issues		
3 January	500 kg at £2.20	1,100
Value of remaining stock	(1,500 kg)	3,100

Average price

Receipts		**£**
1 January	1,000 kg at £2.00 per kg	2,000
2 January	1,000 kg at £2.20 per kg	2,200
Total stock	2,000 kg	4,200
Issues		
3 January	500 kg at £2.10	1,050
Value of remaining stock	(1,500 kg)	3,150

Once again, all these values are correct, depending on the method the organisation uses. It is clearly important that the organisation uses the same method consistently and does not change it unless there is a very good reason.

The information above can now be extended by the transaction of a further 600 kg of materials being issued from stores on 4 January. The three different methods can be used to find out the cost of the materials issued to production and the value of the stock remaining in store:

FIFO

Receipts		£
1 January	1,000 kg at £2.00 per kg	2,000
2 January	1,000 kg at £2.20 per kg	2,200
Total stock	2,000 kg	4,200
Issues		
3 January	500 kg at £2.00	1,000
Value of remaining stock	(1,500 kg)	3,200
Issues		
4 January	500 kg at £2.00	
	100 kg at £2.20	1,220
Value of remaining stock	(900 kg)	1,980

LIFO

Receipts		£
1 January	1,000 kg at £2.00 per kg	2,000
2 January	1,000 kg at £2.20 per kg	2,200
Total stock	2,000 kg	4,200
Issues		
3 January	500 kg at £2.20	1,100
Value of remaining stock	(1,500 kg)	3,100
Issues		
4 January	500 kg at £2.20	1,100
	100 kg at £2.00	1,300
Value of remaining stock	(900 kg)	1,800

Average price

Receipts		£
1 January	1,000 kg at £2.00 per kg	2,000
2 January	1,000 kg at £2.20 per kg	2,200
Total stock	2,000 kg	4,200
Issues		
3 January	500 kg at £2.10	1,050
Value of remaining stock	(1,500 kg)	3,150
Issues		
4 January	600 kg at £2.10	1,260
Value of remaining stock	(900 kg)	1,890

Practice questions

1 A national chain of tyre fitters stocks a popular tyre for which the following information is available:

Average usage   140 tyres per day
Minimum usage   90 tyres per day
Maximum usage   175 tyres per day
Lead time   10 to 16 days
Reorder quantity   3,000 tyres

Based on the data above, at what level of stocks should a replenishment order be issued?

A 2,240.   **B** 2,800.   **C** 3,000.   **D** 5,740.

Based on the data above, what is the maximum level of stocks possible?

A 2,800.   **B** 3,000.   **C** 4,900.   **D** 5,800.

CIMA, Stage 1, May 1996

2 The following details relate to component 1256:

Maximum usage per day   10 units
Minimum usage per day   4 units
Maximum lead time   5 days
Minimum lead time   3 days
Ordering cost   £50 per order
Stock holding cost   £2 per item per year
Annual demand   1,750 units

The budget for December 1995 is currently being revised to take account of these details. The stock is budgeted to be 170 units on 1 December, and the production manager has requested that the stock be at maximum on 31 December 1995.

Assuming that the usage of this component is expected to be 140 units during December, the number of units to be purchased during December is closest to

A 296 units. **B** 304 units. **C** 334 units. **D** 350 units. **E** 474 units.

CIMA, Stage 2, November 1995

3 (a) Explain the meaning of:
  (i) continuous stocktaking, and
  (ii) perpetual inventory

in the context of a material control system.

(5 marks)

(b) A company operates an historic batch costing system, which is not integrated with the financial accounts, and uses the weighted average method of pricing raw material issues. A weighted average price (to 3 decimal places of a pound £) is calculated after each purchase of material.

Receipts and issues of Material X for a week were as follows:

Receipts into stock			Issues to production	
Day	**Kgs**	**£**	**Day**	**Kgs**
1	1,400	1,092.00	2	1,700
4	1,630	1,268.14	5	1,250

At the beginning of the week, stock of Material X was 3,040 kgs at a cost of £0.765 per kg. Of the issues of material on Day 2, 60 kgs were returned to stock on Day 3. Of the receipts of material on Day 1, 220 kgs were returned to the supplier on Day 4. Invoices for the material receipts during the week remained unpaid at the end of the week.

Required:

(i) Prepare a tabulation of the movement of stock during the week, showing the changes in the level of stock, its valuation per kilogram, and the total value of stock held.

(ii) Record the week's transactions in the Material X stock account in the Cost Ledger, indicating clearly in each case the account in which the corresponding entry should be posted.

(9 marks)
(14 marks)

ACCA, Module B, June 1995

4 Costing for Labour

4.1 Introduction

Even in a very small business the minimum information required is the total *cost of labour*. In most businesses management needs a more detailed breakdown of the amounts paid to employees by activity, for each product or service provided, so that they can plan and control costs and make decisions. For example, managers need to know the staff costs in the canteen, the charge out rate for a consultant and the labour costs for undertaking a particular job. Once systems have been established to collected this detailed information, the labour cost of a particular product or service can be calculated. For example, a car manufacturer can establish the labour costs of producing one particular model; a civil engineering company the labour costs of constructing a particular building; a plumber the labour costs of a particular job.

In this chapter, we first consider the different methods which can be used for paying employees. We then go on to look at how the information is recorded and the procedures in the wages office.

4.2 Methods of Employee Remuneration

To understand labour costing it is essential to have some knowledge of the different *methods of employee remuneration* operated. Specific company schemes present a variety of methods, but can be broken down into two main groups: *time-based methods*, where employees are paid at a basic rate per hour for the number of hours worked, and *performance-based methods* or *incentive schemes*, where employees are paid on the basis of output or performance.

Time-based methods

Time-based methods are easy to operate and avoid involving the company in the complicated negotiations which surround most incentive schemes. Time-based methods are very common for clerical work and other activities where it is difficult to measure output with any certainty. It is usual to set a number of normal working hours for a week and any hours worked in excess of this number are classed as overtime. These additional hours are paid at a higher rate – for example, time and a half (1½ times the normal hourly rate).

Activity

A worker who normally works a 40 hour week is paid £5.00 per hour. Overtime is paid at time and a half. In one particular week he works 50 hours. What will his total gross pay be for the week?

You should have experienced little difficulty with this calculation. It also demonstrates why time-based schemes are easy to operate: as long as records are properly maintained of overtime worked it is easy to calculate the labour cost. The calculation is as follows:

	£
40 hours at £5.00 per hour	200.00
10 hours at £7.50 per hour	75.00
Total gross pay	275.00

As there is no pay incentive for high performance with time-based schemes, close supervision and control is required. There is no incentive for workers to increase output and there is a danger that they may unofficially operate slow working in order to obtain overtime. Inefficient and efficient employees are paid the same rate as high performers, which may demotivate the latter.

To encourage good work performance a company may adopt a *high day-rate scheme*. Work studies will establish an attainable output figure above the normal performance and above-normal rates will be paid to workers for achieving this. It is intended that such a scheme will attract higher grade workers by providing an incentive. Problems may arise with high day-rate schemes where the specified output figure is not reached, particularly if the fault is outside the workers' control – for example, material shortages and machine breakdowns. Management must ensure that adequate resources are available so that workers are not prevented from achieving their output figure.

There are circumstances where time-based schemes are appropriate. It is not always possible to measure the output of workers, so no targets of achievement can be set. The nature of the work may be such that care and precision are required and the company does not want workers to rush. It is argued also that time-based schemes do not have any implications of exploitation and are more equitable, thus promoting higher morale and a harmonious industrial relations climate.

Performance-based methods

Performance-based methods or *incentive schemes* relate pay to performance. Because of the intricacies of some production processes, schemes can be quite complex in their nature. However, successful schemes attempt to relate pay directly to employee's performance, be fair and achievable and easy to administer and understand. The implementation of such schemes will require negotiations and agreement with employees and any trade unions. This may take considerable time to achieve, with amendments being made to management's original proposals.

Incentive schemes present advantages by improving morale and increasing production through reward for extra effort. The potential for higher pay may attract more efficient employees and, in reducing the cost per unit, allow a company to be more competitive. There are difficulties in implementing incentive schemes, particularly in determining the required performance levels. Employees may regard specified rates as negotiable and any change in the production process may result in a fresh round of negotiations and possibly disagreements and delays.

There are various types of scheme in operation, many of which are closely tailored to the organisation's own needs. Typical examples of the more straightforward schemes are *straight piecework* and *premium bonus schemes*. *Straight piecework* is where the employee is paid either an agreed rate per unit for the number of units he/she produces or a piecework time allowed for each unit. The worker is paid for the piecework hours of production and piecework time is not the same as actual hours of work.

Activity

The hourly rate for an employee is £5.00 per hour with an agreed rate of production of 250 units per hour. An employee produces 3,000 units in 8 hours. If the employee is paid piecework on the basis of production, the piecework earnings will be the number of units produced multiplied by the rate per unit. As the rate per unit is £0.02 (£5.00 ÷ 250 units) the employee will receive £60.00 (3,000 units × £0.02).

If the calculation is done on piecework hours, it will be:

$$\frac{\text{Units produced}}{\text{Hourly rate of production}} = \frac{3,000}{250} = 12 \text{ piecework hours}$$

12 piecework hours × £5.00 = £60.00

Variations of straight piecework may guarantee a day rate. This minimum rate is paid if piecework earnings fall below it. The advantage is that employees are protected from loss of earnings through no fault of their own – for example, material shortages and machine breakdowns. Another variation is *differential piecework*, where the piecework rate changes at different levels of performance, usually measured as the number of units produced in 1 hour.

Activity

What are the advantages and disadvantages of piecework schemes?

Although piecework schemes may be favoured because of the claimed advantages of high incentives, increased productivity and the possible reduction in the need for close supervision, the disadvantages can be onerous. Negotiations over piecework rates and allowances can become acrimonious and cause much delay and disruption. Schemes can be administratively difficult to monitor and operate and the complexities may lead to incorrect payments to workers. Often control systems have to be implemented to prevent abuse of the scheme.

Premium bonus schemes give a time allowance for a job and the time actually taken is compared with it. A bonus is paid to the workers on the time saved. The bonus is in addition to the normal daily rate and therefore an incentive is offered to the workers for high achievement. As the daily rate is paid even if the time taken exceeds the time allowed, protection is given on the minimum amount of pay the employee receives.

4.3 Recording and Costing Labour

The proper *recording* and payment of employee remuneration and control of *labour costs* are critical activities within a company. Procedures should be implemented and maintained for the following reasons:

- To ascertain the actual number of hours spent by employees on the premises. This permits control of attendance, payment of wages and control of labour costs charged to production activities. The term *gate keeping* is often used to refer to the records of hours spent on the factory premises and in many companies a *clock card* is used with each worker having an individual clock number.
- To allow a detailed analysis of labour costs to show the production and other activities on which the cost was incurred. The time attributed to production activities should be reconcilable with the gate times.

For recording time spent on activities, a system must be devised to provide the maximum information required by the company for the costing system, but not incurring large administrative costs. There are two main methods of recording labour time. One is related to each individual employee through the use of *time sheets*. The other is related to each job through the use of *job cards* or *piecework tickets*:

- *Time sheets* are prepared on a weekly or daily basis. They are frequently used where a service is performed and the client is charged on the basis of the time taken. The employee completes the time sheets himself or herself with the supervisor countersigning them. Daily time sheets encourage accurate recording and control, but lead to high volumes of paperwork and high administrative costs. Weekly time sheets are administratively more economical, but as employees tend to complete them at the end of the week, the accuracy of the information is influenced by their memories or imagination.

- A *job card* refers to a single job or batch. As employees complete their individual tasks on the job they record the time spent. A job card therefore shows a number of different employees' times, reflecting the passage of the job through a series of production processes.
- *Piecework tickets* refer to each stage of manufacture so each job has a number of piecework tickets attached to it. This method increases the amount of paperwork, but permits the piecework tickets to be used promptly for calculating the wages.

Self-check question

What are the main differences between weekly and daily time sheets?

4.4 Wages Office Procedure

The *wages office* must prepare a *payroll* giving details of every employee's pay. The gross wage is calculated from the clock cards for day rate and premium bonus workers and for the calculation of overtime payments. Piecework tickets and job cards are used to calculate payments to workers on incentive schemes. An employee's record card is maintained to show the remuneration details of each employee, including rates, allowances, tax codes and statutory deductions. Figure 4.1 illustrates a typical system for recording and costing labour.

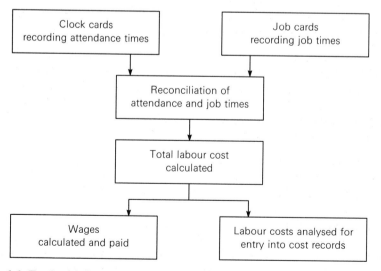

Fig. 4.1 Typical labour recording and costing system

Self-check question

What are the responsibilities of the wages office?

Practice questions

1 How are job cards used within a company?
2 A company operates a piecework scheme where the hourly rate is £6.00 per hour and the agreed rate of production is 600 units per hour. In an 8-hour day a worker produces 7,200 units. Calculate the piecework hours and the worker's pay.
3 What are the advantages and disadvantages of group incentive schemes?

5 Integrated and Interlocking Accounts

5.1 Introduction

All efficiently managed organisations need to keep some form *of financial accounting system*. For some organisations, such as limited companies, there are strict legal requirements that must be adhered to, but even very small businesses need to keep some form of financial records for taxation purposes. In addition to financial accounts, many organisations keep cost accounts. This means that they need two sets of books: a financial accounting system for recording items such as the purchase of raw materials, payment of expenses and revenue collected, and a *cost accounting system* so that the total production costs can be accumulated and allocated to cost units.

There are a number of connections between these two systems and it is important that the records agree. For example, when a business purchases materials and records the transaction in the financial accounting system, those materials form part of the cost of the product in the cost accounting system. In this chapter we explain how *integrated accounts* and *interlocking accounts* are used to ensure that the cost accounting system agrees with the financial accounting system.

5.2 Integrated Accounts

With *integrated accounts*, the financial and cost accounts are combined through one unified accounting system. Only one ledger is kept and this provide financial information for the preparation of financial statements as well as cost information for management. This system has the great advantage of not requiring any reconciliation between the cost profit and the financial profit at the end of a period.

The main *advantages* of integrated accounts are as follows:

- Only one ledger needs to be maintain and no reconciliation between the financial and cost accounts is required.
- The information generated can be used for cost and management purposes as well as for financial reporting purposes.
- The amount of clerical work is reduced and computer applications are easier.

Fig. 5.1 Information flows in an integrated cost accounting system

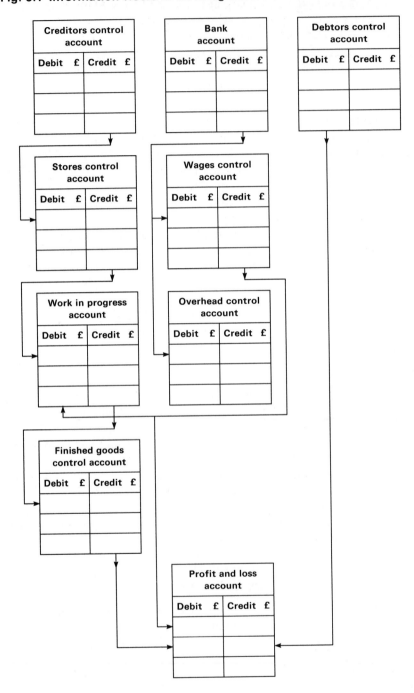

The main *disadvantages* of integrated accounts are:

- The rules relating to stock valuation for the financial accounts which state that stock must be valued at cost or net realisable value, whichever is the lower, may conflict with the methods used for cost valuation.
- Cost and management accounting may require certain treatment of specific items that are not required for financial purposes. For example, overheads are normally charged to production at a predetermined overhead rate (see Chapter 7).

The actual accounts used in any system are likely to vary according to the size of the organisation and the nature of the system. Figure 5.1 gives a simplified example of the flow of accounting information in an integrated system. The overhead control account represents what would be a number of individual overhead accounts, and fixed assets have been ignored for the purpose of simplicity. The general procedure in an integrated accounting system is as follows:

1   When raw materials are purchased the creditors account is credited and the stores control account is debited.
2   Wages are paid and the bank account is credited and the wages control account is debited.
3   As production continues, so materials are issued from stores with a credit to the stores control account and a debit to the work in progress control account. Indirect materials are debited to the production overhead control account.
4   Wages are credited to the wages control account. Direct wages are debited to the work in progress control account and indirect wages are debited to the overhead control account.
5   Completed units are credited to the work in progress control account at production cost and debited to the finished goods control account.
6   The finished goods control account and the overhead control account are transferred to the profit and loss account.
7   By recording sales with a debit to the debtors control account and credit to the profit and loss account, the profit for the period can be calculated.

The following example illustrates how the system works. A company that is operating an integrated accounting system has the following opening balances at the beginning of a financial period:

	£	£
Raw materials	340	
Work in progress	90	
Finished goods	154	
Debtors	490	
Expense creditors		150
Trade creditors (materials)		340
Bank	100	
Fixed assets	600	

During the financial period the following transactions take place:

	£
Purchase of materials	220
Direct wages paid	125
Raw materials issued:	
To production	205
To maintenance	10
Material returns from production	5
Direct wages incurred	136
Administration costs incurred	84
Selling costs incurred	112
Production overhead incurred	207
Sales	840
Receipts from debtors	795
Payments to expense creditors	345
Payments to trade creditors	365
Cost of finished goods sold	515

Notes:
1 Depreciation is charged at 2% of cost.
2 The production overhead was absorbed at 150% of direct wages incurred.
3 Work in progress was valued at £100 at the end of the period.
4 Administration and selling overhead incurred are charged in full.

Stores control account

Debit	£	Credit	£
Balance	340	Work in progress	205
Creditors	220	Production overhead	10
Work in progress	5	Balance c/f	350
	565		565
Balance b/f	350		

Work in progress control account

Debit	£	Credit	£
Balance	90	Stores returns	5
Wages	136	Finished goods	530
Stores	205	Balance c/f	100
Production overhead	204		
	635		635
Balance b/f	100		

Finished goods control account

Debit	£	Credit	£
Balance	154	Cost of sales	515
Work in progress	530	Balance c/f	169
	684		684
Balance b/f	169		

Debtors account

Debit	£	Credit	£
Balance	490	Bank	795
Sales	840	Balance c/f	535
	1,330		1,330
Balance b/f	535		

Expense creditors account

Debit	£	Credit	£
Bank	345	Balance b/f	150
Balance	208	Administration overhead	84
		Production overhead	207
		Selling overhead	112
	553		553
		Balance b/f	208

Trade creditors account

Debit	£	Credit	£
Bank	365	Balance b/f	340
Balance	195	Stores control	220
	560		560
		Balance b/f	195

Bank account

Debit	£	Credit	£
Balance b/f	100	Wages	125
Debtors	795	Trade creditors	365
		Expense creditors	345
		Balance c/f	60
	895		895
Balance b/f	60		

Fixed assets account

Debit	£	Credit	£
Balance	600	Profit and loss	12
		Balance c/f	588
	600		600
Balance b/f	588		

Wages control account

Debit	£	Credit	£
Bank	125	Work in progress	136
Balance	11		
	136		136
		Balance b/f	11

Production overhead control account

Debit	£	Credit	£
Stores	10	Work in progress	204
Expense creditors	207	Balance c/f	13
	217		217
Balance b/f	13		

Administration overhead control account

Debit	£	Credit	£
Expense creditors	84	Profit and loss	84

Selling overhead control account

Debit	£	Credit	£
Expense creditors	112	Profit and loss	112

Sales account

Debit	£	Credit	£
Profit and loss	840	Debtors	840

Cost of sales account

Debit	£	Credit	£
Finished goods	515	Profit and loss	515

Profit and loss account

Debit	£	Credit	£
Cost of sales	515	Sales	840
Administration	84		
Selling overhead	112		
Depreciation	12		
Profit for period	117		
	840		840

Self-check question

What are the advantages and disadvantages of integrated accounts?

5.3 Interlocking Accounts

With *interlocking accounts*, separate financial accounting and cost account ledgers are maintained. There are a number of possible variations, but normally the separate ledgers each have a control account which serves to interlock the two ledgers: a cost ledger control account in the *financial accounting ledger* and a financial ledger control account in the *cost accounting ledger*.

The financial accounting ledger is maintained in the normal way with both debit and credit entries to the financial ledger, but there are no double entries spanning the two ledgers. The financial ledger contains a memorandum account known as the *cost ledger control account* to which are posted all the items that are to be transferred to the cost accounting system. The cost ledger contains all the accounts for costing purposes, such as the stores ledger control account and the wages control account. It also contains a memorandum account known as the *general ledger control account*. This ensures that the cost ledger is self-balancing and is part of its double-entry system. It should also agree, but on opposites sides, with the cost ledger control account in the financial ledger, thus interlocking the two systems.

A typical entry in the financial ledger that interlocks with the cost ledger is the purchase of raw materials. In the financial ledger, the creditors control account is credited and the purchases account is debited. In addition, the cost ledger control account is debited. In the cost ledger, the financial ledger control account is credited and the stores control account is debited. Figure 5.2 shows a simple example of an interlocking cost accounting system.

The following example illustrates the cost ledger entries. A company that is operating an interlocking accounting system has the following opening balances at the beginning of a financial period:

	£	£
Financial ledger control		3,300
Stores ledger control	596	
Work in progress control	1,760	
Finished goods control	944	

The following information is available for the period:

	£
Raw materials purchased	4,180
Direct wages	2,675
Indirect wages	420
Administration expenses	1,186
Selling expenses	725
Production expenses	625
Stores issues – production	2,862
– maintenance	173
Production overheads absorbed	1,140
Factory cost of finished goods	7,395
Cost of finished goods sold	9,162
Sales	10,700

Administration and selling overheads are charged in full for the period.

Financial ledger control account

Debit	£	Credit	£
Sales	10,700	Balance b/f	3,300
Balance c/f	3,146	Purchases	4,180
		Wages	3,095
		Administration expenses	1,186
		Selling expenses	725
		Production expenses	625
		Profit	735
	13,846		13,846
		Balance b/f	3,146

Fig. 5.2 Information flows in an interlocking cost accounting system

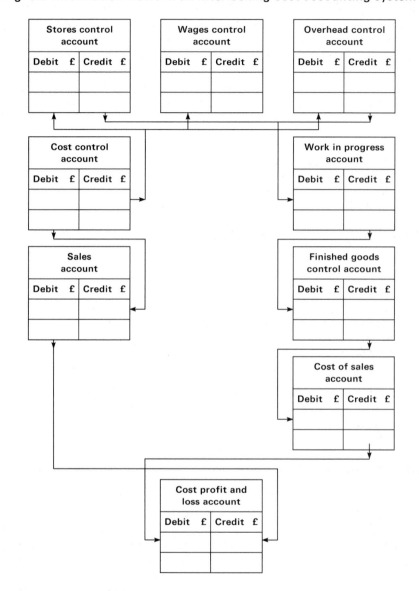

Stores ledger control account

Debit	£	Credit	£
Balance b/f	596	Work in progress	2,862
Financial ledger control	4,180	Production overhead	173
		Balance c/f	1,741
	4,776		4,776
		Balance b/f	1,741

Work in progress control account

Debit	£	Credit	£
Balance b/f	1,760	Finished goods	7,395
Wages	2,675	Balance c/f	1,042
Stores	2,862		
Production overhead	1,140		
	8,437		8,437
Balance b/f	1,042		

Finished goods control account

Debit	£	Credit	£
Balance b/f	944	Cost of sales	9,162
Work in progress	7,395	Balance c/f	363
Administration	1,186		
	9,525		9,525
Balance b/f	363		

Production overhead control account

Debit	£	Credit	£
Wages	420	Work in progress	1,140
Expenses	625	Profit and loss	78
Stores	173		
	1,218		1,218

Administration overhead control account

Debit	£	Credit	£
Financial ledger control	1,186	Finished goods	1,186

Selling overhead control account

Debit	£	Credit	£
Financial ledger control	725	Cost of sales	725

Wages control account

Debit	£	Credit	£
Financial ledger control	3,095	Work in progress	2,675
		Production overhead	420
	3,095		3,095

Cost of sales account

Debit	£	Credit	£
Finished goods	9,162	Profit and loss	9,887
Selling overhead	725		
	9,887		9,887

Profit and loss account

Debit	£	Credit	£
Cost of sales	9,887	Sales	10,700
Production overhead			
under-absorbed	78		
Profit	735		
	10,700		10,700

Closing trial balance

	Debit £	Credit £
Financial ledger control		3,146
Stores ledger	1,741	
Work in progress	1,042	
Finished goods	363	
	3,146	3,146

Self-check question

How would you enter the purchase of raw materials in an interlocking accounting system?

5.4 Reconciliation of the Financial and Cost Ledgers

Some items that appear in the financial accounts do not appear in the cost accounts in an interlocking system. Examples include the purchase of a fixed asset, receipt of dividends and the profit on the sale of fixed assets. In addition, certain items such as depreciation and stock valuations may be treated differently in the two ledgers. Therefore, a periodic *reconciliation* of the profits revealed by the financial and cost ledgers is necessary. The steps to follow are:

1 Begin with the cost profit.
2 Adjust for items appearing in the financial accounts, but not the cost accounts.
3 Adjust for any items appearing in the cost accounts only. This is unusual, but there may be notional charges for such items as rent.
4 Adjust for the different treatment of certain items such as depreciation.

Activity

A company's trading and profit and loss account is as follows:

Trading and Profit and Loss Account for the period ended . . .

	£	£
Sales		37,600
Profits on fixed assets		1,120
Discounts received		135
		38,855
Less purchases	12,604	
Closing stock	2,036	
	10,568	
Direct wages	5,200	
Factory expenses	6,124	
Administration expenses	2,675	
Selling expenses	4,038	
Depreciation	500	29,105
Net profit		9,750

In the cost accounts, the profit is shown as £9,200 based on the following information:

	£
Value of closing stock	2,200
Selling expenses charged	3,600
Depreciation	550
Factory expenses charged	5,971

Reconcile the two figures of profit.

You need to draw up a reconciliation statement as follows:

Reconciliation of profits

	£
Profit as per cost accounts	9,200
Add items not appearing	
Discounts received	135
Profits on fixed assets	1,120
	10,455
Adjust for difference in treatment	
Closing stock	(164)
Selling expenses	(438)
Depreciation	50
Factory expenses	(153)
Profit as per financial accounts	9,750

Practice questions

1 The following data have been taken from the books of CB plc, which uses a non-integrated accounting system:

	Financial accounts £	Cost accounts £
Opening stock of materials	5,000	6,400
Closing stock of materials	4,00	5,200
Opening stock of finished goods	9,800	9,600
Closing stock of finished goods	7,900	7,600

The effect of these stock valuation differences on the profit reported by the financial and cost accounting ledgers is

A the financial accounting profit is £300 greater than the cost accounting profit.

B the financial accounting profit is £2,100 greater than the cost accounting profit.

C the cost accounting profit is £300 greater than the financial accounting profit.

D   the cost accounting profit is £900 greater than the financial accounting profit.

E   the cost accounting profit is £2,100 greater than the financial accounting profit.

CIMA, Stage 2, May 1996

2 In a non-integrated accounting system, the balance shown on the cost ledger control account at the beginning of a financial year is

A   equal to the value of accumulated reserves shown in the financial accounts

B   equal to the value of stocks and work in progress shown in the financial accounts.

C   equal to the value of stocks and work in progress shown in the cost accounts.

D   equal but opposite to the value of the stocks and work in progress shown in the financial accounts.

E   equal but opposite to the value of the stocks and work in progress shown in the cost accounts.

CIMA, Stage 2, November 1995

3 Q Limited uses an integrated standard costing system. In October, when 2,400 units of the finished product were made, the actual material cost details were:

Material purchased	5,000 units @ 4.50 each
Material used	4,850 units

The standard cost details are that 2 units of the material should be used for each unit of the completed product, and the standard price of each material unit is £4.70.

The entries made in the variance accounts would be:

	Material price variance a/c		Material usage variance a/c	
A	Debit	£970	Debit	£225
B	Debit	£1,000	Debit	£225
C	Credit	£970	Debit	£235
D	Credit	£1,000	Debit	£235
E	Credit	£1,000	Debit	£900

CIMA, Stage 2, November 1995

4 (a) Describe briefly THREE major differences between: (i) financial accounting and (ii) cost and management accounting.   **(6 marks)**

(b) Below are incomplete cost accounts for a period:

Stores ledger control account

	£000	
Opening balance	176.0	
Financial ledger control A/c	224.2	

Production wages control account

	£000	
Financial ledger control A/c	196.0	

Production overhead control account

	£000	
Financial ledger control A/c	119.3	

Job ledger control account

	£000	
Opening balance	1,114.9	

The balances at the end of the period were:

Stores ledger	£169.5K
Job ledger	£153.0K

During the period 64,500 kilos of direct material were issued from stores at a weighted average price of £3.20 per kilo. The balance of materials issued from stores represented indirect materials.

75% of the production wages are classified as 'direct'. Average gross wages of direct workers was £5.00 per hour. Production overheads are absorbed at a predetermined rate of £6.50 per direct labour hour.

Required:

Complete the cost accounts for the period. **(8 marks)**

(14 marks)

ACCA, Module B, June 1996

6 Allocation and Apportionment of Overheads

6.1 Introduction

At some point an organisation may wish to know the total cost of a particular product or service. The records kept of direct costs, such as materials and labour, enable these costs to be identified with specific units. However, an organisation also incurs indirect expenses, such as rent and rates, light and heat, insurance and salaries of supervisors. Some method must be found to charge a fair share of these indirect expenses, known as *overheads*, to individual cost units to find the total cost of each unit.

The total cost of a unit may be required so that the company can set the selling price by adding a fixed percentage. This is very useful if the company is doing jobbing work or contract work where each job is different and therefore a common sales price cannot be used. Some people contend that the true profitability of different products cannot be ascertained unless the total cost is known. This is an issue that we will discuss at length in Chapter 16. It is certainly true that for controlling costs, fixing prices, submitting tenders, predicting future activities and making other decisions, management may find that knowledge of the total cost of a product is extremely valuable.

In this chapter we consider the various ways which may be used to share the overheads over the various departments within an organisation. This is known as a process of *allocation* and *apportionment*. One of the main techniques adopted is the use of an *overhead analysis statement*, which we examine. We also explain how the costs of service departments can be shared among the departments that are actually generating cost units.

6.2 Sharing Overheads

If a company has only one department and manufactures only one product or provides only one service, the method of *sharing* the *overheads* for a period of time would be a straightforward task. The total overheads for the period could be divided by the number of cost units produced in that period to give an average overhead cost per unit. This figure can be added to the direct costs per unit to give a total cost. However, in practice, organisations are more complex than that. There may be a number of different departments (which may be called *shops* in some industries) carrying out a range of activities. Some departments, the service cost centres, may not be directly engaged in manufacturing a product or providing a service for external customers, but provide such support as maintenance or the storage of raw materials and finished goods. In addition, the products and services themselves may vary and spend differing lengths of time in the individual departments, thus making unequal demands on resources. In such cases, a way must be found to share the total overheads of the organisation fairly over the departments and then over the cost units passing through them. *Absorption costing* is a technique that allows us to charge overheads to cost units by means of rates separately calculated for each cost centre. It seeks to provide answers to two problems:

- how to share the total overheads of the organisation over the various departments producing the goods and services; and
- how to share the overheads for a particular department over the various cost units passing through it.

We are going to examine the first problem using examples drawn from a manufacturing environment, although absorption costing is used in other industries. In this chapter we look at the *allocation* and *apportionment* of production overheads. In Chapter 7 we discuss how non-production overheads, such as administration and selling overheads, can be shared.

Self-check question

What is absorption costing?

6.3 Classifying and Collecting Overheads

Overheads are those costs which cannot be identified directly through the costing system with a job, product, batch or service, and therefore are the total of indirect materials, indirect labour and indirect expenses. The definition a company uses for a cost unit affects what is classified as an overhead. If a construction company is erecting a new building, it may regard it as the cost unit and costs such as supervision, site administration and power, normally regarded by a manufacturing concern as overheads, will be direct costs for that building. The construction may consist of a number of separate buildings, each regarded as a cost unit in its own right, thus requiring a different definition of overheads. A further example is that of a special machine which may have been purchased. If it is used specifically on one particular job it is a direct cost, but if it is used on a number of jobs it should be considered as an overhead.

Another problem arises where it has been decided to work overtime on a particular job, with a premium paid to the workforce. The overtime premium is a direct cost if the customers request necessitated the overtime working. If the overtime was to permit a general backlog of work to be cleared, the premium should be considered as an overhead cost.

Overhead costs are normally channelled through the accountancy system as part of established procedures. It is usual to *classify* the overheads by *nature* (e.g. indirect materials, depreciation, salaries) and, if possible, by *cost centre*. When the overhead costs have been collected, they fall into two categories. Those which in their entirety can be clearly identified with one cost centre are known as *cost centre direct costs*. Others cannot be identified with only one cost centre and must therefore be shared over the relevant cost centres. These two types of overhead costs require different treatments, known as *allocation* and *apportionment*.

Self-check question

What are overheads?

6.4 Cost Allocation and Apportionment

Overhead costs which can be *allocated* cause few problems and you should tackle these first in an examination question. To allocate an overhead cost, the cost centre must have caused the overhead to have been incurred and the exact amount must be known. The ability to allocate overhead costs depends, to some extent, on the sophistication of the costing system.

However, no matter how good the system is, there will always be a major proportion of overheads which cannot be identified with one department. The process of sharing overhead costs between two or more cost centres, in proportion to the estimated benefit they receive, is known as *cost apportionment.* What constitutes a fair basis on which to apportion the overhead cost differs according to the nature of the overhead and the type of organisation. There are some methods which are widely accepted as equitable. A typical example is rent, where it is normal to share the total cost over the various cost centres on the basis of the floor space occupied. Depreciation may be apportioned on the basis of the book value of the plant and machinery.

Self-check question

What is meant by cost allocation and cost apportionment?

6.5 Overhead analysis

To charge overheads to cost centres a statement known as an *overhead analysis* is prepared. This shows the overheads by their nature (e.g. rent, rates, salaries) and the total cost of each one. The various cost centres are shown and by a process of apportionment and allocation the individual overheads are charged to the cost centres.

The cost centres to which overheads are to be allocated and apportioned in the first instance are *production cost centres* and *service cost centres*. Production cost centres are those where the cost units pass through that centre for work to be carried out on them. Service cost centres, such as the maintenance department, canteen and stores, support the production cost centres, but no cost units pass through them. As all overheads are charged, finally, to the cost units, the total overheads of each of the service cost centres must be shared over the production cost centres. The overhead analysis ensures this in a straightforward and systematic way.

The stages in constructing an overhead analysis are:

1 List overheads vertically by their nature, e.g. rent, salaries.
2 Show cost centres horizontally at the top of the page, both production cost centres and service cost centres.
3 Allocate overheads to those cost centres where the amounts and destinations are known with certainty.
4 Apportion the remaining overheads to all cost centres on the basis of the estimated benefit they receive.
5 Total the overheads for all of the cost centres.
6 Allocate and apportion service cost centres to production cost centres.

Activity

The Rubton Company has a factory with three departments: press shop, assembly shop and canteen. The overhead costs for a 12-month period are as follows:

	£
Rent and rates	60,000
Heat and light	30,000
Repairs to plant and machinery	30,000
Depreciation of plant and machinery	15,000
Salaries	15,000
Stock – fire insurance premium	2,500
Indirect materials	12,500
Indirect wages	14,800

The following additional information is also available:

	Press shop	**Assembly**	**Canteen**
Area (sq ft)	1,500	1,000	500
Number of employees	10	15	5
Indirect wages	£3,000	£3,800	£8,000
Indirect materials	£5,000	£7,500	0
Value of plant	£120,000	£100,000	£80,000
Value of stocks	£75,000	£75,000	–

Construct an overhead analysis.

The first figures to insert in the overhead analysis are those for the overheads which can be allocated to the cost centres – in this case, indirect wages and indirect materials. The other overheads are then apportioned on the basis as shown. In some instances, it may be possible to argue for a different basis of apportionment than that used in this example, although the method shown would appear to be fair.

		Overhead analysis			
Overhead	**Basis**	**Total** £	**Press** £	**Assembly** £	**Canteen** £
Indirect materials	Allocation	12,500	5,000	7,500	
Indirect labour	Allocation	14,800	3,000	3,800	8,000
Rent	Area	60,000	30,000	20,000	10,000
Heat/light	Area	30,000	15,000	10,000	5,000
Repairs	Value	30,000	12,000	10,000	8,000
Depreciation	Value	15,000	6,000	5,000	4,000
Salaries	No. of employees	15,000	5,000	7,500	2,500
Insurance	Value	2,500	1,250	1,250	–
			77,250	65,050	37,500
Canteen	No. of employees	15,000	22,500	(37,500 ——→	
		179,800	92,250	87,550	–

Notes:
1 To apportion the overheads the total figure must be shared in proportion over the three departments. For example, rent is shared on the basis of area so the £60,000 is divided by the total area of 3,000 sq ft area, and the charge per sq ft is multiplied by the space occupied by each department. For the press shop this is £201,500 sq ft.
2 The overheads for the canteen have been apportioned by sharing the total of £37,500 in proportion to the number of employees in the production departments 10:15.

Having allocated and apportioned all the overheads to each of the cost centres, the canteen overheads must be apportioned to the production cost centres. This has been done on the basis of the number of employees in the production cost centres, ignoring those employed in the canteen. This method may be contentious as not all employees will use the canteen, but it is almost certain that the canteen employees themselves will eat there. In the absence of further information, which may be costly to collect, the method used is acceptable because of its simplicity. If a more sophisticated basis is required, there are a number of more rigorous methods to apportion the costs of service cost centres, which are examined in the next section.

6.6 Service Cost Centres

In most companies there are a number of *service cost centres*, such as a maintenance department and stores, supporting the production cost centres. The overheads for these service departments must be apportioned to the production cost centres so that a full charge for all overheads incurred by the company can be made to the cost units. The basis for apportionment should be as fair as possible, but possible bases are as follows:

Basis of apportionment	Service cost centre
No. of employees	Canteen, personnel department
Material requisitions	Stores
Maintenance labour hours	Maintenance department

Before the service departments costs can be apportioned, the total departmental costs must be calculated. There are three different forms of relationship which occur between service departments and/or production departments, and each form requires a different accounting treatment.

Service to production departments only

This is where the service department carries out work for the production departments only and no other service department receives any benefit. Even in the simplest organisation this form of relationship is unlikely to arise, but you may find such a question in the examination. In such an event, the total service department costs are spread over the production departments on a fair basis of apportionment.

Service department for other service and production departments

This is where one service department provides a service for other departments, both production and service, but it is a one-way relationship – the original service department does not get reciprocal support from the other service departments. For example, in an organisation with two service departments in addition to production cost centres, service department *A* may be providing a service to service department *B* as well as production departments, but *B* does not provide a service to A. In this case the costs of service department *A* are apportioned first, to ensure that service department *B* bears a part of its fair share of all overheads. The total cost of service department *B* is then shared over the production cost centres as in the following activity.

Activity

A company has two production departments and two service departments. Department *A* provides services for Department *B*, but the latter only gives support to the production departments. The overheads for both service departments are to be apportioned equally over the departments enjoying their services.

Draw up an overhead analysis that charges the costs of the service departments to the production departments.

Your overhead analysis should look like this:

	Overhead analysis			
	Production dept 1 £	**Production dept 2** £	**Service dept *A*** £	**Service dept *B*** £
Total overheads	10,000	20,000	3,000	2,000
Secondary apportionment:				
Service dept *A*	1,000	1,000	(3,000)	1,000
Subtotal	11,000	21,000	–	3,000
Service dept *B*	1,500	1,500		(3,000)
Production dept overheads	–	–	–	–
Total	12,500	22,500	–	–

Reciprocal services

When two or more service departments provide services for each other, as well as for the production departments, it is known as *reciprocal services*. The total cost of one service department cannot be found until the charge for the second service department is calculated. But the charge for the second service department is not known until a share of the overheads from the first service department has been apportioned to it. There are a number of ways of dealing with this apparently insoluble problem and we will consider them by looking at the simplest first.

With the *elimination method* the cost effects of the reciprocal services are ignored. A specified order of apportioning each department's overheads is used, normally taking the department with the largest overheads, and no return charge is made from other departments. This makes the process very simple. It can be argued that this method leads to inaccuracies and therefore should not be used. However, the process of apportionment is only arbitrary and, unless significant differences are going to arise, the elimination method is acceptable.

The service department with the largest cost is normally apportioned first and thus eliminated from all future calculations. The remaining service departments are then apportioned in a similar manner. Some examination questions may give a specified order for closing the service departments and you should adhere to this.

Activity

Using the following data, apportion the service departments to the production departments using the elimination method.

	Service depts		Production depts	
	1	2	3	4
Overhead costs	£5,000	£3,000	£18,000	£16,000
Proportion for apportioning to:				
Service dept 1	–	10%	40%	50%
Service dept 2	20%	–	40%	40%

The first stage is to apportion service department 1, but you need to remember that the final apportionment of the total overheads for service department 2 is to the production departments in the ratio to the benefits they receive. Your answer should look like this:

Elimination method of apportionment				
	Service depts		Production depts	
	1	2	3	4
	£	£	£	£
Overhead costs	5,000	3,000	18,000	16,000
Apportion service dept 1	(5,000)	500	2,000	2,500
Apportion service dept 2	–	(3,500)	1,750	1,750
Total	–	–	21,750	20,250

The second method is known as the *repeated distribution* or *continuous allotment method.* In this method, the appropriate proportion of the costs of the first service department are apportioned to the second service department, then the costs of this department are apportioned to all the other departments, including the first service department. This process of reapportioning the overheads continues until the amount remaining in any one service department is insignificant. We will use the same data we used for the elimination method to illustrate the repeated distribution method.

Repeated distribution method of apportionment

	Service depts		Production depts	
	1	**2**	**3**	**4**
	£	**£**	**£**	**£**
Overhead costs	5,000	3,000	18,000	16,000
Apportion service dept 1	(5,000)	500	2,000	2,500
Subtotal	–	3,500	20,000	18,500
Apportion service dept 2	700	(3,500)	1,400	1,400
Subtotal	700	–	21,400	19,900
Apportion service dept 1	(700)	70	280	350
Subtotal	–	70	21,680	20,250
Apportion service dept 2	14	(70)	28	28
Subtotal	14	–	21,708	20,278
Apportion service dept 1	(14)	–	7	7
Total	–	–	21,715	20,285

Notes:

1 The total overheads for the two production departments (£21,715 and £20,285) is the same as the commencing figure of overhead for the four departments (£42,000).

2 The first apportionment of service department overheads can be done in any order; it makes no difference to the final result.

3 When the repeated reapportionment reduces the service department overheads to insignificant amounts, they can be rounded up.

Activity

What are the main disadvantages of the repeated distribution method?

One of the main disadvantages that may occur to you after working through the above example is that the repeated distribution method is likely to be very time-consuming. You also need to be confident that the proportioning for apportionment is realistic and up to date. In addition, this method could be costly to operate and the information it provides is of little value to management. If this is the case, it is not worthwhile using.

The third method is the *algebraic method*. In this method, an equation must be constructed for each service department to show the total overhead costs for that department, including its share of other service department overheads. To explain this method we will use the same data we used in the two previous activities.

Let **a** = total overheads for service department 1 when service
department 2 has been apportioned
Let **b** = total overheads for service department 2 when service
department 1 has been apportioned

Therefore, **a** = £5,000 + 0.20**b**
and **b** = £3,000 + 0.10**a**

This data can be rearranged to obtain the following equations:

$$a - 0.20b = £5,000$$
$$b - 0.10a = £3,000$$

The value of either **a** or **b** must be calculated by converting one of them to
the same value and thus cancelling from the equations. This can be done by
multiplying the first equation by 5 and adding the results:

$$5a - b = £25,000$$
$$b - 0.10a = £3,000$$
$$4.9a = £28,000$$
$$a = \frac{£28,000}{4.9}$$
$$a = £5,714$$

Activity

Draw up the overhead apportionment using £5,714 as the first amount to be
apportioned from service department 1.

This may have caused you some problems as the method generates negative
subtotals, but your answer should look like this:

	Service depts		Production depts	
	1	**2**	**3**	**4**
	£	**£**	**£**	**£**
Overhead costs	5,000	3,000	18,000	16,000
Apportion service dept 1	(5,714)	571	2,286	2,857
Subtotal	(714)	3,571	20,286	18,857
Apportion service dept 2	714	(3,571)	1,428	1,429
Total	–	–	21,714	20,286

The repeated distribution method and the algebraic method give approximately the same results, although sometimes there may be a small discrepancy. Examination questions should make it clear which method you should use, but if in doubt, use the method that you know best.

Practice questions

1 Describe the three methods by which service department overheads can be apportioned when there are reciprocal services.

2 Construct an overhead analysis from the following data to find the total overheads of the two production departments. Use the elimination method to apportion the service departments' overheads:

	Overheads for period £
Rent	1,600
Heat and light	160
Depreciation of machinery	2,000
Machinery insurance	80
Indirect materials	100
Indirect labour	400

	Stores	Maintenance dept	Production depts 1	Production depts 2
Area (sq metres)	50	150	300	300
Machine value	–	£5,000	£20,000	£15,000
Indirect materials	£20	£20	£30	£30
Indirect labour	£50	£50	£200	£100
Apportion:				
Maintenance dept	10%	40%	50%	
Stores	50%	50%		

3 A method of dealing with overheads involves spreading common costs over cost centres on the basis of benefit received. This is known as

A overhead absorption.
B overhead apportionment.
C overhead allocation.
D overhead analysis.

CIMA, Stage 1, November 1995

7 Overhead Absorption

7.1 Introduction

In Chapter 6 we looked at methods for collecting overheads to the production departments, but two problems remain. First, a suitable method for charging the overheads to the individual cost units passing through the departments must be found, and this leads to the solution to the second problem, which is calculating the total cost of a particular job or an individual item.

Overhead absorption or *overhead recovery* is a method of charging a fair proportion of the overheads to cost units. This is done by calculating the *overhead absorption rate* which means taking the overhead for a particular cost centre and dividing it by the number of units of the absorption base. The units of the absorption base need not be the same as the cost units. Overhead absorption is of great importance when the products or services are not similar and yet pass through the same departments. In the course of manufacture these dissimilar cost units make different demands on the production resources for unequal lengths of time. The amount of overhead charged to the individual cost unit should reflect these differing demands made on the resources.

In this chapter, we discuss the various bases of absorption that can be used to charge overheads to cost units. We demonstrate how these are applied and look at the use of predetermined overhead rates and some of the problems which can arise.

7.2 Bases of Absorption

If all cost units were identical, the cost centre overhead could be divided by the number of cost units to share it fairly. In practice, there is often a problem of dissimilar cost units and a way must be found of absorbing or recovering the overhead into the various cost units to reflect the demands made by each cost unit on the production facilities. Because companies differ in the nature of their production and the sophistication of their record keeping, there are a number of absorption rates and the most appropriate one must be selected. The various bases of absorption are shown using the following data:

Production department 1 for the month of January

Total cost centre overhead (TCCO)	£10,000
Number of cost units	£1,000
Direct labour hours	2,500
Machine hours	500
Direct wages	£5,000
Direct materials	£2,000
Prime cost	£7,000

The *cost unit overhead absorption rate* can be found by using the following formula:

$$\frac{\text{TCCO}}{\text{Number of cost units}}$$

The advantage of using this absorption rate is that it is easy and very accurate. However, the disadvantage is that cost units must be identical or capable of conversion. Inserting the figures into the formula:

$$\frac{£10,000}{1,000} = £10 \text{ overhead per unit}$$

The *direct labour hour overhead absorption rate* is found by applying the following formula:

$$\frac{\text{TCCO}}{\text{Number of labour hours}}$$

The advantage of using this absorption rate is that it reflects the direct relationship between the passage of time and the overhead cost. In addition, the method can be used with incentive scheme payments and other statistics can be made readily available for other costing purposes. The disadvantages are that records must be maintained and greater clerical work is required. Inserting the figures into the formula:

$$\frac{£10,000}{2,000} = £4 \text{ overhead per direct labour hour}$$

The following formula is used to calculate the *machine hour overhead absorption rate*:

$$\frac{\text{TCCO}}{\text{Number of machine hours}}$$

The advantage of using this absorption rate is that there is a direct relationship between the passage of time and the overhead cost and this base should be used when machine hours predominate in the cost centre.

However, the disadvantage is that records must be maintained and greater clerical work is required. Inserting the figures into the formula:

$$\frac{£10,000}{£500} = £20 \text{ overhead per machine hour}$$

The *direct wage percentage overhead absorption rate* can be calculated using the following formula:

$$\frac{\text{TCCO}}{\text{Direct wages}}$$

The advantage of using this absorption rate is that it is quick and easy to apply. However, the disadvantage is that it takes no account of the fact that workers' rates of pay and speeds of operation may vary. Inserting the figures into the formula:

$$\frac{£10,000}{£5,000} = 200\% \text{ of direct wage cost or £2 overhead charge for every £1 of direct wages}$$

The following formula is used to calculate the *materials cost percentage overhead absorption rate*:

$$\frac{\text{TCCO}}{\text{Direct materials}}$$

The advantage of using this absorption rate is that it is quick and easy to apply, but the disadvantages are that no element of time is taken into account and if two jobs take the same time, but one contains more expensive materials, the overhead charge will differ. Inserting the figures into the formula:

$$\frac{£10,000}{£2,000} = 500\% \text{ of material cost or £5 overhead charge for every £1 of direct materials}$$

The *prime cost percentage overhead absorption rate* can be found by applying the following formula:

$$\frac{\text{TCCO}}{\text{Prime cost}}$$

The advantage of using this absorption rate is that it is quick and easy to apply, but it compounds the disadvantages of the direct wage percentage and material cost percentage overhead absorption rates above. Inserting the figures into the formula:

$$\frac{£10,000}{£7,000} = 143\% \text{ of prime cost or £1.43 overhead charge for every £1 of prime cost}$$

Self-check question

Describe three overhead absorption rates and their respective advantages and disadvantages.

7.3 Applying Absorption Rates

Having demonstrated the calculation of the different bases of absorption, we are now ready to *apply* these principles to an example of a particular job carried out by a company.

Activity

Job No. 633 passes through only one production department. Calculate the overhead absorption rate the six units of base discussed in section 7.2 from the following information:

Job No. 633

Direct material cost	£50
Direct wages paid (£2 per hour)	£30
Time taken on machine	10 hours

Production department information for period

No. of direct labour hours	4,000
No. of machine hours	3,000
Direct wages paid	£8,000
Direct materials	£6,000
No. of cost units	500
Total overheads for period	£12,000

We will calculate the overhead absorption rates in the same order as they were described in section 7.2:

Cost unit overhead absorption rate:

$$\frac{£12,000}{500} = £24 \text{ for each cost unit}$$

Direct labour hour overhead absorption rate:

$$\frac{£12,000}{4,000} = £3 \text{ overhead for each direct labour hour and as}$$
15 hours were worked on the job, the total overhead charge will be £45

Machine hour overhead absorption rate:

$$\frac{£12,000}{3,000} = £4 \text{ overhead for each machine hour and as 10 hours were worked on the job, the total overhead charge will be } £40$$

Direct wage percentage overhead absorption rate:

$$\frac{£12,000}{8,000} = 150\% \text{ of direct wage cost and as this is } £30 \text{ the overhead charge will be } £45$$

Direct material percentage overhead absorption rate:

$$\frac{£12,000}{6,000} = 200\% \text{ of direct material cost and as this is } £50 \text{ the overhead charge will be } £100$$

Prime cost percentage overhead absorption rate:

$$\frac{£12,000}{14,000} = 85\% \text{ of prime cost and as this is } £80 \text{ the overhead charge will be } £68$$

The next step is to apply one of the overhead absorption rates to Job No. 633 to calculate the total cost. The costs of the job, before charging overheads, are as follows:

Job No. 633	
	£
Material cost	50
Wage cost	30
Prime cost	80

Activity

If the cost unit overhead absorption rate is used the charge for overheads will be £24, giving a total cost for the job of £104. If, however, the direct material overhead absorption rate is used the total cost for the job would be £180. Depending on which rate is adopted a different total cost is found. Which is the right one?

The answer is that theoretically they are all right, but the company must decide which particular overhead absorption rate it will consistently adopt. When the information is available, it is best to select a rate which is related to some aspect of time. In this example direct labour hours or machine hours could be selected. As more labour hours are available in the production department for the period than machine hours, it would appear that the company incurs the overhead primarily to provide labour. Using the direct labour hour overhead absorption rate, the total cost is:

Job No. 633	
	£
Material cost	50
Wage cost	30
Prime cost	80
Overhead	45
Total cost	125

Having selected a particular rate for one department the company should consistently apply this unless there is a revision of policy. It is perfectly normal to have different bases of absorption in different departments. For example, in the same company the machine hour overhead absorption rate may be used in the machine shop and a direct labour hour rate in the assembly department.

In unsophisticated costing systems a *blanket-wide* or *factory-wide overhead absorption rate* may be used. Overheads will not be compiled for each separate department and the standard rate is applied, irrespective of the department through which the cost unit passes. This makes for considerable ease in application and a saving in clerical work. However, there is a considerable loss in accuracy because the overheads charged to the product do not normally represent fairly the resources drawn from the different departments. It is not recommended that you use a blanket rate.

Self-check question

What is a blanket or factory-wide overhead absorption rate, and what are its disadvantages?

7.4 Predetermined Overhead Absorption Rates

In section 7.3 it was implied that the overhead absorption rates were based on actual costs. In practice, it is normal to use *predetermined overhead absorption rates*. In other words, prior to the start of an accounting period the budgeted overheads are determined and the budgeted units of base. This allows a predetermined rate to be calculated at the beginning of a period and applied throughout.

Activity

What are the advantages of using predetermined overhead absorption rates?

There are two reasons for not using actual figures. First, the collection, analysis and absorption of overheads to products or jobs takes a considerable time. The figures may not be finalised until the end of the financial year and clearly it is not possible to wait until the actual figures are known before invoicing customers, submitting estimates and generally carrying out the management function. Secondly, if the industry is seasonal, short-term fluctuations in activity will be smoothed out by using predetermined rates.

7.5 **Underabsorption or overabsorption**

Because predetermined rates are used, it is highly unlikely that the actual overheads for the period will be the same as those charged to the production process on the predetermined basis. The difference can be because the actual overheads are not the same as the budget or because the amount of the base of absorption differs from the budget, or a combination of these two factors. If the overheads charged to production are higher than the actual overheads for the period, this is referred to as *overabsorption* (i.e. too much overhead has been charged). When the overheads absorbed into production are lower than the actual figures it is known as *underabsorption*.

Activity

Using the following data calculate the predetermined overhead absorption rate and the amount of underabsorption at the year-end:

Cost centre X: Period 2		
	Budget	**Actual**
Overheads	£12,000	£11,642
Direct labour hours	4,000	3,700

The first stage is as follows:

$$\text{Direct labour hour overhead absorption rate} = \frac{£12,000}{4,000}$$

$$= £3 \text{ per hour}$$

The overheads absorbed into production are calculated at £3 per hour multiplied by the actual activity:

	£
Overhead absorbed (£33,700 hours	11,100
Actual overheads incurred	11,642
Underabsorption	542

The final profit for the period can be ascertained only by adjusting the figures by the amount of overhead underabsorbed. Assuming the figures as shown below, the underabsorption would be treated as follows:

Cost centre X: Period 2	
	£
Direct materials	8,000
Direct labour	10,000
Absorbed overheads	11,100
Calculated production cost	29,100
Overheads underabsorbed	542
Total production cost to profit and loss account	29,642

The underabsorption or overabsorption of overheads is known only when the actual production and actual overheads for a period have been calculated. Although underabsorbed or overabsorbed overheads must finally be brought into the calculation of the profit figure, a *suspense account* may be opened to transfer the periodic adjustments.

Activity

A medical practice in the private sector recovers overheads on chargeable consultancy hours. The budgeted overheads were £615,000 and actual consultancy hours were 32,150. Overheads were underabsorbed by £35,000. If the actual overheads were £694,075, what was the budgeted overhead absorption rate per hour?

If you assume that x = the budgeted overhead absorption rate per hour the equation is as follows:

$$£694,075 - 32,150x = £35,000$$
$$£659,075 = 32,150x$$
$$x = £20.50$$

7.6 **Non-production Overheads**

The examples we have used so far have concentrated on production overheads which are the indirect costs associated with the factory. Part of the total cost of a product is made up of non-production overheads, such as *administration* costs and *selling* costs. Although these may be substantial, many companies do not follow the same procedures for absorbing these indirect costs as with production overheads. Different methods are used and the guiding principle is to be consistent.

If possible, it is best to apportion *administration overheads* between production and selling before the allocation and apportionment of production overheads to cost centres. These apportioned administrative costs can then be incorporated into the selling and production overheads and be absorbed or computed in the usual way.

Selling overheads cannot be added to the cost of a product until the product is actually sold. The overheads can normally be absorbed on a valuation basis; factory cost is a good measure. The selling overhead absorption rate (SOAR) can be calculated as a percentage to be added to the factory cost as follows:

$$\text{SOAR} = \frac{\text{Total selling overheads}}{\text{Total factory cost of sales}}$$

Self-check question

How would you charge non-production overheads?

Practice questions

1 A large firm of solicitors use a job costing system to identify costs with individual clients. Hours worked by professional staff are used as the basis for charging overhead costs to client services. A predetermined rate is used derived from budgets drawn up at the beginning of each year commencing on 1 April.

In the year to 31 March 1996, the overheads of the solicitors' practice, which were absorbed at a rate of £7.50 per house of professional staff were overabsorbed by £4,760. Actual overheads incurred were £742,600. Professional hours worked were 1,360 over budget.

The solicitors' practice has decided to refine its overhead charging system by differentiating between hours of senior and junior professional staff respectively. A premium of 40% is to be applied to the hourly overhead rate for senior staff compared with junior staff.

Budgets for the year to 31 March 1997 are as follows:

Senior professional staff hours	21,600
Junior professional staff hours	79,300
Practice overheads	£784,000

Required:

(a) Calculation for the year ended 31 March 1996:
  (i) Budgeted professional staff hours
  (ii) Budgeted overhead expenditure.

(5 marks)

(b) Calculate, for the year ended 31 March 1997, the overhead absorption rates (to three decimal places of a £) to be applied to:
  (i) Senior professional staff hours
  (ii) Junior professional staff hours.

(4 marks)

(c) How is the change in method of charging overheads likely to improve the firm's job costing system?

(3 marks)

(d) Explain briefly why overhead absorbed using predetermined rates may differ from actual overhead incurred for the same period.

(2 marks)

(14 marks)

ACCA, Module B, June 1996

2 TRI-D has three production departments – Extrusion, Machining and Finishing – and a service department known as Production Services which works for the production departments in the ratio of 3:2:1.

The following costs and relevant data, which represent normal activity levels, have been budgeted for the period ending 31 December 1996:

	Extrusion	Machining	Finishing	Production Services	Total
Costs	**£000**	**£000**	**£000**	**£000**	**£000**
Direct wages	58	72	90	–	220
Direct materials	40	29	15	–	84
Indirect wages	15	21	8	58	102
Depreciation					84
Rates					22
Power					180
Personnel					60
Insurance					48
Other data:					
Direct labour hours	7,250	9,000	15,000		31,250
Machine hours	15,500	20,000	2,500	2,000	40,000
Floor area (m²)	800	1,200	1,000	1,400	4,400
Fixed assets	£160,000	£140,000	£30,000	£70,000	£400,000
Employees	40	56	94	50	240

REQUIREMENTS:

(a) Prepare an overhead analysis sheet for TRI-D Ltd for the period ending 31 December 1996.

(10 marks)

(b) Calculate appropriate overhead absorption rates for the Extrusion, Machining and Finishing Departments.

(3 marks)

(c) The following data are available for the actual results of the Extrusion Department for the period ending 31 December 1996:

Actual overheads	£211,820
Actual labour hours	7,380
Actual machine hours	16,250

Calculate the under/over recovery of overheads for the Extrusion Department.

(2 marks)
(Total marks=15)

CIMA, Stage 1, November 1996

3 QRS Limited has three main departments – Casting, Dressing and Assembly – and for period 3 has prepared the following production overhead budgets for an output level of 110,000 units:

Department:	Casting	Dressing	Assembly
Production overheads	£225,000	£175,000	£93,000
Expected production hours	7,500	7,000	6,200

During period 3, actual results were as follows for an output level of 117,500 units:

Department:	Casting	Dressing	Assembly
Production overheads	£229,317	£182,875	£94,395
Production hours	7,950	7,820	6,696

REQUIREMENTS:

(a) Calculate predetermined departmental overhead absorption rates for period 3.

(3 marks)

(b) Calculate the under/over absorption of overheads for EACH department for period 3 and suggest possible reasons for the value of under/over absorbed overheads you have calculated for the CASTING department.

(7 marks)

(c) Analyse the values of under/over absorbed overheads you have calculated for DRESSING and ASSEMBLY and briefly discuss whether the calculated values assist departmental management with the operations of their departments or in the control of their overheads.

(5 marks)
(Total marks=15)

CIMA, Stage 1, November 1995

8 Job and Batch Costing

8.1 Introduction

Some organisations carry out their activities at the specific orders of clients, such as a building firm that builds a house to meet the particular requirements of a client or an electrician who repairs a washing machine. In this chapter we shall be looking at the two main specific-order costing methods used by these types of businesses, *job costing* and *batch costing*.

Specific-order costing is a costing process that assesses the individual costs of performing each particular job. It is used in organisations where different products are manufactured and also in service organisations where the cost of each service provided is required. A *job* is an identifiable discrete piece of work carried out by an organisation. For costing purposes, a job is usually given a job number which enables the costs to be charged to the number so that all the individual costs for a job can be collected. The costs incurred in carrying out a job are usually analysed into the constituent costs, such as direct materials costs, direct labour costs and overheads.

Job costing is used when customers specify their requirements and usually the job is short and small. Job costing is likely to be used by small businesses such as landscape gardeners, electricians, plumbers, decorators, small printing firms and small builders. The purpose of job costing is to establish the profit or loss for each separate job. The records maintained also serve for estimating the costs of future jobs and setting the price to be quoted to customers. For jobs which are incomplete at the end of an accounting period, job costing provides a Work-in-progress valuation for the balance sheet.

Batch costing is used when a quantity of identical units are processed on the premises as a batch. The batch is treated as a single job and all the costs charged to it. The total costs for the batch may then divided by the number of good units in the batch to give an average cost per unit if this information is required.

It is not unusual for a business that is using job or batch costing to use *cost plus pricing* where the selling price is calculated by adding a fixed percentage (margin) to the cost of the job. This approach has a number of weaknesses as there is no incentive to control the cost of the job, it ignores market conditions and the total costs are dependent on the method of overhead recovery. However, it is simple to apply and where competitive pricing is not an issue, it allows the business to ensure that it recovers its costs.

In this chapter we look first at the procedures involved and how job costs are collected. We then go on to examine how the cost of a job or batch is calculated.

8.2 **Job Costing Procedures**

Job costing is used when customers specify their requirements and the job is relatively small and short in duration. It is often carried out in the factory or workshop, although very small jobs may be carried out on the client's premises. The type of *job costing* adopted depends on the complexity of the organisation and the sophistication of its recording system, but in all forms of job costing rigorous costing procedures are needed. The main stages are as follows:

1   The customer informs the company of the specific requirements.
2   The estimating department prepares an *estimate*, quoting a selling price to the customer.
3   If the customer accepts the estimate and places an order, a *works order* with an identifying number is raised.
4   A *materials requisition note* is prepared so that materials can be drawn from the stores department.
5   A *purchase requisition note* is sent to the purchasing department for any special materials and equipment that may be required.
6   Traditionally, a *job card* is raised. This shows the written instructions for the operations to be carried out for the completion of a job. The instructions are now likely to be in the form of a computer printout.
7   If workers with special skills are needed, a *labour requirement note* is sent to the personnel department.
8   The job is entered into the *production schedule* with a starting date that will allow completion by the agreed delivery date.

Self-check question

What are the eight main stages in job costing?

8.3 **Collecting Job Costs**

Failure to maintain adequate records of all the costs relating to a specific job means that the profit or loss for the job cannot be calculated and future estimates based on past records will be inaccurate. All systems used to collect job costs concentrate on identifying the materials and labour for each job and recording them on a *job cost sheet*. Although many businesses have now adopted computerised systems, the principles remain the same.

Job costing is usually combined with absorption costing and all the examples in this chapter are based on that assumption. A simple system for collecting costs has the following characteristics:

1   A *materials requisition note* is sent to the stores department identifying the materials required for the job. The materials requisition note is used to cost the materials to the job cost sheet.
2   A *job card* is given to the worker who is performing the first operation. the starting and finishing times for that operation are clocked onto the ticket and the same procedure is followed for subsequent operations. Finally, the job card is sent to the cost office where the time is costed and entered on the job cost sheet.
3   *Direct expenses* are entered on the job cost sheet from the invoices or an analysis of the cash book.
4   The cost of *direct materials* and *direct labour* as recorded on the *job cost sheet* is charged to the *job account*.
5   The job account is charged with an appropriate share of the *production overheads*, usually on the basis of predetermined overhead absorption rates.
6   If the job has not been completed at the end of an accounting period, it is valued at *production cost* on the balance sheet.

Self-check question

What are the six main features of a system for collecting job costs?

8.4 Job Cost Cards or Job Cost Sheets

Job cost cards and *job cost sheets* are the key documents in a job costing system. The example below would be used for relatively small jobs. For larger jobs only the summary figures would be entered on the job card from an analysis schedule. If the business has a number of very small jobs it is not practical to keep a separate job cost sheet for each job. Instead, a *general jobbing account* is kept to which all the costs of the jobs are charged.

Self-check question

What are the main features of a job cost card to be used for relatively small jobs?

8.5 Costing a Job or Batch

Costing a batch is very similar to *costing a job*, and the same procedures are followed, treating the batch as a separate, identifiable job. The costs are

JOB COST CARD													
Customer . . . . Delivery date.													
Job No. . . . . Start date.													
Job description . . . . Order No.													
Invoice price. Despatch note No.													
MATERIALS					DIRECT WAGES				DIRECT EXPENSES			OVERHEADS		
Date	R. Note	Qty	Price	Cost	Date	Hours	Rate	Cost	Date	Ref	Cost	Unit of Base	Rate	Cost

SUMMARY

£   p

Direct materials
Direct wages
Direct expenses   _____

Prime cost
Factory overhead   _____

Factory cost
Admin & selling
overhead   _____

Total cost
INVOICE PRICE   _____

PROFIT   _____

Fig. 8.1 Job cost card

collected in the same way as for job costing. When the batch has been completed, the total batch cost is divided by the number of good units in the batch to give an average cost per unit if this information is required.

We have now explained all the various stages and are ready to apply them to an example. If the company is operating absorption costing, it is important to work out the predetermined overhead rates and to include a share of the overheads in the cost of the job or batch.

Activity

The following information refers to a company in the jobbing industry using absorption costing:

Department	Budgeted overheads £	Absorption base
Machine shop	12,000	3,000 machine hours
Press shop	7,000	2,000 labour hours
Assembly dept	6,000	2,500 labour hours

Administration and selling overheads are calculated at 25% of factory cost. An order has been placed for Job No. A24 with a selling price of £6,500. The following information relates to that job.

Direct materials	£1,415
Direct labour:	
Machine shop	50 hours at £6.00 per hour
Press shop	80 hours at £5.00 per hour
Assembly	100 hours at £3.50 per hour

Time booked in the machine shop for the job is 210 machine hours. Calculate the total cost of the job.

The first step to work out the overhead absorption rates:

$$\text{Machine shop} \quad \frac{£12,000}{3,000} = £4.00 \text{ per machine hour}$$

$$\text{Press shop} \quad \frac{£7,000}{2,000} = £3.50 \text{ per labour hour}$$

$$\text{Assembly} \quad \frac{£6,000}{2,000} = £2.40 \text{ per labour hour}$$

Total cost of Job No. A24

	£	£
Direct materials		1,415
Direct wages:		
Machine shop	300	
Press shop	900	
Assembly	350	1,550
Prime cost		2,965

Factory overheads:

Machine shop (210£4.00)	840	
Press shop (180£3.50)	630	
Assembly (100£2.40)	240	1,710
Factory cost		4,675
Administration and selling overheads	1,169	
Total cost		5,844
Profit		656
Selling price		6,500

Practice questions

1 State which of the following are characteristics of job costing:

(i) homogeneous products,
(ii) customer-driven production,
(iii) complete production possible within a single accounting period.

A (i) only
B (i) and (ii) only
C (ii) and (iii) only
D (i) and (iii) only
E All of them.

(CIMA, Stage 2, May 1995)

2 A company absorbs overheads on machine hours which were budgeted at 11,250 with budgeted overheads of £258,750. Actual results were 10,980 hours with overheads of £254,692. Overheads were

A under-absorbed by £2,152.
B over-absorbed by £4,058.
C under-absorbed by £4,058.
D over-absorbed by £2,152.

(CIMA, Stage 1, November 1997)

3 A firm makes special assemblies to customers' orders and uses job costing. The data for a period are:

	Job No. AA10 £	Job No. BB15 £	Job No. CC20 £
Opening WIP	26,800	42,790	0
Material added in period	17,275	0	18,500
Labour for period	14,500	3,500	24,600

The budgeted overheads for the period were £126,000.

What overhead should be added to job number CC20 for the period?

A £24,600.   **B** £65,157.   **C** £72,761.   **D** £126,000.

Job number BB15 was completed and delivered during the period and the firm wishes to earn $33\frac{1}{3}\%$ profit on sales.

What is the selling price of job number BB15?

A £69,435.   **B** £75,521.   **C** £84,963.   **D** £138,870.

What was the approximate value of closing work in progress at the end of the period?
A £58,575.   **B** £101,675.   **C** £147,965.   **D** £217,232.

(Total marks = 20)

CIMA, Stage 1, November 1997

9 Contract Costing

9.1 Introduction

Like job costing and batch costing, *contract costing* is also used when customers specify their requirements. However, contract costing is a costing technique applied to large, long-term contracts, such as construction and civil engineering projects, where the contract is conducted off the contractor's premises, in some cases abroad. The client appoints a contractor and a formal contract is drawn up which includes details of what work is to be carried out, the method and timing of payments and any financial penalties that can be invoked if the work is not completed to the required standard and in the agreed time. Contract costing allows the relevant costs for each contract to be identified and collected, and the profit or loss to be calculated on a contract at the end of a financial period. On uncompleted contracts at the end of the financial period, only a proportion of the profit is transferred.

In this chapter we begin by looking at the main features of contract costing and the procedures involved. We then go on to describe how complete and incomplete contracts are costed.

9.2 Main Features

The *main features* of contract costing are as follows:

1 Each contract takes a long time to complete and may span more than one accounting period.
2 Most materials are ordered specifically for each contract.
3 Most labour costs, including staff such as site clerks and security guards whose wages are normally regarded as indirect costs, are direct costs to the contract.
4 Most expenses, such as site electricity and telephones, are direct costs to the contract.
5 A method must be found to charge plant and machinery used on site to the contract and the most appropriate is usually a time basis.
6 Nearly all the overhead costs can be identified as head office costs.
7 An architect or surveyor inspects the work periodically and issues certificates to the contractor which detail satisfactorily completed work. Such work is valued at selling price and the contractor sends the certificate to the client with an invoice to obtain interim payments.
8 The contract often states that the client can withhold a proportion of the contract value for a period after final completion. This is known as *retention monies* and until the date when this is finally settled the contractor must make good any defects appearing in the work.

9   Because of the conditions on site and the involvement of non-clerical staff, great attention must be paid to collecting prime documentation and controlling costs.

Self-check question

What is an architect's certificate and what are retention monies?

9.3 **Contract Costing Procedures**

The general *procedure* for contract costing is as follows:

1   A separate *account* for each contract is opened. This is charged with all the costs and credited with the contract price. Each contract account is regarded as a separate profit and loss account. The profit or loss on each account is transferred to the main profit and loss on contracts account.

2   *Materials* are charged either direct from the invoice or, if drawn from stores, from a materials requisition note. Any materials returned to stores from site are credited to the contract

3   All *labour* must be charged to each contract. If employees are working on a number of contracts at the same time, they must complete time sheets for each contract.

4   *Direct expenses* can be charged directly from invoices submitted to the company. In the construction industry, a significant amount of the work may be completed by subcontractors and these are regarded as direct expenses.

5   Any *plant and machinery* costs are charged to the contract in a number of different ways, depending on the circumstances. If it is hired, the cost is a direct expense. If it is owned, but on site short-term it is charged at an hourly rate for each item. If it is owned but is on site long-term the contract is charged with the value of the plant on arrival at the site and credited with its depreciated value when it is removed.

6   *Overhead costs* are usually added on the basis of a predetermined overhead rate. If a contract is unfinished at the end of the financial period, head office general costs are not added and only production overheads are included in the value of any work in progress.

7   The *contract price* is credited to the contract account from the architect's certificate and any profit or loss transferred to the profit and loss on contracts account. An agreed percentage should not be transferred until all defects have been remedied and retention monies received.

Self-check question

What are the main stages in contract costing?

9.4 **Completed Contracts**

We will now use an activity to illustrate the costing for a completed contract.

Activity

Kennet Construction Ltd has just completed the conversion of a house into flats for a client in the financial year and the period for retention monies has been satisfied. The following information is available at the end of the financial period:

Contract No. 866 Chilton Flats

	£000
Value of materials delivered to site	230
Wages	250
Subcontractors' charges	30
Site expenses	20
Plant transferred to site	160
Materials returned to stores	30
Plant removed from site (depreciation value)	124
Head office charges (10% of wages)	25
Value of work certified	750

Using this information, draw up a contract account for contract 866.

Your contract account should look like this:

Contract account No. 866

	£000		£000
Materials	230	Materials to stores	30
Wages	250	Plant transferred	124
Plant to site	160	Cost of contract c/d	561
Subcontractors	30		
Site expenses	20		
Head office charges	25		
	715		715
Cost of contract b/d	561	Value of work certified	750
Profit on contract	189		
	750		750

The profit on the contract of £189,000 will be transferred to the main profit and loss account. the value of the work certified of £750,000 will be debited to the client's account, and this is shown as a debtor in the balance sheet until payment has been received.

9.5 **Incomplete Contracts**

A particular problem of long-term projects is the determination of annual profits to be taken to the profit and loss account when the contract is *incomplete*. This requires the valuation of work in progress at the end of the financial year. When work has been done, but has not yet been certified, it is valued at cost, without any profit element. The estimated profit for the entire contract is first calculated by deducting the total estimated costs of the contract from the total value of the contract. The total estimated costs of the contract comprise the actual costs incurred to date, the estimated costs to completion and the estimated future costs of any rectification and guarantee work. The amount of profit to be taken in the financial period is then calculated by applying the following formula:

$$\text{Profit to date} = \frac{\text{Cost of work completed}}{\text{Total estimated costs of contract}} \times \frac{\text{Estimated}}{\text{contract price}}$$

If it is calculated that by deducting the total estimated costs form the value of the contract there is a loss rather than a profit, the loss should be shown in full in the accounts for the period.

We will now use an activity to illustrate the costing for an incomplete contract.

Activity

Kennet Construction has a long-term contract to construct a new shopping precinct in Burden. At the end of the financial period, 31 December, the following information is available:

Contract No. 211 Burden Precinct

	£
Materials purchased for contract	125,160
Materials from stores	22,240
Operating costs of plant and machinery	11,470
Book value of plant to site 1 January	96,420
Wages	43,120
Subcontractors' charges	20,000
Site salaries	10,000
Site expenses	16,200
Materials returned to stores	1,230
Book value of plant removed from site	10,640
Materials on site at 31 December	10,020
Book value of plant on site at 31 December	74,240
Cost of work in progress not certified at 31 December	32,580
Total contract value	500,000
Value of work certified at 31 December	250,000
Estimated costs to complete contract	220,000

Using this information, draw up the contract account.

Your contract account should look like this:

Contract account No. 590

	£		£
Materials purchased	125,160	Materials to stores	1,230
Materials from stores	22,240	Plant transferred	10,640
Plant operating costs	11,470	Materials on site c/d	10,020
Plant to site	96,420	Plant on site c/d	74,240
Wages	43,120	Work in progress c/d	32,580
Subcontractors' costs	20,000	Cost of work certified	215,900
Site salaries	10,000		
Site expenses	16,200		
	344,610		344,610
Cost of work certified b/d	215,900	Value of work certified	250,000
Profit on contract to date	16,718		
Profit in suspense c/d	17,382		
	250,000		250,000
1 January			
Materials b/d	10,020	Profit in suspense b/d	17,382
Plant b/d	74,240		
Work in progress b/d	32,580		

Notes:
1 The cost of work certified (£215,900) is the net balance on the first part of the contract account.
2 The cost of work not certified (the work in progress of £32,580) is added to the cost of work certified (£215,900) to give the cost of all work done to date (£248,480).
3 The profit for the period is calculated as follows:

	£	£
Contract value		500,000
Costs to date	248,480	
Estimated future costs	220,000	468,000
Estimated total profit		31,520

4 As the contract is not yet finished, it would be wrong to take the full amount of estimated profit of £31,520 and only a proportion should be recognised in the profit and loss account. There are a number of

ways in which this can be calculated and the one used in this example uses costs as follows:

Profit for period

$$= \frac{\text{Cost of work done}}{\text{Estimated total costs}} \times \text{Estimated total profit}$$

$$= \frac{£248,480}{£468,480} \times £31,520$$

$$= £16,718$$

5 The profit in suspense is calculated as follows:

		£
	Value of work certified	250,000
Less	Cost of work certified	215,900
		34,100
Less	Profit in period	16,718
	Profit in suspense	17,382

Practice questions

1 HR Construction plc makes up its accounts to 31 March each year. The following details have been extracted in relation to two of its contracts:

	Contract A	Contract B
Commencement date	1 April 1994	1 December 1994
Target completion date	31 May 1995	30 June 1995
Retention %	4	3
	£000	**£000**
Contract price	2,000	550
Materials sent to site	700	150
Materials returned to stores	80	30
Plant sent to site	1,000	150
Materials transferred	(40)	40
Materials on site 31 March 1995	75	15
Plant hire charges	200	30
Labour cost incurred	300	270
Central overhead cost	75	18
Direct expenses incurred	25	4
Value certified	1,500	500
Cost of work not certified	160	20
Cash received from client	1,440	460
Estimated cost of completion	135	110

Depreciation is charged on plant using the straight-line method at the rate of 12% per annum.

REQUIREMENTS:

(a) Prepare contract accounts, in columnar format, for EACH of the contracts A and B, showing clearly the amounts to be transferred to profit and loss in respect of each contract.

(20 marks)

(b) Show balance sheet extracts in respect of EACH contract for fixed assets, debtors and work in progress.

(4 marks)

(c) Distinguish between job, batch and contract costing.
Explain clearly the reasons why these methods are different.

(6 marks)
(Total marks = 30)

CIMA, Stage 2, May 1996

2 (a) PZ plc undertakes work to repair, maintain and construct roads. When a customer requests the company to do work, PZ plc supplies a fixed price to the customer, and allocates a works order number to the customer's request. This works order number is used as a reference number on material requisitions and timesheets to enable the costs of doing the work to be collected.

PZ plc's financial year ends on 30 April. At the end of April 1997, the data shown against four of PZ plc's works orders were:

Workers order number	488	517	518	519
Date started	1/3/96	1/2/97	14/3/97	18/3/97
Estimated completion date	31/5/97	30/7/97	31/5/97	15/5/97
	£000	£000	£000	£000
Direct labour costs	105	10	5	2
Direct material costs	86	7	4	2
Selling price	450	135	18	9
Estimated direct costs to complete orders:				
Direct labour	40	60	2	2
Direct materials	10	15	1	1
Independent valuation of work done up to 30 April 1997	350	30	15	5

Overhead costs are allocated to works orders at the rate of 40% of direct labour costs. It is company policy not to recognise profit on long-term contracts until they are at least 50% complete.

REQUIREMENTS:

(i) State, with reasons, whether the above works orders should be accounted for using contract costing or job costing.

(4 marks)

(ii) Based on your classification at **(i)** above, prepare a statement showing CLEARLY the profit to be recognised and balance sheet work in progress valuation of EACH of the above works orders in respect of the financial year ended 30 April 1997.

(10 marks)

(iii) Comment critically on the policy of attributing overhead costs to works orders on the basis of direct labour cost.

(6 marks)

(b) Explain the main features of process costing. Describe what determines the choice between using process costing or specific-order costing in a manufacturing organisation.

(10 marks)
(Total marks = 30)

CIMA, Stage 2, May 1997

10 Continuous-Operation Costing

10.1 Introduction

Continuous-operation costing is a system of costing applied to industries where the method of production is in continuous operation – for example, electricity generation and bottling. This costing system is essentially a form of *average costing*, which is a method of obtaining unit costs in which the items produced have a high degree of homogeneity. The unit cost is obtained by dividing the total production cost by the number of items produced.

There are three methods of continuous-operation costing. In this chapter we look at *output costing* and *service costing; process costing* is examined in Chapter 11. Output costing, which has some of the features of job costing or batch costing (see Chapter 8) insofar as the aim is to calculate the cost per unit. However, output costing is used where standardised goods or services are produced from a single operation over a period of time.

Service costing is used when specific functions or services, such as a canteen or personnel department, are costed. It can be used to ascertain the cost of a service provided internally or a service provided for external customers. Process costing is used where production is carried out in a series of stages or processes. Costs are accumulated for the whole production process and average unit costs of production computed at each stage. Special rules are applied to the valuation of work-in-progress, normal and abnormal losses, and it is usual to distinguish between the main product of the process, by-products and joint products.

10.2 Output Costing

Output costing is used when basically only one product is being manufactured, although various types or grades of the product may be made. It is commonly used in highly mechanised industries, such as quarrying and cement manufacture. Costs are collected for the financial period, usually by nature, and the total is divided by the number of units produced to give an *average cost per unit*. Any partly completed units at the end of the financial period are usually ignored, as they are likely to be insignificant compared with the total number of whole units produced. In addition, the amount of unfinished units tends to be constant at the end of each period.

The *cost statements* used by companies vary according to the nature of the industry and the information needs of managers. To allow some control, it is normal to show the costs classified by their nature for the period and the cost per unit. It is useful if some basis of comparison is also given, such as the results for the previous period or the budgeted figures. The following example shows a unit cost statement for 1 kg of material being produced:

Unit cost statement for January
(Total units produced 10,000)

		Cost per kg	
Item	**Cost**	**Actual**	**Budget**
	£	**£**	**£**
Wages and salaries	25,000	2.50	2.55
Materials	40,000	4.00	4.02
Packaging	2,000	0.20	0.21
Transport	3,500	0.35	0.33
Depreciation	4,500	0.45	0.45
Electricity	8,000	0.80	0.75
Rates and rent	7,500	0.75	0.75
Repairs and maintenance	1,500	0.15	0.12
Total cost	92,000	9.20	9.18

Self-check question

What is output costing?

10.3 Service Costing

Service costing is used when specific services or functions are to be costed, such as service centres, departments or functions. The services may be offered to external parties, such as hotel accommodation or car hire, or the business may be a manufacturing organisation which needs to know the cost of services provided internally, such as the canteen, stores or maintenance department. The main problem is identifying a *cost unit* so that the service being provided can be measured – for example, a hotel may decide on an occupied bed night; a bus company on a passenger mile. If particular industries have agreed on common cost units, it is possible to make *inter-company comparisons*.

Many of the organisations using service costing are large, national businesses. Rigorous systems and procedures are therefore needed to collect and analyse the costs. Such organisations are often subject to fluctuating demands for their services – for example, there are peak periods of demand during the day for electricity, water, bus and rail services. This fluctuating demand means that managers will need information to distinguish between *fixed costs* and *variable costs* (see Chapter 13) and we will be examining how these costs are treated in Chapter 11. However, not all service organisations use service costing because if the services provided do not have a high degree of homogeneity, a form of *job costing* (see Chapter 8) must be used. This is the case with the services provided by accountants and architects, for example, where services are tailored to the needs of individual clients.

There are a number of features associated with service costing. Usually the cost of direct materials is relatively small compared with direct labour and overhead costs. The service may not be a revenue-earner, so the purpose of service costing is not to establish a profit or a loss, but to provide information to managers for the purpose of cost control and the predicting future costs.

A simple example of service costing in operation is that of a company canteen. The organisation needs to know the cost of running the canteen and the average cost per meal. A monthly statement is drawn up showing the various costs. Typically, these would include the following:

- *Labour costs* – Hourly paid staff need to complete time sheets to provide this information; the salaries of any supervisors and managers would be regarded as fixed costs.
- *Food and beverages* – These costs are collected from the suppliers' invoices. A separate stores may be in operation for food and beverage supplies which will require the usual controls and procedures (see Chapter 9).
- *Consumables* – These are items such as crockery, cutlery and cleaning materials which all require regular renewal.
- *Ovens, equipment and furniture* – A depreciation charge is made for these fixed assets.
- *Occupancy or building costs* – Some apportionment is made so that the canteen carries a fair share of the costs incurred through the space it occupies (see Chapter 15).

All these costs are recorded for the month to give a total cost figure for running the canteen. By dividing this figure by the number of meals serviced during the period, the average cost per meal can be calculated.

Activity

A training college in the tourism industry has annual running costs per student of £800,000. It provides a basic training course which can be taken full-time, block release or as a sandwich course. The following table gives details of the courses and the student numbers.

Mode of study	No. of students	No. of attendance days
Full-time	60	125
Block release	300	34
Sandwich	180	85

Determine a suitable cost unit for the training college and calculate the cost per unit.

Although it is possible to use a student as a cost unit, this would not provide a meaningful figure because of the different modes of study. Therefore, it would be more useful to use a student day as the cost unit by multiplying the number of students by the number of attendance days for each mode of study, as follows:

Mode of study	No. of students	No. of attendance days	Student day
Full-time	60	125	7,500
Block release	300	34	10,200
Sandwich	180	85	15,300
			33,000

$$\text{Cost per student day} = \frac{£800,000}{33,000} = £24.24$$

Practice question

State which of the following are characteristics of servicing costing:

(i) high levels of indirect costs as a proportion of total costs.
(ii) use of composite cost units.
(iii) use of equivalent units.

A (i) only
B (i) and (ii) only
C (ii) only
D (ii) and (iii) only
E All of them.

CIMA, Stage 2, May 1995

11 Process Costing

11.1 Introduction

Process costing is a method of costing applied to production when the process is carried out in a series of chemical or operational stages. The finished output at one stage of production becomes the input for the next stage in the process. At the end of all the stages the completed production is sold or transferred to finished goods stock. This type of production is often found in chemical works, oil refineries and paint manufacturers.

Costs are accumulated for the whole production process and average unit costs of production are computed at each stage in the production process. In this chapter we look at the main features of process costing and the special rules applied to the valuation of *work in progress (WIP)* and *wastage*. Work in progress is also sometimes referred to as *work in process (WIP)*.

11.2 Main Features

For each stage in the process, both direct costs – such as materials and labour – and production overheads are charged. By dividing the costs on one process by the number of units, the average cost per unit is calculated. Cost units which are similar in nature pass through each of the production processes. It is essential that appropriate cost units are chosen (see Chapter 13). For a liquid product the cost unit might be a litre; for a solid product a kilogram or a tonne would be more appropriate. As cost units move from one process to another, the costs incurred accumulate and are transferred with them. This is illustrated in Figure 11.1.

Although the actual method of process costing varies from one organisation to another, the *main features* of process costing systems are as follows:

- There are separate processes which can be defined easily and the costs collected to them.
- The output from one process forms the input of the next process.
- Both direct costs and overheads are charged to the processes.
- Costs are accumulated in respect of cost units as production goes through the various processes.
- The average unit cost is calculated by dividing the total cost of a process for a period of time by the number of cost units for the period.

The average unit cost can be expressed as a formula:

$$\text{Average cost per unit} = \frac{\text{Costs incurred during period}}{\text{Number of units produced}}$$

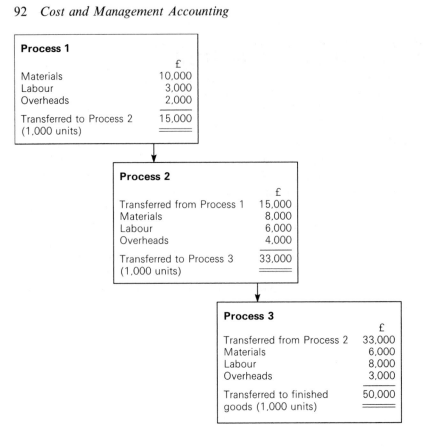

Process 1

	£
Materials	10,000
Labour	3,000
Overheads	2,000
Transferred to Process 2 (1,000 units)	15,000

Process 2

	£
Transferred from Process 1	15,000
Materials	8,000
Labour	6,000
Overheads	4,000
Transferred to Process 3 (1,000 units)	33,000

Process 3

	£
Transferred from Process 2	33,000
Materials	6,000
Labour	8,000
Overheads	3,000
Transferred to finished goods (1,000 units)	50,000

Activity

Production for January at Brilliant Paints was 50,000 completed units. The following cost information is also available:

	£
Direct materials	5,000
Direct labour	3,500
Production overheads	1,500
Total costs for period	10,000

Calculate the average cost per unit.

All you need to do is insert the figures into the formula:

$$\frac{£10,000}{50,000} = £0.20$$

Of course, at the end of the period it is likely that there will be some units which are not yet complete because they have only been partly processed. This balance of unfinished work remaining in the production operation is known as *work in progress* or *work in process (WIP)*. The costs incurred for the period relate to all the units, whether completed or only partly completed. To find out the average cost per unit when there are partly completed units we must first convert them to *equivalent units*; in other words, equivalent of whole units. For example, if there were 2,000 partly finished units in WIP which are 50% complete, they would be counted as 1,000 equivalent units (2,000 × 50%). We can now adjust the formula for calculating the average cost per unit for the period as follows:

Average cost per unit =

$$\frac{\text{Costs incurred during period}}{\text{Completed units produced} + \text{Equivalent units in WIP}}$$

Activity

In February Brilliant Paints produced 55,000 completed units. WIP was 2,000 units which were 50% complete. The following cost information is also available:

	£
Direct materials	5,500
Direct labour	4,000
Production overheads	1,500
Total costs for period	11,000

Calculate the average cost per unit.

You calculate the answer by substituting the figures in the adjusted formula:

$$\frac{£11,000}{55,000 + (2,000 \times 50\%)} = £0.196$$

11.3 Cost Elements

The costs incurred in production comprise the usual elements of direct materials, direct labour and production overheads. When WIP is examined at the end of a period the degree of completion may vary for each cost element. For example, the units may be almost complete as far as materials are concerned, but further substantial labour and overhead costs may be incurred in order to complete the units. In such cases, the cost elements must be treated separately in order to find out the number of equivalent units before the average cost per unit can be calculated.

Activity

Moving on to the month of March, the following cost figures are available for Process No. 1 at Brilliant Paints:

	£
Direct materials	8,050
Direct labour	12,375
Production overheads	8,400

There are 5,000 completed units and 1,000 units in WIP. The units in WIP are 75% complete for materials, 50% complete for labour and 25% for production overheads. Calculate the average cost per unit.

Using the formula, you should not have had too much difficulty with this activity. Using the formulae, you first need to calculate the value of WIP for each of the cost elements as follows:

Cost element	Formula	Cost per unit £
Direct materials	$\dfrac{£8,050}{5,000 + (1,000 \times 75\%)}$	1.40
Direct labour	$\dfrac{£12,375}{5,000 + (1,000 \times 50\%)}$	2.25
Production overheads	$\dfrac{£8,400}{5,000 + (1,000 \times 25\%)}$	1.60
Total cost per unit		5.25

		£	£
Direct materials	750 equivalent units @ £1.40	1,050	
Direct labour	500 equivalent units @ £2.25	1,125	
Production overheads	250 equivalent units @ £1.60	400	2,575
Value of completed units	5,000 units @ £5.25		26,250
			28,825

You may have noticed that the value of WIP (£2,575) plus the value of the completed units (£26,250) equals the total cost incurred for Process No. 1 for March (£28,825). This is a check which should always be carried out.

So far we have considered only the first process. Let us take the above figure of 5,000 completed units at the end of March for Process No. 1 and add information concerning the second stage of production.

Activity

At the end of April the following cost information is available:

	£
Direct materials	6,000
Direct labour	3,800
Production overheads	2,850

There were 4,500 completed units transferred to stock and 500 units in WIP which were 50%. Calculate the value of WIP and the completed production transferred to finished goods store at the end of April.

There are two points to note here. First, Process No. 2 starts with the 5,000 units transferred from Process No. 1 at the end of March. Secondly, when calculating the number of equivalent units, there will be no further materials costs incurred, as materials were needed at the start of the process. WIP is therefore 100% complete as far as direct materials are concerned. To tackle the calculations in a logical way, the information can be drawn up in the form of a table:

Process No. 2 Costs for April

Cost element	Total costs £	No. of completed units	Equivalent units in WIP	Total effective units	Cost per unit £	Value of WIP £
Previous process costs	26,250	4,500	500	5,000	5.25	2,625
Direct materials	6,000	4,500	500	5,000	1.20	600
Direct labour	3,800	4,500	250	4,750	0.80	200
Production overheads	2,850	4,500	250	4,750	0.60	150
	38,900				7.85	3,575

	£
Value of completed units (4,500 @ £7.85)	35,325
Add Value of WIP	3,575
	38,900

This example illustrates a number of important points. The first and second columns in the table are straightforward; the third column shows the number of completed units transferred to finished goods stock. The fourth column shows the number of equivalent units in WIP. There are 500 units in WIP and for previous process costs and materials costs the units are 100% complete. By definition, previous process costs are always complete. In this example, the materials were added at the beginning of the process. This means that even when there are partly finished units in WIP at the end of the period, the units must be complete as far as the material cost element is concerned. This is a favourite examination topic and the following rules should be applied:

1   If any cost elements are added at the start of the process, no further costs of this nature will be incurred.
2   If any cost elements are added at the end of the process, as the units in WIP have not reached this stage, no part of the cost element can be included in WIP.
3   Having calculated the number of equivalent units this is added to the number of completed units to give the number of total effective units. The total cost for each element in the second column is divided by the number of total effective units to give the cost per unit in the sixth column. To find the value of WIP, the number of equivalent units in WIP for each element is multiplied by the cost per unit.
4   The final stage is to calculate the value of the completed units at the bottom of the table and add the value of WIP. These total of these two figures must agree with the figure of total costs as shown in the second column.

11.4 Valuation of Work in progress

Closing WIP for a process at the end of one period forms the opening WIP for the same process at the start of the next period. This raises the problem of how WIP should be valued. Certain assumptions can be made to decide the method of valuation. Management may assume that the units comprising WIP are completed during the current period and use the *first in, first out (FIFO)* method (see Chapter 14). Alternatively, it may be assumed that the partly finished units forming the opening WIP are mixed with the current period's production and as it is not known which units are completed at the end of the period the *average cost method* can be used.

Activity

Brilliant Paints has three production processes. For the month of December the opening WIP for Process No. 2 was 300 units (50% complete) valued at £4,500. At the start of the period there were 900 completed units transferred from the first process which were valued at £2,700. The total costs for Process No. 2 for the month were £8,100. At the end December 1,000 completed unit were transferred to Process No. 3 and the closing WIP was 200 units which were 25% complete. Use this information to calculate the value of closing WIP using FIFO.

The various calculations can be broken down into a number of steps as follows:

1 Number of effective units produced by Process No. 2 during December:

		Units
	Closing WIP (200 × 25%)	50
Add	Completed units transferred to Process No. 3	1,000
		1,050
Less	Opening WIP (300 × 50%)	150
	Effective units manufactured in period	900

2 Costs incurred in period to produce 900 effective units:

		£
	Transferred from Process No. 1	2,700
Add	Other costs incurred in period	8,100
		10,800

3 Valuation of closing WIP:

$$\frac{\text{Costs incurred in period}}{\text{No. of effective units}} = \frac{£10,800}{900} = £12 \text{ per unit}$$

No. of equivalent units in closing WIP (200 × 25%) = 50
Value of closing WIP = 50 units @ £12 = £600

4 Value of 1,000 completed units transferred to Process No. 3:

		£
	Value of opening WIP	4,500
Add	Costs transferred from Process No. 1	2,700
	Other costs incurred in period	8,100
		15,300
Less	Value of closing WIP	600
	Value of completed units transferred to Process No. 3	14,700

In the average cost method, the opening WIP valuation plus the period costs are used to calculate the average cost per unit. The same average cost per unit is used to value both the closing WIP and the completed units. The steps are as follows:

1 Total number of effective units:

		Units
	Completed units transferred to Process No. 3	1,000
Add	Closing WIP (200 × 25%)	50
		1,050

2 Total costs incurred:

		£
	Opening WIP valuation	4,500
Add	Costs transferred from Process No. 1	2,700
	Other costs incurred in period	8,100
		15,300

3 Valuation of closing WIP:

$$\text{Average cost per unit} = \frac{\text{Total costs incurred}}{\text{Total number of effective units}}$$

$$= \frac{£15,300}{1,050} = £14.5714$$

Closing WIP $= (200 \times 25\%) \times £14.5714 = £728.57$

4 Valuation of 1,000 completed units transferred to Process No. 3:

		£
	Transferred to Process No. 3	
	(1,000 units @ £14.5714)	14,571.40
Add	Value of closing WIP	728.57
	Value of completed units transferred to	
	Process No. 3	15,299.97

The above examples demonstrate the input of the different WIP valuations on the value of completed units transferred to the next process. The consequence is that under the two different methods the final profit for the business will also differ. Therefore, once a policy has been established, it is essential to use the specified method consistently.

Self-check question

Describe two methods for valuing closing work in progress.

11.5 Waste

Even in a highly efficient production process there is likely to be some *waste* or spoilage. This is the amount of material lost as part of a production process. Acceptable levels of waste, known as *normal loss*, are part of the cost of production and are allowed for in the product costs. It is possible for losses to take place at any point in the process. Where waste occurs part-way through a process, some of the loss is charged to WIP. If the loss takes place at the end of a process, perhaps at the final inspection stage, only units which have been completed during the period are charged with the loss. The procedure for dealing with normal loss occurring at the end of the process is as follows:

1 Complete a table for process costs as explained in Section 11.4.
2 The third column of the table should show all the completed units, both the good units and those which have been designated as normal loss.
3 Complete the table and use the cost per unit to calculate the value of the normal loss.
4 Divide the value of the normal loss by the number of good completed units and add to the original cost per unit to obtain a revised cost per unit.

Activity

Brilliant Paints has provided the following cost information for the period:

	£
Materials (added at start of process)	18,000
Direct labour	31,000
Production overheads	15,725

There were 2,000 units of closing WIP at the end of the period. which were 50% complete as far as labour costs were concerned and 25% complete with regard to production overheads. There were 18,000 completed units of which 1,000 units were scrapped. Using this information, construct a table to calculate the process costs.

Your table should look like this:

Cost element	Total costs £	No. of completed units	Equivalent units in WIP	Total effective units	Cost per unit £	Value of WIP
Direct materials	18,000	18,000	2,000	20,000	0.90	1,800
Direct labour	31,350	18,000	1,000	19,000	1.65	1,650
Production overheads	15,725	18,000	500	18,500	0.85	425
	65,075				3.40	3,875

Normal loss process costs for period

Value of normal loss (1,000 units @ £3.40 allocated to 17,000 units)	£3,400 / 17,000	0.20
Revised cost per unit		3.60

	£
Value of completed units (17,000 units @ £3.60)	61,200
Add Value of WIP	3,875
	65,075

Abnormal loss is the loss arising from a manufacturing or chemical process through abnormal waste, shrinkage, seepage or spoilage in excess of the normal loss. It may be expressed as a weight or volume, or in other units appropriate to the process, and is usually valued on the same basis as the good output. An *abnormal gain* is an unexpected surplus of output that may occur if the actual loss is less than the normal loss. The abnormal losses must carry their share of the costs of the normal losses. It is important to do this calculation before working out the value of the abnormal loss to be charged to the profit and loss account. The procedure is as follows:

1   Complete a table for process costs as explained in Section 11.4.
2   The third column of the table should show all the completed units: the good units, those which have been designated as normal loss and the abnormal loss.
3   Complete the table and use the cost per unit to calculate the value of the normal loss.
4   Divide the value of the normal loss by the number of good completed units and abnormal loss units and add to the original cost per unit to obtain a revised cost per unit.
5   Multiply the revised cost per unit by the number of units of abnormal loss to obtain the value of the abnormal loss to be charged to the profit and loss account.

Activity

Brilliant Paints has provided the following cost information for the period:

	£
Materials (added at start of process)	50,000
Direct labour	47,500
Production overheads	18,000

There were 2,000 units of closing WIP at the end of the period. which were 75% complete as far as labour costs were concerned and 50% complete with regard to production overheads. There were 8,000 completed units. Normal loss is 500 units, but actual waste in the period was 750 units. Using this information, construct a table to calculate the process costs.

If you were able to follow the procedure for calculating normal loss, you should not have had too many problems with this activity. Check your answer against the following:

Abnormal loss process costs for period

Cost element	Total costs £	No. of completed units	Equivalent units in WIP	Total effective units	Cost per unit £	Value of WIP
Direct materials	50,000	8,000	2,000	10,000	5.00	10,000
Direct labour	47,500	8,000	1,500	9,500	5.00	7,500
Production overheads	18,000	8,000	1,000	9,000	2.00	2,000
	115,500				12.00	19,500

Value of normal loss	£6,000	0.80
(500 units @ £12.00 allocated	7,500	
to 7,500 remaining units)		
Revised cost per unit		12.80

	£
Value of completed units	92,800
(7,250 units @ £12.80)	
Add Value of WIP	19,500
Value of abnormal loss charged to	3,200
profit and loss account	115,500
(250 units @ £12.80)	

Practice questions

1 PQR Limited produces two joint products – P and Q – together with a by-product R, from a single main process (process 1). Product P is sold at the point of separation for £5 per kg whereas product Q is sold for £7 per kg after further processing into product Q2. By-product R is sold without further processing for £1.75 per kg.

Process 1 is closely monitored by a team of chemists who planned the output per 1,000 kg of input materials to be as follows:

Product P	500 kg
Product Q	350 kg
Product R	100 kg
Toxic waste	50 kg

The toxic waste is disposed of at a cost of £1.50 per kg, and arises at the end of processing. Process 2, which is used for further processing of product Q into product Q2, has the following cost structure:

Fixed costs	£6,000 per week
Variable costs	£1.50 per kg processed

The following actual data relate to the first week of accounting period 10:

Process 1

Opening work in process	Nil
Materials input 10,000 kg costing	£15,000
Direct labour	£10,000
Variable overhead	£4,000
Fixed overhead	£6,000

Outputs:

Product P	4,800 kg
Product Q	3,600 kg
Product R	1,000 kg
Toxic waste	600 kg
Closing work in process	Nil

Process 2

Opening work in process	Nil
Input of product Q	3,600 kg
Output of product Q2	3,600 kg
Output of product Q2	3,300 kg
Closing work in process	300kg, 50% converted.

Conversion costs were incurred in accordance with the planned cost structure.

REQUIREMENTS:

(a) Prepare the main process account for the first week of period 10 using the final sales value method to attribute pre-separation costs to joint products.
(12 marks)

(b) Prepare the toxic waste accounts and process 2 account for the first week of period 10.
(9 marks)

(c) Comment on the method used by PQR Limited to attribute the pre-separation costs to its joint products.
(4 marks)

(d) Advise the management of PQR Limited whether or not, on purely financial grounds, it should continue to process product Q into product Q2.
  (i) if product Q could be sold at the point of separation for £4.30 per kg and
  (ii) if 60% of the weekly fixed costs of process 2 were avoided by not processing product Q further.
(5 marks)
(Total marks = 30)
CIMA, Stage 2, May 1995

2 Summarised below is data for two production processes in a factory for the month just ended:

Process 1:
  Materials, £6,335
  Labour and overheads, £7,677

Five per cent of input units are expected to be rejected; rejects occur at the end of the process, 190 units failed inspection in the morninth and were rejected. After inspection, units are transferred immediately to the next process.

Process 2
  Opening work in process, 500 units: £3,576
  Completed output from Process 1, 4,110 units
  Additional materials, £11,672
  Labour and overheads, £9,485
  Closing work in process, 400 units

The FIFO method is used to value completed production. There are no losses in the process. Work in process is 100% complete as to materials, and both opening and closing work in process were 50% complete as to labour and overheads:

Required:
(a) Prepare the Process 1 account for the month just ended

(7 marks)

(b) Prepare the Process 2 account for the month just ended

(9 marks)

ACCA, Module B, June 1997

12 By-product Costing and Joint Product Costing

12.1 Introduction

In process costing it is usual to distinguish between the main product of the process and *by-products* or *joint products*. By-products are the output of a process that have secondary economic significance to the main product of the process and they may require further processing to make them marketable. Joint products are the output of a process in which there is more than one product and all the products have similar or equal economic importance. They use the same commonly processed materials up to a certain point (the *split-off point*), although they may require further processing to make them marketable.

By-products and joint products are very common in the meat, oil refining, chemical and mining industries. Because the definition of the terms depends on the perceived significance of the sales value of the products, companies tend to have differing views as to whether a product can be regarded as a by-product or a joint product.

In this chapter we describe how by-products can be costed and two different bases of apportionment that can be used to cost joint products.

12.2 By-products

By-products have a small sales value and there is little advantage in maintaining a complex costing system for them. It is usual to select a way of dealing with by-product costs that is simple, even if this means that relatively insignificant problems are ignored. There are three main methods of costing by-products:

1   No attempt is made to distinguish between the main product and the by-product. Any sales value from the by-product is added to the sales of the main product and all costs are set against this to show the total profit. The view is taken that as there is a common process it is unrealistic to attempt to attribute a proportion of the costs to the by-product.
2   If the sales value of the by-product is very small it may be shown directly in the profit and loss account as 'other income'. Any costs incurred after

the split-off point to bring the by-product into a saleable condition are deducted from its income before showing in the profit and loss account.
3 The preferred method is to deduct the sales value of the by-product less any costs incurred after the split-off point from the total cost of production.

Activity

The following information is available from Paisley Poultry Ltd:

Costs of production for period	£200,000
Opening stock	Nil
Closing stock of main product	5% of production
Sales revenue of main product	£220,000
Net sales value of by-product	£2,200
Subsequent costs of by-product	£200

Draw up a by-product costing statement using the preferred method **(3)** described above.

Your costing statement should look like this:

By-product costing statement

	£	£
Sales of main product		200,000
Cost of production (£200,000 – £2,000)	198,000	
Less Closing stock (5%)	9,990	
Cost of sales		188,100
Profit		31,900

12.3 Joint Products

Joint products are the output of a process in which more than one product is produced from the same process, but all the products use the same commonly processed materials up to a certain point known as the *split-off point*. All the products have significant sales value, but may require further processing to make them marketable. Figure 12.1 illustrates the processing of joint products.

The common costs incurred up to the split-off point must be apportioned is some way between the joint products. Subsequent costs arising after that

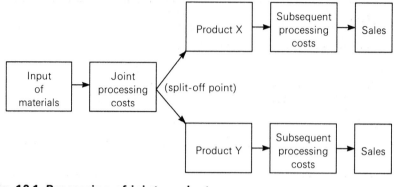

Fig. 12.1 **Processing of joint products**

point relate to each specific product and do not require apportionment. There are two methods by which common costs can be apportioned:

- the *physical units basis of apportionment*, which apportions the costs according to the physical weight or volume of the products; and
- the *sales value basis of apportionment*, which apportions the costs in proportion to the relative sales value of the products.

Both methods allow a closing value to be placed on the closing stock of each of the joint products and permit the costs and profits of each of the joint products to be determined. In addition they both provide management information. It is important to remember that one product cannot be manufactured independently of the other; the profit of one product is affected by the way the common costs are apportioned.

Self-check question

What is the difference between joint products and by-products?

12.4 Physical Units Basis of Apportionment

The *physical units basis of apportionment* can be used only when the joint products separate after the split-off point into comparable states. Therefore, this method cannot be used if one product is a solid and the other a gas after the separation point, for example. In addition, if the products have very different sales values this is not reflected in the attributable profits and could lead to one product appearing to be very profitable and the other less so. The physical units basis of apportionment is easy to apply; the joint costs are simply apportioned on the basis of the output of each product to the total output measure by weight or volume.

Activity

The following information is available for the period:

Joint processing costs	£6,000
Output of joint product *A*	2,000 kg
Output of joint product *B*	10,000 kg
Sales value of product *A*	£1.10 per kg
Sales value of product *B*	£0.55 per kg

Draw up a joint product costing statement using the physical units basis of apportionment.

Your costing statement should look like this.

Joint product costing statement
Physical units basis of apportionment

	Product *A*	Product *B*	Total
Output	2,000 kg	10,000 kg	12,000 kg
	£	£	£
Sales	2,200	5,500	7,700
Apportioned costs	1,000	5,000	6,000
Profit	1,200	500	1,700
Profit/sales percentage	54.5%	9.1%	22.1%

The apportioned costs for Product *A* are calculated as follows:

$$\frac{\text{Product } A \text{ output}}{\text{Total output}} = \frac{2,000 \text{ kg}}{12,000 \text{ kg}}$$

The profit/sales percentage for Product *A* is calculated as follows:

$$\frac{\text{Product } A \text{ profit}}{\text{Product } A \text{ sales}} \times 100 = \frac{£1,200}{£2,200} \times 100 = 54.5\%$$

12.5 Sales Value Basis of Apportionment

The advantage of the *sales value basis of apportionment* is that it gives the same profit/sales percentage for each product. As managers often operate on an assumed relationship between costs and profits, this method is widely used. In applying this method, the joint costs are apportioned in the proportion that the total sales value of each product bears to the total sales value for all output of the joint processes. The selling price per unit is not used to apportion.

Activity

Using the same data as in the previous activity, draw up a joint product costing statement using the sales value basis of apportionment.

Your joint costing statement should look like this:

Joint product costing statement
Sales value basis of apportionment

	Product *A* £	Product *B* £	Total £
Sales	2,200	5,500	7,700
Apportioned costs	1,714	4,286	6,000
Profit	486	1,214	1,700
Profit/sales percentage	22.1%	22.1%	22.1%

The apportioned costs for product A are calculated as follows:

$$\frac{\text{Product } A \text{ sales}}{\text{Total sales}} \times \text{Joint processing costs}$$

$$= \frac{£2,200}{£7,000} \times £6,000 = £1,714$$

Whichever method is used, the total profit remains the same, but the profit per product can be significantly different.

Some products incur further costs after the split-off point to put them into a saleable condition. This means that there is no sales value at the split-off point which can be used to apportion costs. If it is not possible to determine what the relative sales value should be at the split-off point, the subsequent processing costs should be *deducted* from the final sales value to give a *notional sales value* at the split-off point. The notional sales value is then used to apportion costs in the way described.

Practice questions

1 (a) Distinguish between the cost accounting teatment of joint product and of by-products.

(3 marks)

(b) A company operates a manufacturing process which produces joint products A and B, and by-product C.

Manufacturing costs for a period total £272,926, incurred in the manufacture of:

Product A – 16,000 kgs (selling price £6.10kg)
B – 53,200 kgs (selling price £7.50/kg)
C – 2,770 kgs (selling price £0.80/kg)

Required:
Calculate the cost per kg (to 3 decimal places of a pound £) of Products A and B in the period, using market values to apportion joint costs.

(5 marks)

(c) In another of the company's processes, Product X is manufactured using raw materials P and T which are mixed in the proportions 1:2.
　　Material purchase prices are:

　　P　£5.00 per kilo
　　T　£1.60 per kilo

Normal weight loss of 5% is expected during the process.
　　In the period just ended 9,130 kilos of Product X were manufactured from 9,660 kilos of raw materials. Conversion costs in the period were £23,796. There was no work in process at the beginning or end of the period.

Required:
Prepare the Product X process account for the period.

(6 marks)
(14 marks)

ACCA, Module B, June 1995

2 XYZ plc, a paint manufacturer, operates a process costing system. The following details relate to process 2 for the month of October 1997:

Opening work in progress	5,000 litres fully complete as to transfers from process 1 and 40% complete as to labour and overhead, valued at £60,000.
Transfer from process 1	65,000 litres valued at cost of £578,500
Direct labour	£101,400
Variable overhead	£80,000
Fixed overhead	£40,000
Normal loss	5% of volume transferred from process 1, scrap value £2.00 per litre
Actual output	30,000 litres of Paint X (a joint product) 25,000 litres of Paint Y (a joint product) 7,000 litres of by-product Z
Closing work in progress	6,000 litres fully complete as to transfers from process 1 and 60% complete as to labour and overhead.

The final selling prices of products X, Y and Z are:

Paint X	£15.00 per litre
Paint Y	£18.00 per litre
Product Z	£4.00 per litre

There are no further processing costs associated with either Paint X or the by product, but Paint Y requires further processing at a cost of £1.50 per litre.
　　All three products incur packaging costs of £0.50 per litre before they can be sold.

REQUIREMENTS:

(a) Prepare the process 2 account for the month of October 1997, apportioning the common costs between the joint products, based upon their values at the point of separation.

(20 marks)

(b) Prepare the abnormal loss/gain account showing clearly the amount to be transferred to profit and loss account.

(4 marks)

(c) Describe one other method of apportioninhg the common costs between the joint products, AND explain why it is necessary to make such apportionments, and their usefulness when measuring product profit-ability.

(6 marks)
(Total marks = 30)

CIMA, Stage 2, November 1997

13 Marginal Costing

13.1 Introduction

This chapter investigates the impact of changes in the volume of activity undertaken by a business on costs and profits. To examine these changes and the financial implications, a technique known as *marginal costing* (also known as *variable costing*) is used. Marginal costing principles are also used in *cost–volume–profit (CVP) analysis* and *break-even analysis*, which we shall be looking at in Chapter 15.

In marginal costing variable costs are charged to cost units and the fixed costs for the period are written off in full, without attempting to charge them to individual cost units. Thus, marginal costing is differs considerably from absorption costing, the other major technique for ascertaining the cost of a unit (see Chapter 7).

In this chapter we describe the purpose of marginal costing and the terms used. We then go on to explain how marginal costing is used to provide managers with information for decision-making and control.

13.2 Purpose of Marginal Costing

The *purpose* of marginal costing is to provide information to managers that is useful for making a number of *short-term decisions*, such as:

- setting the selling price of products, particularly in times of trade depression and when introducing new products;
- evaluating proposed closure or temporary cessation of part of the business activities;
- determining whether it is preferable to manufacture a component or to buy it from another company;
- deciding the value of accepting a special order or contract;
- comparing different methods of manufacture.

Because of the immense value of the information supplied to management by marginal costing, its use is more widespread than the above list indicates. It is used by companies operating a flexible budgetary control system and it may underpin medium-term and long-term corporate planning. In addition, it is also the basis of cost–volume–profit (CVP) analysis, which is used for short-term planning.

The theory behind marginal costing is simple to understand and the principles can easily be applied to straightforward problems. Although in practice there are some difficulties and limitations to marginal costing, it is nevertheless a very useful technique.

Despite the fact that absorption costing is the basis of all financial accounting statements, the information it provides can be misleading when managers are making decisions in certain circumstances.

Activity

David Huish has a business supplying handmade rocking chairs. The selling price of each chair is £100 and the market is such that he can sell 5 chairs in one week. The wood costs £20 per chair and David pays a craftsman £40 for each chair he makes. David rents a small showroom for £150 per week. What is his weekly profit?

The answer is £50, which you can work out by drawing up a simple profit statement:

Profit statement for 1 week (5 chairs)		
	£	**£**
Sales		500
Materials	100	
Wages	200	
Rent	150	450
Profit		50

The above statement includes all the costs and gives us a total profit figure. As he has sold 5 chairs, the profit for each chair, based on the above information, is £10. But what if he only makes and sells 3 chairs one particular week; what will his profit be then? Using the information that the profit for 1 chair is £10, we may conclude that the profit for the week will be £30. The following profit statement gives a very different picture:

Profit statement for 1 week (3 chairs)		
	£	**£**
Sales		300
Materials	60	
Wages	120	
Rent	150	330
Loss		(30)

From this simple example, it is easy to appreciate how a loss was made on 3 chairs instead of the anticipated profit of £30. The rent of £150 remains the same each week irrespective of the number of chairs made and sold. The rent is known as a *fixed cost* which is not influenced by changes in the level of activity. However, direct wages and material costs vary in proportion to changes in the level of activity. It is this difference in the way that some costs vary with changes in the level of activity and some costs remain fixed which is the basis underlying marginal costing. By differentiating between *fixed* and *variable costs*, managers can be given information for planning and decision-making.

13.3 Definition of Terms

Marginal costing has very few technical *terms*, but it is important to understand them in context in order to answer questions correctly. The key terms are:

- *Variable costs* are those costs which, in total, tend to follow the level of activity in the short-term. As activity increases, measured possibly by production or sales levels, so variable costs increase in total. As activity decreases, so variable costs decrease in total.
- *Fixed costs* are those costs which, in total, tend to remain the same, irrespective of changes in the level of activity in the short-term. For example, the rent of the factory or the salary bill is unlikely to change solely because the level of activity has temporarily changed one week.
- *Contribution* is the difference between the sales value and the variable costs incurred in achieving those sales. The contribution can be calculated for one unit or for any chosen level of sales. A complete understanding of what is meant by the term 'contribution' is essential.
- *Marginal costing* is the application of the principle that only variable costs are charged to the cost units. The fixed costs for a particular period must be written off against the total contribution for that period to arrive at the profit or loss for the period.
- A *marginal cost* is regarded by the accountant as the average variable cost and is assumed to be constant in the short-term. Accountants tend to use the terms 'marginal cost' and 'variable cost' interchangeably, but some argue that it is preferable to adhere to the term variable cost.

Self-check question

What is contribution?

Marginal costing involves making some *general assumptions*. Although they may be relaxed in particular circumstances, the following assumptions are normally applied:

- Costs can be defined either as fixed or variable and they behave in a consistent fashion.
- There is a linear relationship between costs and revenue, at least over the range of activity being considered.
- No changes in the efficiency of production methods are introduced.
- There are no changes in stock levels, or stock is valued at marginal cost.

13.4 **Cost Behaviour**

It is important to note that in the definitions of fixed and variable costs the words 'in total' are used. The variable cost per unit remains constant, but the total variable cost increases as activity increases. In the example of the rocking chairs, the material cost per chair is £20. This is a variable cost because as the number of chairs made increases or decreases, so the total material cost changes. Figure 13.1 shows what happens to costs when activity changes. This is known as *cost behaviour*.

Activity

A company finds that actual output is lower than budgeted output. Which of the following actual costs would you expect to be lower than the budgeted costs?

a Variable costs per unit
b Total variable costs
c Fixed costs per unit
d Total fixed costs

You can use Figure 13.1 to answer this question. It is only the total variable costs which will be lower if actual output is lower than budgeted. Whether a specific type of cost is fixed or variable depends on the particular circumstances. A prime example is direct wages, sometimes termed operatives' wages. Accountants normally deem wages to be a variable cost in the absence of information to the contrary. However, in some organisations activity may decrease for a short period, but the wages bill is not reduced in any way because the workforce is retained until business picks up. Unless there is information indicating an alternative treatment, the list of common costs in Figure 13.2 indicates how they should be regarded.

Fig. 13.1 Cost behaviour

	Increased activity	Decreased activity
Fixed costs:		
In total	unchanged	unchanged
Per unit	decreased	increased
Variable costs:		
In total	increased	decreased
Per unit	unchanged	unchanged

Cost element	Fixed cost	Variable cost
Rent	✔	
Direct materials		✔
Direct labour		✔
Advertising	✔	
Salesmen's commission		✔
Depreciation	✔	
Metered power supply		✔
Warehouse wages	✔	
Machine operators' wages		✔
Rates	✔	
Lubricants	✔	
Accountants' salaries	✔	

Fig. 13.2 Identifying fixed and variable rates

Some costs do not change in total in direct relationship to changes in the level of activity, neither do they remain fixed. Such costs are known as *semi-variable costs*, as they contain both fixed and variable cost elements. To deal with semi-variable costs the fixed cost element must be identified and added to other fixed costs, and the variable cost element added to other variable costs. There are a number of methods for separating the fixed and variable elements, but the following method is the simplest.

The first step is to identify the total semi-variable costs for two different levels of production as in the following data:

Production level Units	Semi-variable costs £
6,000	8,000
16,000	13,000

The increase in units of 10,000 has brought about an increase in costs of £5,000. This increase in costs is due entirely to changes in the variable cost element as fixed costs do not change in total. The variable cost per unit is therefore:

$$\frac{£5,000}{10,000} = £0.50 \text{ per unit}$$

The variable costs can now be calculated for each level of activity and deducted from the total semi-variable cost to give the total fixed cost (which should be the same at the different activity levels):

Production level Units	Semi-variable costs £	Variable costs £	Fixed costs £
6,000	8,000	3,000	5,000
16,000	13,000	8,000	5,000

Activity

The following data relates to the overhead expenditure of a contract cleaners at two levels of activity:

Square metres cleaned	12,750	15,100
Overheads	£73,950	£83,585

If 16,200 square metres are to be cleaned, what is the estimate of overheads?

The first step is to find the variable overhead per square metre which is calculated by dividing the extra overhead cost of £9,635 by the extra square metres cleaned of 2,350. This gives the variable cost at £4.10 per square metre. For cleaning 12,750 square metres the total variable overhead cost will be 12,750, which gives £52,275. Taking this from the total overhead cost of £73,950 gives a result of £21,675 for the fixed overhead. Therefore, 16,200 metres will be:

	£
Fixed overhead	21,675
Variable overhead (16,200 × £4.10)	66,420
Total overheads	88,095

13.5 Contribution

The *contribution per unit* is calculated by deducting the unit marginal cost from the unit selling price. The total contribution is calculated by deducting the total variable costs from the total sales. Contribution is not profit because no regard has been paid to the fixed costs of the organisation. The contribution can be considered as a contribution to the fixed costs of the organisation and, when these have been completely covered, to profit. Unless a particular activity gives a contribution – i.e. the selling price is higher than the variable costs – that activity will never make a profit because the fixed costs still have to be borne. If you know the contribution per unit from any activity, it is simple to calculate the profit for a company.

Activity

A company manufactures an item with variable costs of £1.60 per unit and a selling price of £2.20 per unit. In January, it manufactures 2,000 units and the fixed costs for the month amount to £900. What is the profit for the month?

The calculation is straightforward. First you need to find out the contribution per unit:

	£
Selling price per unit	2.20
Variable costs per unit	1.60
Contribution per unit	0.60

Now you can work out the profit for the period:

	£
Total contribution for January	
(2,000 units × £0.60)	1,200
Total fixed costs for January	900
Profit for January	300

As sales and contribution are always in direct proportion to each other, a ratio can be calculated by expressing the contribution as a percentage of sales. This is known as the *profit/volume (P/V) ratio* or the *contribution ratio* and is used in subsequent sections on decision-making, but at the simplest level the contribution for a product can be quickly calculated at any given level of sales by using the ratio.

In the previous activity the contribution was 60p per unit and the selling price was £2.20 per unit. The P/V ratio is:

$$\frac{\text{Contribution}}{\text{Selling price}} = \frac{£0.60}{£2.20} \times 100 = 27.27\%$$

The contribution at any given level of sales can be found by using the formula:

Contribution = Sales × P/V ratio

Thus, in this example the sale of 2,000 units at £2.20 each gives a contribution of £4,400 × 27.27% = £1,200.

13.6 Marginal Cost Statements

When drawing up information in the form of a *marginal costing statement*, it is useful to show the figures per unit as well as the total level of activity for the period.

Activity

Keytone Ltd manufactures an article with a selling price of £10.00 per unit. The variable costs per unit are £3.00 for direct materials, £2.00 for direct labour and £2.00 for variable overheads. In the month of January sales are 4,000 units and the fixed costs are £10,000 for the month. Construct a marginal costing statement.

Keytone Ltd
Marginal costing statement for the month of January

	Total production 4,000 units £	£	Figures for 1 unit £	£
Sales		40,000		10
Variable costs:				
Direct materials	12,000		3	
Direct labour	8,000		2	
Overheads	8,000	28,000	2	7
Contribution		12,000		3
Total fixed costs		10,000		
Total profit		2,000		

From the figures for one unit you can calculate that the P/V ratio is 30%, so the total contribution with sales of £40,000 is £12,000 as shown on the statement.

Practice questions

1 If actual output is lower than budgeted output, which of the following costs would you expect to be lower than the original budget?

A Total variable costs
B Total fixed costs
C Variable costs per unit
D Fixed costs per unit

ACCA, Module B, December 1996

2 XYZ Limited currently produces two sizes of machines – the Minor and the Major. Various forecasts have been prepared for 1995 which are summarised below.

Budget costs for 1995:

	£
Direct materials	2,700,000
Direct labour	1,560,000
Variable overhead	3,120,000
Fixed overheads	4,200,000

The product details for 1995 are as follows:

	Minor	Major
Forecast selling price/unit	£60	£95
Forecast sales volume (units)	120,000	70,000

Each unit of Major needs 1.5 times the amount of materials as a Minor and twice as much labour. Variable overheads are always absorbed in proportion to labour.

In the following year, 1996, it is proposed to launch a luxury version of the Major to be called the Major Plus. The Major Plus is expected to sell at £125 per unit and to have estimated direct unit costs of £24 materials and £17 labour and to increase fixed costs by £600,000 per year.

The forecast sales volumes for 1996 are:

	Units
Minor	120,000
Major	40,000
Major Plus	40,000

REQUIREMENTS:

(a) Prepare a projected profit and loss acount for 1995 on marginal costing principles, showing the performance of the products.

(6 marks)

(b) Prepare a projected profit and loss account for 1996 on marginal costing principles, showing the performance of the products.

(5 marks)

(c) Comment briefly on the position revealed by your statements.

(4 marks)
(Total marks = 15)

CIMA, Stage 2, November 1995

14 Marginal Costing and Decision-Making

14.1 Introduction

Marginal costing is a very valuable *decision-making* technique. It helps management to set prices, compare alternative production methods, set production activity levels, close production lines and choose which of a range of potential products to manufacture. Moreover, the principles of marginal costing can be easily applied to straightforward problems, and although there are some difficulties and limitations to marginal costing, it is nevertheless a very useful technique.

In Chapter 13 we described how the contribution per unit is used to calculate the profit for the organisation. In this chapter we examine the effect of *limiting factors* on contribution and show how products can be *ranked* to determine which is the most profitable, thus aiding managers in deciding which products to manufacture. We also look at how marginal costing can be used to decide whether to accept a *special order* or whether to *manufacture* or *buy* a component.

14.2 Limiting Factors

The concept of contribution is useful for decision-making purposes, although there are occasions when it is necessary to modify the concept. This is because an organisation does not have unlimited growth potential; there are nearly always constraints. The main limitation on a company's growth is often the sales it can achieve, as the market will accept only a certain quantity of the product. However, an organisation can also be limited in its activities by the scarcity of some economic factor of production, such as a shortage of direct labour, materials or limited plant capacity. When a key factor constrains the growth of the company, this factor is known as the *limiting factor* or *principal budget factor*. Management must identify the limiting factor at any one time and arrange production so that the contribution per unit of limiting factor is maximised.

Activity

LDC Ltd has found an extremely rare mineral. The total world supply is only 20,000 tonnes. The company has a choice of using the mineral in the manufacture of either of two products, the details of which are:

	Product *A*	Product *B*
	£	£
Selling price per unit	6.00	4.00
Variable costs per unit	2.00	2.50
Contribution per unit	4.00	1.50
Tonnes of material required	4	1

Which product should the company manufacture?

As Product *A* gives a greater contribution per unit it would appear to be the better choice. But a limiting factor of materials is in operation. In this instance a tonne can be used as a unit of the limiting factor. Product *A* gives a contribution of only £1.00 per tonne of material, whereas Product *B* gives a contribution of £1.50 per tonne. If the rule is applied to maximise the contribution per unit of limiting factor, Product *B* will be the better choice. By doing so, the total contribution from 20,000 tonnes of material available will be £30,000 compared with the possible total contribution from Product *A* of £20,000.

14.3 Ranking of Products

A company may have the choice of manufacturing alternative products. There are a number of different ways the products can be ranked to determine which would be the most profitable for the company to manufacture. The method to be used depends on the circumstances.

Activity

Juno Ltd has the choice of manufacturing one of two products. Based on the following information, rank the two products and decide which is preferable.

	Product *A*	Product *B*
	£	£
Selling price per unit	15	30
Variable costs per unit:		
Materials	5	12
Labour	4	7
Overheads	1	3
Total cost	10	22
Contribution per unit	5	8

There are four methods you can use to rank the products:

1 If there is no limitation on the sales of either of the units and no limiting factor operating on the resources used, the products can be ranked by the absolute size of the *contribution per unit*, and Product *B* would be selected.

2 If there is a maximum sales income which can be achieved from either product, the *profit/volume ratio* should be used to rank them. In this example, if sales of £50,000 could be achieved of either Product *A* or Product B, the calculation using the following formula is:

$$\text{Profit/volume ratio} = \frac{\text{Contribution}}{\text{Sales}} \times 100$$

Product *A* $\frac{£5}{£15} \times 100 = 33.3\%$ Product *B* $\frac{£8}{£30} \times 100 = 26.7\%$

Therefore, with sales of £50,000 the contribution from Product *A* is £16,650, but £13,350 from Product *B*, the company should choose Product *A*.

3 If the sales in units for each product are unequally limited, ranking should be by the *total contribution*. For example, if sales of either 10,000 units of Product *A* or 6,000 units of Product *B* could be achieved, Product *A* should be selected as this gives a total contribution of £50,000 compared with £48,000 from Product *B*.

4 If a limiting factor is in operation, the products should be ranked by the *limiting factor*. For example, assuming that the same material is used for both products, differing only in the quantity used, the contribution per unit of limiting factor should be calculated.

	Product A	Product B
	£	£
Contribution per unit	5.00	8.00
Material cost per unit	5.00	12.00
Contribution per £1 of materials	1.00	0.66

Product *A* should be selected as it gives a higher contribution per unit of limiting factor.

14.4 Ceasing an Activity

A typical examination question asks you to decide whether, on the basis of the data provided, one of the company's activities should be *ceased*. The solution to this problem is to lay out the information in the form of a *marginal cost statement*.

Activity

Benjak plc operates from one factory and manufactures 3 products. The profit and loss account for the year ended 31 December shows that Product 3 has made a loss.

Profit and loss account for the year ended 31 December

	Product 1 £	Product 2 £	Product 3 £
Sales	100,000	70,000	130,000
Direct materials	32,000	16,000	54,000
Direct labour	22,000	20,000	58,000
Variable overheads	10,000	8,000	6,000
Fixed overheads	25,000	16,000	30,000
Total costs	89,000	60,000	148,000
Profit/(loss)	11,000	10,000	(18,000)

Should Product 3 be dropped from the range? This would not affect the sales of the other products.

The solution to this question is to assume that, in the absence of information to the contrary, fixed costs will remain the same in total for the company, even if one of the products is dropped. What must be calculated is the contribution, if any, each product makes to those total fixed costs. The figures need to be redrafted to show this information.

Marginal cost statement for the year ended 31 December

	Product 1 £	Product 2 £	Product 3 £	Total £
Sales	100,000	70,000	130,000	300,000
Direct materials	32,000	16,000	54,000	102,000
Direct labour	22,000	20,000	58,000	100,000
Variable overheads	10,000	8,000	6,000	24,000
Total variable costs	64,000	44,000	118,000	226,000
Contribution	36,000	26,000	12,000	74,000
Less Total fixed costs				71,000
Profit				3,000

You can see from the marginal cost statement that Product 3 makes a contribution of £12,000 to fixed costs. If Product 3 was dropped, that contribution would be lost and the company would make a total loss of £9,000. The general rule is that if an activity makes a contribution towards fixed costs, it is worthwhile continuing. However, there are exceptions to this rule, which are examined in Chapter 15.

14.5 **Accepting a Special Order**

Deciding whether to accept a *special order* is another area where marginal costing can be helpful.

Activity

A company manufactures a product with variable costs of £8.00 per unit and a selling price of £10.50. A customer asks if they can have 2,000 units in addition to their ordinary order, but at a special price of £10.00 per unit. Should the company agree?

This problem raises complex issues on relationships with customers and the likely reaction of competitors, but from the financial point of view the solution is simple. As the variable costs of the product are £8.00, any selling price above this amount will give a contribution. The general rule is that if an activity gives a contribution, it is worthwhile undertaking. On financial grounds it is worthwhile accepting the order at the reduced selling price.

It would not make financial sense to agree to sell the product at a price less than the variable costs. To do so would mean a negative contribution. Similarly, if the company could supply the additional 2,000 units at £10.00 only by reducing its present sales at £10.50, it would be reducing its total contribution by accepting the order, and therefore should not do so.

14.6 **Making or Buying a Product**

Sometimes a business has to decide whether to *make* a product or *buy* it direct from another company. This often occurs when the item is a component which is assembled as part of another product. Marginal costing can be used to assist the decision.

Activity

A company can make a component with variable costs of £9.00 per unit or buy it from another manufacturer at £10.00 per unit. What would you advise?

If the company has idle capacity, it should make the product itself as the variable cost of £9.00 is lower than the buying price of £10.00. Fixed costs are excluded from the comparison, as it is assumed that they will continue even when factory facilities are idle. The only additional costs incurred by the company in making the component will be the £9.00 variable costs per unit. The rule that it is more profitable to manufacture if the variable costs are lower than the buying price holds true only if there is idle capacity. If the part can be made internally only by dropping production of another product, further analysis is required.

Activity

Bruton plc can make a component in 6 hours with variable costs of £10.00. The supplier's price for the component is £20.00. If Bruton decides to make the component it can do so only by sacrificing production of its main product, Keto. Keto takes 25 hours to make and has variable costs of £150.00 and a selling price of £200.00. What is the correct financial decision?

On the face of it the company should make the component since the variable costs are lower than the price at which it can be bought. However, if it makes the component the company will lose the contribution from Keto which is £50.00 for 25 hours or £2.00 per hour. The calculation is:

<table>
<tr><th colspan="2" align="center">Cost of making the component</th></tr>
<tr><td></td><td align="center">£</td></tr>
<tr><td>Variable costs</td><td>10.00</td></tr>
<tr><td>Lost contribution (6 hours @ £2.00)</td><td>12.00</td></tr>
<tr><td></td><td>22.00</td></tr>
</table>

As the supplier's price is only £20.00, it is financially more worthwhile for Bruton to buy the component rather than make it. This decision has been arrived at by bringing the lost contribution from Keto into the calculation. This is using the concept of *opportunity cost* which represents the value of the benefit given up in favour of an alternative course of action.

Practice questions

1 Z Limited manufactures three products, the selling price and cost details of which are given below:

	Product X £	Product Y £	Product Z £
Selling price per unit	75	95	95
Costs per unit:			
Direct materials (£5/kg)	10	5	15
Direct labour (£4/hour)	16	24	20
Variable overhead	8	12	10
Fixed overhead	24	36	30

In a period when direct materials are restricted in supply, the most and the least profitable uses of direct materials are

	Most profitable	Least profitable
A	X	Z
B	Y	Z
C	X	Y
D	Z	Y
E	Y	X

CIMA, Stage 2, May 1995

2 P Limited is considering whether to continue making a component or buy it from an outsider supplier. It uses 12,000 of the components each year.
The internal manufacturing cost comprises:

	£/unit
Direct materials	3.00
Direct labour	4.00
Variable overhead	1.00
Specific fixed cost	2.50
Other fixed costs	2.0
	12.50

If the direct labour were not used to manufacture the component, it would be used to increase the production of another item for which there is unlimited demand. The other item has a contribution of £10.00 per unit but requires £8.00 of labour per unit.
The maximum price per component at which buying is preferable to internal manufacture is

A	£8.00
B	£10.50
C	£12.50
D	£13.00
E	£15.50

CIMA, Stage 2, May 1996

3 M plc makes two products – M1 and M2 – budgeted details of which are as follows:

	M1	M2
	£	**£**
Selling price	10.00	8.00
Costs per unit:		
Direct materials	2.50	3.00
Direct labour	1.50	1.00
Variable overhead	0.60	0.40
Fixed overhead	1.20	1.00
Profit per unit	4.20	2.60

Budgeted production and sales for the year ended 31 December 1998 are:

Product M1   10,000 units
Product M2   12,500 units

The fixed overhead shown above comprises both general and specific fixed overhead costs. The general fixed overhead cost has been attributed to units of M1 and M2 on the basis of direct labour cost.

The specific fixed cost totals £2,500 per annum and relates to product M2 only.

Both products are available from an external supplier. If M plc could purchase only one of them, the maximum price which should be paid per unit of M1 or M2 instead of internal manufacture would be

	M1 **£**	*M2* **£**
A	4.60	4.40
B	4.60	4.60
C	5.80	4.40
D	5.80	4.60
E	5.80	5.60

If only product M1 were to be made, the number of units to be sold to achieve a profit of £50,000 per annum (to the nearest unit) would be

A 4,074.
B 4,537.
C 13,333.
D 13,796.
E none of the above.

CIMA, Stage 2, November 1997

4 The following details relate to products made by K Limited:

	L **£**	*M* **£**	*N* **£**
Selling price per unit	60	85	88
Direct materials per unit	15	20	30
Direct labour per unit	10	15	10
Variable overhead per unit	5	8	10
Fixed overhead per unit	10	16	20
	40	59	70
Profit per unit	20	26	18

All three products use the same direct labour and direct materials, but in different quantities.

In a period when the material used on these products is in short supply, the most and least profitable use of the material is

	Most profitable	Least profitable
A	N	L
B	N	M
C	L	M
D	M	L
E	M	N

CIMA, Stage 2, November 1996

5 Z plc manufactures three products which have the following selling prices and costs per unit:

	Z1 £	Z2 £	Z3 £
Selling price	15.00	18.00	17.00
Costs per unit:			
Direct materials	4.00	5.00	10.00
Direct labour	2.00	4.00	1.80
Overhead:			
Variable	1.00	2.00	0.90
Fixed	4.50	3.00	1.35
	11.50	14.00	14.05
Profit per unit	3.50	4.00	2.95

All three products use the same type of labour.
In a period in which labour is in short supply, the rank order of production is:

	Z1	Z2	Z3
A	1st	2nd	3rd
B	3rd	2nd	1st
C	2nd	1st	3rd
D	1st	3rd	2nd
E	2nd	3rd	1st

CIMA, Stage 2, November 1997

15 Break-even Analysis

15.1 Introduction

Break-even analysis is concerned with predicting costs, volume and profit as the level of activity changes. The theory of break-even analysis is derived from the principles of *marginal costing* and the assumptions and definitions of fixed and variable costs and their behaviours discussed in earlier chapters are used. Break-even analysis can be conducted by constructing a chart or applying a formula. A *break-even chart* shows the approximate profit or loss at different levels of activity. A formula is frequently used to calculate the *break-even point* which is the level of activity at which the company makes neither profit nor loss, but breaks even.

Because break-even analysis uses assumptions of cost behaviour, it has some *limitations*. One of the most important limitations is that fixed and variable costs change their behaviour over a certain range of activity. For example, if production is doubled more factory space will be required with an increase in the associated fixed costs. Variable costs may also be affected if, for example, the company enters into bulk-buying of materials at a discount.

The identification of the break-even point is not the sole purpose of break-even analysis. The behaviour of costs and profits at various levels of activity is of great importance to management and this information can be provided through the use of break-even analysis. However, the term *cost–volume–profit (CVP) analysis* is often preferred because it emphasises the changes in relationships at different levels of activity. In this chapter we use the terms 'break-even analysis', but you should be aware of the alternative term.

15.2 Constructing a Break-even Chart

All costs must be divided into their fixed and variable elements and some appropriate measure of activity must be selected. If possible, the unit of output should be used, although percentages of total capacity or other measures may have to be adopted. With information on fixed and variable costs, selling price and volumes, a *break-even chart* can be constructed, as in the following activity.

Activity

A company manufactures a single product with a maximum production capacity of 2,000 units. The variable costs incurred are £5.00 per unit; the product sells at £10.00 each. During the financial period the fixed costs are £5,000. Construct a break-even chart.

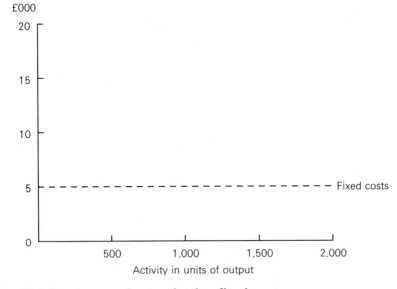

Fig. 15.1 Break-even chart – plotting fixed costs

The first stage is to draw on graph paper the horizontal axis marked with the levels of activity and the vertical axis with values in £ for costs and revenues. The first line can then be drawn, which is the fixed cost line. Fixed costs are the same whatever the level of activity, so the line will be parallel to the horizontal axis. In this example the fixed costs are £5,000 at nil output and the same figure at 2,000 units (see Figure 15.1).

Variable costs must now be added to the fixed costs to give a *total cost line*. By drawing up a simple table, the total costs for different activity levels can be calculated and plotted on the graph:

Units £	Fixed costs £	Variable costs £	Total costs £
0	5,000	0	5,000
500	5,000	2,500	7,500
1,000	5,000	5,000	10,000
1,500	5,000	7,500	12,500
2,000	5,000	10,000	15,000

You can see from the table that at nil activity the total costs are equal to the fixed costs as no variable costs have been incurred. When plotting the total costs on the graph only two points need be plotted, those at nil activity and maximum activity, as the total cost line is a straight line. At this stage you may prefer to plot all the points calculated to minimise the possibility of error (see Figure 15.2).

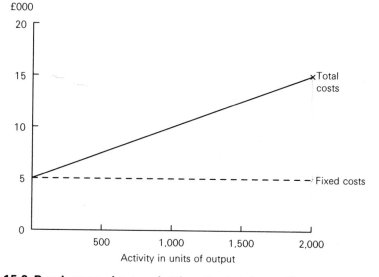

Fig. 15.2 Break-even chart – plotting the total cost line

The final stage is to plot the revenue line. At nil activity there is no revenue. At 2,000 units activity is 2,000 × £10.00 per unit £20,000. The point at which the total cost line and revenue line intersect is the *break-even point*, which is the level of activity where neither profit nor loss is made – in this instance 1,000 units (see Figure 15.3).

Fig. 15.3 Break-even chart – plotting the revenue line

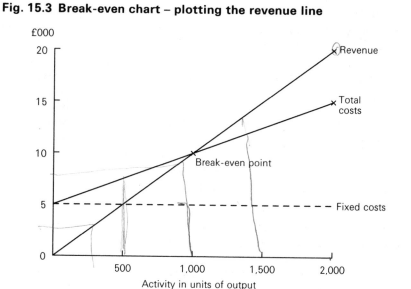

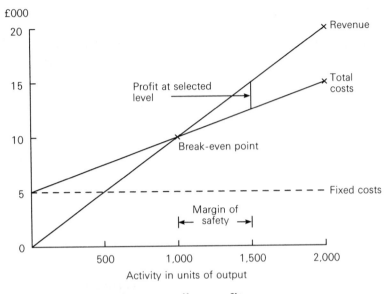

Fig. 15.4 Break-even chart – reading profit

At this stage, a small calculation can be made to prove that the break-even point is 1,000 units:

	£	£
Revenue (1,000 units @ £10.00)		10,000
Fixed costs	5,000	
Variable costs (1,000 @ £5.00)	5,000	10,000
Profit/(loss)		0

If we want to know what the profit is at a selected level of activity, the figure can be read from the graph. If the selected level of activity is 1,500 units, the total costs at this level are £12,500 and the revenue is £15,000. The profit figure of £2,500 is obtained by deducting the total costs from revenue (see Figure 15.4).

The difference in activity levels between the break-even point and the selected level of activity is known as the *margin of safety*. In this example, the margin of safety is 500 units – in other words, the company can drop 500 units from the selected level of activity before it starts to enter a loss.

Self-check question

What is the margin of safety?

15.3 Using Formulae

You will have realised from the last example that constructing a break-even chart can lead to some inaccuracies because of the lack of precision in drawing the chart. Instead of drawing a chart, *formulae* can be used to calculate the answers. The formulae in this section are for an organisation with a single product or an unvarying mix of sales and they are applied to the data given in section 15.2.

The break-even point can be expressed either in terms of units or sales value. To find the break-even point in units, the first stage is to calculate the contribution per unit:

	£
Selling price per unit	10.00
Variable costs per unit	5.00
Contribution per unit	5.00

The formula is:

$$\text{Break-even point} = \frac{\text{Fixed costs}}{\text{Contribution per unit}}$$

Inserting the figures into the formula:

$$\frac{£5,000}{£5.00} = 1,000 \text{ units}$$

Although this is the same answer as we arrived at by constructing the break-even chart, you can see that with more complex figures a greater degree of accuracy can be achieved by using the formula.

It may be that you want to know what the level of sales must be to break even. One way to do this is to multiply the number of units at break-even point by the selling price per unit. With 1,000 units selling at £10.00 each a total sales value of £10,000 would have to be achieved to break even.

Another method is to use the following formula:

$$\text{Sales value at break-even point} = \frac{\text{Total fixed cost} \times \text{Sales value}}{\text{Total contribution}}$$

The amounts for sales value and contribution can be at the maximum level of activity, or per unit, or any other level. The formula is based on the profit/volume ratio which we discussed in Chapter 13:

$$\frac{\text{Contribution}}{\text{Selling price}}$$

Inserting the figures into the formula:

$$\frac{£5,000 \times £10.00}{£5.00} = £10,000$$

Once the formulae for calculating the break-even point are understood, it is simple to calculate any other level of activity. In the examples above we have been attempting to find the level of activity which will allow recovery of the fixed costs. If we wish to recover more than the fixed costs – i.e. to have some profit – the formula is:

$$\text{Selected level of activity} = \frac{\text{Fixed costs} + \text{Target profit}}{\text{Contribution per unit}}$$

If the business wants to make a profit of £2,500, the level of activity will be:

$$\frac{£5,000 + £2,500}{£5.00} = 1,500 \text{ units}$$

Or in terms of sales value:

$$\frac{£7,500 \times £10.00}{£5.00} = £15,000$$

15.4 Limitations of Break-even Analysis

Although break-even analysis can be a useful tool, it has a number of *limitations* which affect its value. These disadvantages can be grouped under three broad headings:

- *Measuring activity* – If the company is manufacturing a single, identifiable product, the *measure of activity* is simply the unit of output. Frequently this situation does not exist and alternative measures must be found. If there are a number of products, direct labour hours may be used as a measure of activity, although this raises problems of plotting the revenue line. If the sales mix is constant, activity may be usefully measured in £ of sales.
- *Managerial decisions* – Although costs may be identified as fixed or variable, management can take *decisions* which will affect this division. Labour is often regarded as a variable cost, but in times of temporary shortages of work, management may determine to retain labour at their normal pay rates so that the workforce is available when business picks up. Such a policy makes labour a fixed cost. Another example of the impact of managerial decision-making is the change to subcontract services. If a company provides its own service internally – for example, computer services – there will be a high element of fixed cost. If management decides to scrap its own service and hire outside services, it becomes primarily a variable cost.
- *The relevant range* – The assumptions made about cost behaviour hold true only within a certain limited range of activity, known as the *relevant range*. Outside this range, variable costs may not give a straight line – for example, labour may be working overtime at enhanced pay rates, thus

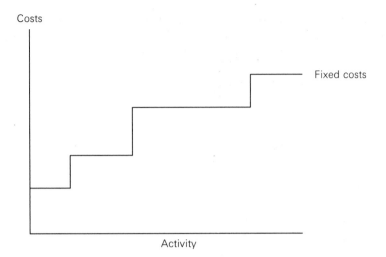

Fig. 15.5 Possible fixed cost behaviour

causing variable costs to develop a curve; direct materials may be purchased at a discount once the company exceeds a certain order limit. Fixed costs may change at different levels of activity. Over the entire range of activity a company can achieve some of the fixed costs are likely to increase incrementally. For example, an increase in production may require larger stores facilities and greater maintenance provision with higher fixed costs.

Figure 15.5 shows how costs can behave over the complete range of activities and decisions should be made concerning those levels of activity only within the relevant range. Within this range, it is assumed that costs will behave in the predicted fashion.

Self-check question

What is the relevant range?

15.5 Alternative Break-even Charts

The break-even charts constructed so far in this chapter are often referred to as traditional break-even charts. The fixed line is plotted first and the variable costs are added to this to plot the total cost line. There are alternatives to this chart which use the same underlying principles and data, but present the information in a different way.

The *contribution break-even chart* is designed so that the contribution figure at various levels of activity can be read easily. The variable costs are plotted first and the fixed costs added to them to give the total cost line. The

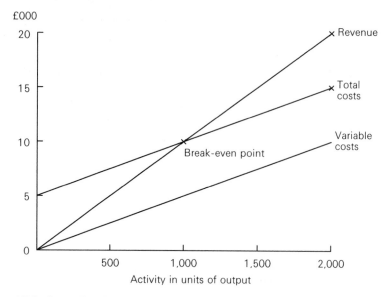

Fig. 15.6 Contribution break-even chart

Fig. 15.7 Profit chart

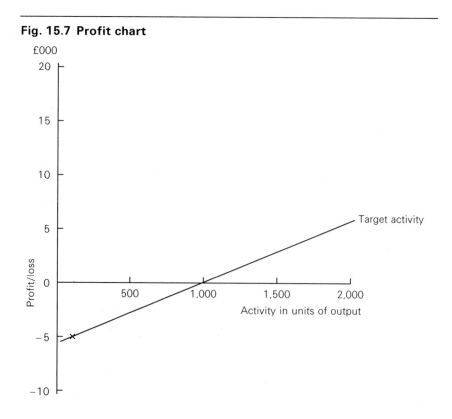

difference between the variable cost line and the income line represents the contribution wedge. In Figure 15.6, the same figures are used as in the previous examples in this chapter.

Profit may be the most significant figure for management, but in the two variations of the break-even chart examined, profit can be calculated only by reading the income and total costs figures and making a deduction. The *profit chart* concentrates upon profit and the fixed, variable and total cost lines are not shown. The horizontal axis shows the levels of activity, but the vertical axis shows profits and losses. The profit line is drawn from zero activity, where losses must be equal to fixed costs, and through the break-even point.

Practice questions

1 The following statistics have been taken from the information system of PZ Limited for the last five years:

	1990	1991	1992	1993	1994
Activity index	100	98	101	103	106
Cost index	100	105	109	113	115
Total costs (£)	70,000	73,080	76,518	79,778	81,880
Sales (£)	100,000				
Profit (£)	30,000				

Notes:
1 The activity index measures the volume of sales/production.
2 The cost index is representative of the costs incurred by PZ Limited and measures the effects of inflation on costs over the 5-year period.
3 The activity index for 1995 is forecast as 110.
4 The cost index for 1995 is forecast as 117.

REQUIREMENTS:
(a) (i) Calculate, using the high and low points method, the forecast fixed and variable costs of PZ Limited for 1995.

(8 marks)

(ii) Prepare a break-even chart for 1995, assuming that selling prices will be 20% higher than those of 1990.

(10 marks)

(b) Comment critically on the use of the high and low points method to separate fixed and variable costs.

(7 marks)

(Total marks = 25)

CIMA, Stage 2, November 1995

2 H Limited manufactures and sells two products – J and K. Annual sales are expected to be in the ratio of J:1 K:3. Total annual sales are planned to be £420,000. Product J has a contribution to sales ratio of 40% whereas that of product K is 50%. Annual fixed costs are estimated to be £120,000.

The budgeted breakeven sales value (to the nearest £1,000)

A   is £196,000.
B   is £200,000.
C   is £253,000.
D   is £255,000.
E   cannot be determined from the above data.

CIMA, Stage 2, May 1995

3 A Limited makes a single product which it sells for £10 per unit. Fixed costs are £48,000 per month and the product has a contribution to sales ratio of 40%.
In a period when actual sales were £140,000, A Limited's margin of safety, in units, was

A 2,000.   **B** 6,000.   **C** 8,000.   **D** 12,000.   **E** 14,000.

CIMA, Stage 2, November 1995

4 Z plc operates a single retail outlet selling direct to the public. Profit statements for August and September 1996 are as follows:

	August £	September £
Sales	80,000	90,000
Cost of sales	50,000	55,000
Gross profit	30,000	35,000
Less:		
Selling and distribution	8,000	9,000
Administration	15,000	15,000
Net profit	7,000	11,000

REQUIREMENTS:
(a) Use the high and low points technique to identify the behaviour of
  (i)   Cost of sales,
  (ii) Selling and distribution costs, and
  (iii) Administration costs.

(4 marks)

(b) Using the graph paper provided, draw a contribution break even chart and identify the monthly break even sales value, and area of contribution.

(10 marks)

(c) Assuming a margin of safety equal to 30% of the break even value, calculate Z plc's annual profit.

(2 marks)

(d) Z plc is now considering opening another retail outlet selling the same products. Z plc plans to use the same profit margins in both outlets and has estimated that the specific fixed costs of the second outlet will be £100,000 per annum.
Z plc also expects that 10% of its annual sales from its existing outlet would transfer to this second outlet if it were to be opened.

REQUIREMENT:
Calculate the annual value of sales required from the new outlet in order to achieve the same annual profit as previously obtained from the single outlet.

(5 marks)

(e) Briefly describe the cost accounting requirements of organisations of this type.

(4 marks)
(Total marks = 25)

CIMA, Stage 2, November 1996

16 Absorption Costing and Marginal Costing Compared

16.1 Introduction

Absorption costing, which we discussed in Chapter 7, is a technique which charges fixed costs to products or cost units. The fixed overheads are either allocated or apportioned to cost centres. An *overhead absorption rate* is then used to charge the production cost centre costs to the cost units passing through them. Although the process is arbitrary, the result is that a cost unit is charged with what is deemed to be a fair share of the fixed overhead.

Marginal costing, which we discussed in Chapter 14, is concerned with the way that costs behave when there are changes in activity levels. Costs are divided into variable and fixed costs. Only variable costs are charged to the cost units and the contribution is calculated by deducting the variable costs from the revenue. Fixed costs are regarded as *period costs* unaffected by changes in the level of activity. The fixed costs are deducted from the total contribution for a period to arrive at the profit or loss for the period.

Both techniques have *advantages* and *disadvantages*. In addition, both absorption costing and marginal costing can have a significant impact on the *valuation of stock* and the reporting of *period profits*, and we examine these aspects in this chapter.

16.2 Main Features of the Techniques

A comparison of the main features of the two costing techniques permits a fuller discussion of their respective advantages and disadvantages. The main features of *absorption costing* are:

- All costs are charged to the cost unit, and a profit can be ascertained for each unit.
- The total profit is equal to the sum of the profits from the individual cost units.
- As output changes, the total cost per unit changes because fixed costs are spread over the different number of units.
- The valuation of work in progress (WIP) and finished stock includes a share of fixed costs and are therefore valued at full production cost.

The main features of *marginal costing* are:

- Only variable costs are charged to each cost unit and the contribution is ascertained for each unit.
- The total profit is equal to the total contribution less the fixed costs for the period.
- As output changes the variable costs and contribution per unit are constant.
- The valuation of WIP and finished stock is at variable production cost; there is no inclusion of any fixed cost.

Self-check question

What are the main features of absorption and marginal costing?

16.3 **Main Arguments for Using Each Technique**

The following list of arguments in favour of absorption costing must be balanced by the subsequent list in favour of marginal costing. It is important to remember that absorption costing is not necessarily 'better' than marginal costing, or vice versa. Although some practitioners assert that one technique is superior to another, it is a matter of examining the circumstances in each case.

The main arguments for using *absorption costing* are as follows:

- Fixed costs represent a sacrifice to ensure production can take place and therefore should be included.
- Changes in production level, particularly when they are significant, have an impact on fixed costs, and decisions should take this into account.
- In the long term, fixed costs must be recovered for the organisation to make a profit; and concentrating on recovering the variable cost per unit may obscure this fact.
- Writing off fixed costs in the period in which they incur can lead to the reporting of losses, but the company may have been producing goods for stock for sale later in the year, such as seasonal products for Christmas. Therefore, a proportion of the fixed costs should be included in the stock valuation to give a more accurate representation.
- When capital expenditure is high, no knowledge of true product profitability can be ascertained unless fixed costs are included.
- The separation of costs into their fixed and variable elements is not always possible.
- *Statement of Standard Accounting Practice 9, Stock Valuation*, recommends absorption costing for stock valuation for financial accounts.

The main arguments for using *marginal costing* are as follows:

- Fixed costs are a period cost rather than a product cost; therefore they should be written off in the period in which they occur.
- Production impacts only on variable costs and therefore this is where the concentration should be.
- Pricing decisions are improved, because management can determine the level at which a contribution is made.
- Changes in volume of activity do not affect the unit cost as only variable costs are involved and there is no spreading of fixed costs.
- Underabsorption or overabsorption of overheads does not arise.
- The arbitrary apportionment of fixed costs is avoided.

Self-check question

What are the main arguments for using absorption and marginal costing?

16.4 Valuation of Stock Using the Two Techniques

If there is no stock or no change in stock levels at the beginning and end of a period, the two techniques give the same figure of profit for the period. If there are changes in the stock levels, the *valuation of stock* differs between absorption and marginal costing, and this is reflected in the period profit figure.

Activity

Fion Ltd manufactures a product, Edita, which has a selling price of £6.00 each. For the month of January the figures are:

Total number of units manufactured	10,000
Total number of units sold	9,000
Production costs:	
Variable costs	£25,000
Fixed	£10,000
Fixed selling costs	£16,000

Calculate the profit for January using the two techniques.

You need to start by drawing up an *absorption cost statement*. You will remember that in absorption costing fixed costs are charged to products or cost units. The fixed overheads are either allocated or apportioned to cost centres. An overhead absorption rate is then used to charge the production cost centre costs to the cost units passing through them:

Absorption cost statement for the month of January

	£	£
Sales		54,000
Production costs:		
Variable	25,000	
Fixed	10,000	
		35,000
Less Closing stock	3,500	31,500
Gross profit		22,500
Less Fixed selling costs		16,000
Profit		6,500

In absorption costing the value of the closing stock is calculated by multiplying the number of units by the total cost of each unit. The total cost consists of fixed and variable costs, so the total production cost of one unit is £35,000 divided by 10,000 units.

Next, you need to draw up a *marginal cost statement*, using the same data. You will remember that only variable costs are charged to the cost units and the contribution is calculated by deducting the variable costs from the revenue. Fixed costs are deducted from the total contribution for a period to arrive at the profit or loss for the period:

Marginal cost statement for the month of January

	£	£
Sales		54,000
Variable costs of production	25,000	
Less Closing stock	2,500	22,500
Contribution		31,500
Less Fixed costs for period:		
Production	10,000	
Selling	16,000	26,000
Profit		5,500

In marginal costing, the value of the closing stock is calculated by multiplying the number of units (1,000) by the variable cost per unit only (£2.50). This is found by dividing the variable costs of production of £25,000 by the total number of units produced of 10,000.

In absorption costing a proportion of the fixed costs incurred in January is transferred to the following period in the stock valuation, whereas in marginal costing the total of the fixed costs are charged to production in the period in which they are incurred. If at the end of a period there is an increase in the stock held by the company, the reported profit will be higher under absorption costing because of the treatment of fixed costs than under marginal costing. Over a long period of time, total profits for the company will be the same under absorption costing and marginal costing because total costs will be the same. It is the profit for the separate accounting periods which will differ.

Practice question

1 When comparing the profits reported under marginal and absorption costing during a period when the level of stocks increased,

A absorption costing profits will be higher and closing stock valuations lower than those under marginal costing.

B absorption costing profits will be higher and closing stock valuations higher than those under marginal costing.

C marginal costing profits will be higher and clsoing stock valuations lower than those under absorption costing.

D marginal costing profits will be lower and closing stock valuations higher than those under absorption costing.

E there is no difference in the profit report or the valuation of closing stock between the two systems.

CIMA, Stage 2, May 1996

17 Budgetary Control

17.1 Introduction

Managers are concerned for the future success of their company. Therefore, they need to assess the challenges and opportunities facing them and set goals. These are usually expressed in financial terms. They also need to monitor the progress of the organisation towards these goals and take action to improve performance or revise goals if they have become unrealistic. Known formally as *budgetary control,* this is the process by which financial control can be exercised within an organisation, using predetermined *budgets* for income and expenditure for each function of the organisation.

A budget is a financial or quantitative statement prepared in advance of a specified accounting period. These budgets are compared with actual performance to establish any variances, so that individual managers can remedy any divergence from the plan or revise the plan if necessary. The budget normally gives the income and/or the expenditure, including any capital expenditure, needed during a financial period to achieve the given objective. The period of time for which the budget is intended is known as the *budget period* and the budget must be prepared and approved before this period of time. Managers normally consider their plans and objectives over a long time of, say, 5 years. These long-range plans are broken down into periods of 1 year and budgets drawn up in detail, normally subdivided into months, so that monitoring and control can be conducted.

Budgets are drawn up showing the income or expenditure for individual functions of the organisation – for example, sales budget, production budget. As well as these functional budgets there are budgets for capital expenditure, stock holdings and cash flow. All the budgets are interrelated and incorporated into a *master budget* which consists of the budgeted operating statements and balance sheet.

In all but the smallest of organisations, budgetary control is a major technique for *planning and control.* Individual function managers are made responsible for the controllable activities within their budgets and are expected to take action to remedy unacceptable adverse variances. There are very few managers who do not encounter a budgetary control system during their career. Budgetary control is used in service and manufacturing businesses, as well as not-for-profit organisations. Apart from the government's budgets, some of the most publicly announced budgets are those of major films, where even the credits at the end of the film give the name of the accountant.

In this chapter, we discuss the purpose of budgetary control and describe the budgetary control process and the interrelationship of budgets. We then go on to examine the main requirements of an effective budgetary control system, together with the advantages and disadvantages of budgetary control.

17.2 **Purpose of Budgetary Control**

The overall *purpose* of budgetary control is to help managers to plan and control the use of resources. However, there are a number of other, more specific, purposes:

- A formal system of budgetary control enables an organisation to carry out its planning in a systematic and logical manner.
- Control can be achieved only by setting a plan of what is to be accomplished in a specified time period and managers regularly monitoring progress against the plan, taking corrective action where necessary.
- By setting plans, the activities of the various functions and departments can be coordinated. For example, the production manager can ensure that the correct quantity is manufactured to meet the requirements of the sales team, or the accountant can obtain sufficient funding to make adequate resources available to carry out the task, whether this is looking after children in care or running a railway network.
- A budgetary control system is a communication system which informs managers of the objectives of the organisation and the constraints under which it is operating. The regular monitoring of performance helps keep management informed of the progress of the organisation towards its objectives.
- By communicating detailed targets to individual managers, motivation is improved. Without a clear sense of direction, managers will become demotivated.
- By setting separate plans for individual departments and functions, managers are clear about their responsibilities. This allows them to make decisions, as long as they are within their budget responsibilities, and avoids the need for every decision to be made at the top level.
- By comparing actual activity for a particular period of time with the original plan any variance (difference), expressed in financial terms, is identified. This enables managers to assess their performance and decide what corrective action, if any, needs to be taken.
- By predicting future events, managers are encouraged to collect all the relevant information, analyse it and make decisions in good time.
- An organisation is made up of a number of individuals with their own ambitions and goals. The budgetary control process allows these individual goals to be modified and integrated with the overall objectives of the organisation. Thus, it encourages consensus. Managers can see how their personal aims fit into the overall context and how they might be achieved.

Activity

Give an example of a budget.

A *cash flow forecast* is a good example of a budget. You will have met this if you have done financial accounting. A cash flow forecast is a statement which shows the amount of cash which is expected to come in and go out during some period in the future. It is usually drawn up for each month over a 12-month period, and shows the monthly cash inflows and outflows, as well as the net cash flows and the cumulative cash position. A cash flow forecast is not a tool for control because it is only a plan. In order to achieve control, comparison must be made with the actual figures.

17.3 **The Budgetary Control Process**

The *process* of preparing budgets for each of the functions and other activities in an organisation and drawing up a master budget can take a number of months. During preparation of the budgets it is important to identify any *limiting factor* or *principal budget factor*, and to ensure the best coordination of the various functions. A limiting factor, as we saw in Chapter 14, is a factor – such as a shortage of materials or inadequate plant capacity – that prevents the company from achieving higher levels of performance in the budget period, and decisions must be taken at an early stage to minimise the impact of any limiting factor. Once a limiting factor has been identified and individual functional budgets are being set, it is important to ensure that coordination of functions takes place. It would not make sense, for example, to set a sales budget with a sales volume in excess of existing plant capacity, unless decisions were made on improving capacity, subcontracting work or cutting back on the sales budget.

Self-check question

What is a limiting factor or principal budget factor?

It is essential that budgetary control and the preparation of budgets is not regarded as the sole responsibility of the accounting function. The whole management team should be involved, with the accounting function normally providing a coordinating role and providing quantitative and financial data when needed. A *budget committee* may be formed, made up of the functional or departmental managers and chaired by the chief executive. The management accountant usually occupies the role of committee secretary, and he or she coordinates and assists in the preparation of the budget data provided by each manager. The budget committee reviews the budgets submitted by individual managers and ensures that each has the following characteristics:

- The budget conforms to the policies formulated by the owners or directors.
- It shows how the objectives are going to be achieved and recognises any constraints under which the organisation will be operating.
- It is realistic.
- It integrates with the other budgets.
- It reflects the responsibilities of the manager concerned.

If a budget does not display all these characteristics, it will need to be revised. This may affect other budgets and there may need to be negotiations between the managers concerned to introduce the necessary budget changes. When the budgets have been approved by the budget committee, they are submitted to the directors for approval prior to the commencement of the budget period. If the directors accept the budget, it is then adopted by the organisation as a whole and becomes the working plan.

The budgets must be communicated to managers before the start of the appropriate financial period, called the *budget period*, so that they know what the plans are for their own departments and can implement them. Some organisations adopt the top-down approach to budget-setting: the owners or directors decide the individual plans for each department and function, and these plans are given to the individual managers to implement. Other organisations use the bottom-up approach to budget-setting: individual managers construct their own budgets which are given to the owners or directors who coordinate the individual budgets into a master budget. These are the two extremes and most organisations fall somewhere between the two, often with functional heads identifying possible targets in broad terms at an early stage and the board considering these before detailed budgets are constructed.

If there is no formal system of planning and control in an organisation, there will be an informal system. In small organisations, managers may be responsible for all the stages. In larger organisations, there is probably a formal system with a greater division of responsibility at each stage. Assumptions and predictions are normally made at board level following consultation throughout the organisation.

Collecting information to measure actual performance is part of the accounting function and accountants are also responsible for issuing financial statements which compare the actual performance with the plan. At this stage most managers find that they have a role in explaining any differences which have taken place between the plan and actual, and suggesting the appropriate course to pursue.

17.4 **Interrelationship of Budgets**

Budgets are drawn up for individual departments and functions (for example, the sales budget and the production budget), as well as for capital expenditure, stock holding and cash flow. Although budgets for such activities as research and administration are not totally connected to the other budgets, they must be kept within limits directed by general policy. All the budgets are interrelated and incorporated into a *master budget*, which includes a budgeted profit and loss account and balance sheet. Figure 17.1 shows the interrelationship of budgets in a simple organisation.

Fig. 17.1 Interrelationship of budgets

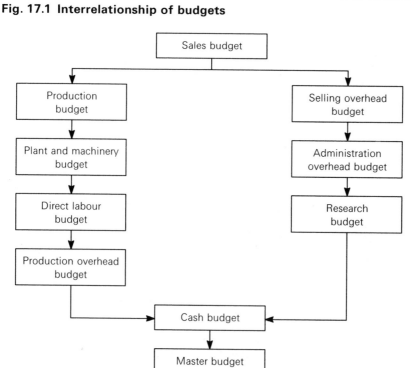

Notes:

1 The *sales budget* is set first and shows what quantities can be sold and at what price.
2 The production budget is based on the sales budget, but policy changes on stock levels could lead to volume changes compared to the sales budget.
3 The *production budget* may reveal immediate plant shortages which have to be incorporated into a capital expenditure budget. A capital expenditure budget is required on a long-term basis in any event.
4 General policies dictate the limits of *administration budgets* and *research budgets*, but they bear some relationship to the sales budget.
5 The individual budgets are assembled and incorporated into the *master budget*.

The following activity shows how the budgets are linked.

Activity

Portalight Ltd manufactures torches. The sales director has estimated that the following quantities will be sold over the next 6 months:

	January	February	March	April	May	June
Sales	1,000	1,200	1,500	1,600	1,600	1,750

The production department will manufacture the torches in the month before the sales take place and it has been agreed that a buffer stock of 200 torches will be maintained. On 1 December there is a stock of 100 torches. How many torches must the production department manufacture each month?

The best way to tackle this problem is to draw up a table giving all the information:

	December	January	February	March	April	May	June
Opening stock	100	1,200	1,400	1,700	1,800	1,800	1,950
Production	1,100	1,200	1,500	1,600	1,600	1,750	
Sales		1,000	1,200	1,500	1,600	1,600	1,750
Closing stock	1,200	1,400	1,700	1,800	1,800	1,950	

Having calculated the number of torches which must be produced, we need to consider the decisions that the production manager now take and which budgets will be affected. The most immediate decisions concern whether there is sufficient machine capacity to make the torches and whether there is sufficient labour. It may be that more machines and labour are required in the busy months and more space will be required in the factory; therefore all these budgets will be affected. The accountant will be concerned with the cash requirements for any changes and will want to ensure that the implications of these decisions are shown in the cash budget. It is because of the interrelated nature of budgets that a change in any one can affect all the other budgets.

17.5 Main Requirements of an Effective Budgetary Control System

Sometimes management implements a system of budgetary control, but becomes disillusioned with it: the disadvantages seem to outweigh the advantages. There is no single model of a perfect budgetary control system, and each organisation needs a system that meets its own particular needs. However, the following list shows the main requirements for an *effective system of budgetary control*:

- A sound and clearly defined organisation with the managers' responsibilities clearly indicated.
- Effective accounting records and procedures which are understood and applied.
- Strong support and the commitment of senior managers to the system of budgetary control.
- The education and training of managers in the development, interpretation and use of budgets.
- The revision of the original budgets where circumstances show that amendments are required to make them appropriate and useful.
- The recognition throughout the organisation that budgetary control is a management activity and not an accounting exercise.
- An information system which provides data for managers so that they can make realistic predictions.
- The correct integration of budgets and their effective communication to managers.
- The setting of budgets which are reasonable and achievable.
- The participation of managers in the budgetary control system.

Self-check question

What are the main requirements of an effective system of budgetary control?

17.6 Advantages and Disadvantages of Budgetary Control

When an organisation has an effective budgetary control system, internal planning and control should be improved, which must be a considerable advantage.

Activity

What other advantages might there be and what are the disadvantages of a budgetary control system?

The main *advantages* are as follows:

- Decisions are based on the examination of future problems in sufficient time for the organisation to take corrective action.
- With clearly defined objectives and the monitoring of achievement, motivation of the entire management team is improved.
- Plans can be reviewed regularly in the light of changing circumstances and can be amended where appropriate.
- The resources of the organisation are given the fullest and most economical use.
- The activities of all the various functions in the organisation are properly coordinated.
- Capital and effort are put to the most profitable use.

There are, however, quite a number of potential drawbacks with a budgetary control system; how damaging they are depends on the way the system is operated. The main *disadvantages* are as follows:

- The process of drawing up budgets is time-consuming and managers may be deflected from their prime responsibilities of running the organisation.
- The future is always uncertain and budgets may be unrealistic. This can lead to poor control and the disillusionment of managers.
- Budgets may be imposed by top management with no consultation; consequently managers may feel demotivated.
- Managers may consider the budgets as 'being set in stone' and instead of taking effective and sensible decisions when the circumstances warrant it, may be constrained by the original budget

---

Practice questions

1 The following details have been extracted from the debtor collection records of C Limited:

Invoices paid in the month after sale	60%
Invoices paid in the second month after sale	25%
Invoices paid in the third month after sale	12%
Bad debts	3%

Invoices are issued on the last day of each month.
  Customers paying in the month after sale are entitled to deduct a 2% settlement discount.
  Credit sales values for June to September 1995 are budgeted as follows:

June	July	August	September
£35,000	£40,000	£60,000	£45,000

The amount budgeted to be received from credit sales in September 1995 is

A £47,280. **B** £47,680. **C** £48,850. **D** £49,480. **E** £50,200.

CIMA, Stage 2, May 1995

2 The following extract is taken from the production cost budget of S Limited:

Production (units)	2,000	3,000
Production cost (£)	11,100	12,900

The budget cost allowance for an activity level of 4,000 units is

A £7,200.
B £14,700.
C £17,200.
D £22,200.
E none of these values.

CIMA, Stage 2, May 1995

18 Budgets

18.1 Introduction

Management may prepare *budgets* for the organisation as a whole and for particular aspects of it. There may be budgets for *functions* such as production, cash, capital expenditure, personnel and for other activities. Despite the apparent differences in the nature of the activities, the basic principles in setting and operating the budgets are the same. The plans and policies established by the owners and directors must be converted into detailed plans covering all aspects of the organisation's activities. These are normally broken down on a monthly basis for a year or a longer period. Initially the plans may be in quantitative terms – for example, the number of products to be made or the quantity of materials to be ordered. However, they will be converted into financial terms to form the *budgetary control system*. Next, the detailed plans must be translated into actions for each manager to pursue.

Most plans cover a period of 1 year, although activities such as capital expenditure and research may be for 5 years or longer. For effective monitoring and control the annual budget plans are divided into shorter, usually monthly, periods. This is known as *phasing the budget*. Normally it is insufficient to take the annual figure and divide by 12 to give the monthly figures, as most businesses experience peaks and troughs during the year which need to be reflected in the monthly budget figures.

In this chapter, we start by explaining how *variance analysis* is conducted. Next we look at *cash budgets* and *production budgets*. This is followed by a discussion of the difference between *fixed budgets* and *flexible budgets*.

18.2 Variance Analysis

Variance analysis is the investigation of the factors which have caused the differences between the actual figures and the budgeted figures. The differences are known as *variances*. Actual progress is measured from the beginning of the budget period, which is usually a year. Each month, the actual figures are compared with the plan and reported to the managers responsible.

If the actual costs are lower than the budgeted costs, there will be a *favourable variance*, and this will result in a higher final profit. But if the actual costs are higher than the budgeted costs, the variance is known as an *adverse variance*, which will result in a lower profit. As well as *cost variances*, there may also be *income variances*. If actual income is higher than budgeted income, there will be a favourable variance and this will result in a higher final profit. On the other hand, if actual income is lower than budgeted income, there will be an adverse variance which will result in a lower final profit. Adverse variance figures are usually shown in brackets.

The following example shows the key information contained in a budget report. This report is for one period only, but in many companies the monthly budget report gives the figures for the entire year divided into months, the actual figures to date and a cumulative column which shows the actual totals compared with the budget totals for the year to date.

Budget report for the month of January

	Budget £	Actual £	Variance £
Income:			
Product *A*	25,000	24,500	(500)
Product *B*	18,000	17,200	(800)
Product *C*	19,000	19,600	600
Total income	62,000	61,300	(700)
Costs:			
Salaries	28,400	29,000	(600)
Expenses	12,500	12,000	500
Administration	1,800	1,700	100
Miscellaneous	700	300	400
Total costs	43,400	43,000	400
Profit	18,600	18,300	(300)

Self-check question

What is the purpose of variance analysis?

18.3 Cash Budgets

Cash is the most essential resource of a business. Without sufficient cash, a business will be unable to operate. An excess of cash means that there is inefficiency and a subsequent impairment of profitability. Even small companies without a budgetary control system will have some form of *cash budget*. A cash budget shows the cash (including cheques) coming into the organisation and the cash going out. The cash coming in is known as *positive cash flow* and the cash going out is known as *negative cash flow*. The difference between these two flows is known as the *net cash flow*.

Activity

Jane Castle starts a small business called Trek-Kit selling outdoor leisure clothing with £5,000 savings she has in the bank. The sales and purchases for the first 3 months are as follows:

	Sales £	Purchases £
January	10,000	5,000
February	12,000	6,000
March	18,000	9,000

Jane has to pay for the purchases in the month in which they are made. Of her sales, 50% of the customers pay cash and the remainder pay in the month following the month of sale. She rents a shop for £2,500 quarterly payable on the first day of the quarter. The running costs of the shop are £1,000 per month, payable in the month after the month in which they occur. She pays wages of £500 per month payable in the month. Draw up a cash budget for the 3-month period.

Using the information you have been given you need to draw up a cash budget. The exact form of the cash budget varies from one organisation to another, but the following layout is typical. The cash budget is drawn up for the year and divided into monthly or even weekly amounts. In this activity, you need to show only the first 3 months, as follows:

Trek-Kit

Cash budget for the period January to March

	January £	February £	March £
Cash in:			
Cash sales	5,000	6,000	9,000
Credit sales	0	5,000	6,000
Total cash in	5,000	11,000	15,000
Cash out:			
Purchases	5,000	6,000	9,000
Rent	2,500	0	0
Running costs	0	1,000	1,000
Wages	500	500	500
Total cash out	8,000	7,500	10,500
Balance b/f	5,000	2,000	5,500
Net cash flow	(3,000)	3,500	4,500
Balance c/f	2,000	5,500	10,000

The last three rows show how much Jane starts the month with (her £5,000 savings in January), the net cash flow for the month and the balance at the end of the month which is carried forward as the opening balance for the next month. Jane's cash budget shows that she will need at least £3,000 savings to start the business because of the negative cash flow in January. As she has £5,000 in the bank, the business appears viable. In February and March there are positive cash flows and Jane should be deciding before the budget period starts how the surplus cash flows should be used.

18.4 Production Budgets

There are two main considerations when deciding on the level of production. The first concerns the *production levels* in each subperiod and whether they will be even or uneven. Assuming an annual budget, most companies prefer to manufacture the same quantities each month to arrive at the annual figure. This even flow ensures that labour and machines are employed at optimum capacity. In seasonal industries it may be necessary to have an uneven production flow, with peaks and troughs during the year. The second is the amount of *stock* to be held. This depends on a number of factors including the cash available, storage capacity, delivery times, possibility of shortages, etc.

If the level of sales is a limiting factor and a decision has been taken on the level of stockholding, with *uneven* production flows a simple calculation is required to determine the production levels for each period.

Activity

Wheelers plc manufactures bicycle locks and has decided that the stock level should not fall below 500 units. At the beginning of January the company has 600 units in stock and the budgeted sales for the month are 2,000 units. What should the production level for the month be?

The calculation is as follows:

		Units
	Closing stock required at end of January	500
Add	Budgeted sales for the month	2,000
		2,500
Less	Opening stock at beginning of month	600
	Production requirement for the month	1,900

If production flows are *even* (in other words, the company wishes to produce the same quantity each month), and the minimum stock level has been decided, the problem is to determine the opening quantity of stock to ensure that sales needs are met.

Activity

Weatherproof Ltd manufactures window frames and has set a monthly production level of 50 units and does not want the stock level to fall below 100 units. The sales budget shows the following figures:

	Units
January	40
February	40
March	60
April	80
May	100
June	60

What should the opening stock in January be so that the company can meet its sales targets?

The way to tackle this problem is to set out the known information in the form of a simple budget, leaving spaces to calculate the missing figures:

	January	**February**	**March**	**April**	**May**	**June**
Opening stock						
Production	50	50	50	50	50	50
Total						
Less Sales	40	40	60	80	100	60
Closing stock						

As the stock level must not fall below 100 units, we can start by inserting this figure as the opening stock in January and carry the calculations through to the end. The closing stock at the end of one month becomes the opening stock at the beginning of the next month:

	January	**February**	**March**	**April**	**May**	**June**
Opening stock	100	110	120	110	80	30
Production	50	50	50	50	50	50
Total	150	160	170	160	130	80
Less Sales	40	40	60	80	100	60
Closing stock	110	120	110	80	30	20

The budget shows us that an opening stock of 100 units would be insufficient; this means that in three of the months stocks fall below the minimum level. June is the month with the lowest stock of only 20 units and a further 80 units are required to meet the stockholding of 100 units. Therefore the opening stock in January must be 180 units.

18.5 **Fixed and Flexible Budgets**

A *fixed budget* is a budget which is not changed once it has been established, regardless of changes in activity level. It may be revised if the situation so demands, but a fixed budget is not changed solely because the actual activity level differs from the budgeted activity level. This can be a considerable disadvantage because a fixed budget may show an adverse variance on costs which is simply due to an increase or decrease in variable costs. As you will remember, total variable costs increase or decrease in proportion with changes in activity level. The *disadvantage* of fixed budgeting is that if actual activity fluctuates from the planned level, the budget may become irrelevant.

A *flexible budget* changes in accordance with activity levels, and reflects the different behaviours of fixed and variable costs. Therefore, in a flexible budget, any cost variance can be assumed to be due to an increase or decrease in fixed costs. A flexible budget may be used at the planning stage to illustrate the impact of achieving different activity levels. It can also be used at the control stage at the end of a month to compare the actual results with what they should have been. The following activity shows the importance of flexible budgeting.

Activity

Portalight Ltd's budget for January is based on an output of 1,000 torches. The following budget report shows the budgeted and actual figures for the month when 1,100 torches were sold:

	Portalight Ltd			
	Budget report for January			
	Budget		**Actual**	
	£	**£**	**£**	**£**
Sales		1,500		1,650
Variable costs	750		880	
Variable overheads	250		260	
Fixed overheads	200		200	
Total costs		1,200		1,340
Profit		300		310

The managing director has been sent the above budget statement and is delighted that the actual profit is £10 above the budget. Write a brief report to the managing director explaining why he should not be so pleased with the results. Support your report with calculations.

After all the work you have done on marginal costing, the words *variable costs* should immediately have alerted you to the problem of comparing the actual results with the original budget when there has been a change in activity level. In this case, the number of torches sold was 1,100 compared with the planned amount of 1,000. Although the sales department must be congratulated on achieving increased sales, the company needs to construct a flexible budget to see if they have controlled their variable costs. This is done by multiplying the planned variable costs per unit by the actual level of production.

The variable costs were originally set at £750 for 1,000 torches, which is 75p per torch. The variable overheads were originally set at £250 for 1,000 torches, which is 25p per torch. If we assume that as the number of torches manufactured increases, the total variable costs increase, the flexible budget compared with the actual results is as follows:

Portalight Ltd

Budget report for January

	Flexible budget £	£	Actual £	£
Sales (at £1.50 per unit)		1,650		1,650
Variable costs (1,100 × 75p)	825		880	
Variable overheads (1,100 × 75p)	275		260	
Fixed overheads	200		200	
Total costs		1,300		1,340
Profit		350		310

The flexible budget shows that at an output of 1,100 torches, a profit of £350 should have been made. A comparison of the figures shows that although variable overheads have been reduced, there is an overspend on variable costs which should be investigated.

The *advantages* of flexible budgeting over fixed budgeting are that flexible budgeting provides clearer information to management for decision-making and control purposes. By comparing the actual results with what should have been achieved at that level of activity, a more accurate measure is given.

Practice questions

1 You are the assistant management accountant of ZED plc. Preliminary discussions concerning the company budgets for the year ended 30 June 1999 have already taken place, and the sales and production directors have produced the following forecasts:

Sales Director:
'I forecast that the total sales for the year will be 24,00 units of product *A* if we continue to sell them at £10.00 per unit for the first six months of the year and increase the price to £11.00 per unit thereafter. I estimate the quarterly sales to be:

July–September	7,200 units
October–December	3,000 units
January–March	4,800 units
April–June	9,000 units

This represents a 20% increase over our present quarterly sales targets, and I expect that within each quarter the monthly demand will be equal. We can also sell up to 2,000 units of product *B* per month at a selling price of £8.00 per unit. This is a less profitable product, so we should concentrate on product *A*.'

Production Director:
'Our maximum capacity is at present limited by the available machine hours. Each unit of product *A* requires 2 machine hours, and on this basis we can usually produce 2,000 units per month. However, because of employee holidays in August, the number of machine operators is reduced, and in that month we can produce only 1,000 units. We have placed an order for new semi-automatic machines which are being installed in August 1998. These should be capable of producing a further 2,000 units per month starting on 1 September 1998.

Product *B* requires 4 machine hours per unit. The quantity that we can produce is limited because of the demands on the available machine time by making product *A*.'

You have predicted the costs per unit of the two products for the 1999 budget year as follows:

	A £/unit	*B* £/unit
Direct materials	1.50	1.60
Direct labour	2.50	3.00
Variable overhead	1.50	3.00
	5.50	7.60

REQUIREMENTS:
(a) Use the above information to calculate the extent of the limiting factor during the budget period.

(5 marks)

(b) Prepare monthly sales and production budgets, expressed in units, for the period JULY TO DECEMBER 1998, based upon the limiting factor you determined in (a) above. Assume that stocks of products *A* and *B* cannot be held, and that ZED plc wishes to concentrate on production of product *A*.

(8 marks)

(c) Prepare monthly sales and production budgets, express in units, for the period JULY TO DECEMBER 1998, based upon the limited factor you determined in (a) above. Assume that stocks of products *A* and *B* can now be held, and assume that ZED plc decided to sell equal quantities of product *A* and product *B* each month.

(10 marks)

(d) Determine the effect on profits of the change in sales mix proposed in part
(c) above.

(2 marks)
(Total marks = 25)

ACCA, Module B, June 1996)

2 A fixed budget is

A   a budget for a single level of activity.
B   used when the mix of products is fixed in advance of the budget period.
C   a budget which ignores inflation.
D   used only for fixed costs.
E   an overhead cost budget.

CIMA, Stage 2, May 1997

19 Standard Costing – Materials and Labour

19.1 Introduction

Standard costing is a method of financial control that compares predetermined and actual costs. Standard costing is a system of financial control which is closely associated with *budgetary control*. Many organisations use both systems, although one can be used without the other. However, it is less common to find a standard costing system in operation without a budgetary control system being present.

Budgetary control is applied to departments, budget centres and the organisation as a whole, and is a technique which can be used in any organisation, whether it is a business, charity, university, hospital, etc. Standard costing is mainly applied to products and processes. Therefore it is a technique that is more commonly used in manufacturing organisations, although it may also be useful in service industries. As in a budgetary control system, it allows the comparison of predetermined costs and income with the actual costs and income achieved. Any *variances,* or differences, can then be investigated. Managers within the organisation can be held responsible for these variances and, by analysing the reasons for the variances, control can be achieved.

In this chapter we begin by looking at how standards are set. We then explain how variance analysis is conducted and look in detail at materials variances and labour variances. In the next chapter we discuss overhead variances and sales variances.

19.2 Setting Standards

The predetermined costs are known as *standard costs*. These are the costs which are incurred under defined working conditions. The standard cost is calculated from technical specifications, which give the quantity of materials, labour and other elements of cost required, and relate them to the prices and wages it is anticipated will be in place for the period in which the standard cost is to be used. It is usual to measure the time in which it is planned to complete a certain volume of work in *standard hours* or *minutes.* This means that a standard hour is a measure of production output, rather than a measure of time.

Activity

A company has set 1 standard hour's production at 500 units. In a 7 hour day, 4,000 units are produced. What is this output in standard hours?

You will have needed to make the following calculation to answer this question:

$$\frac{4{,}000 \text{ units}}{500 \text{ units per standard hour}} = 8 \text{ standard hours' production}$$

The type of standards used depends on the philosophy of the organisation. We can define a standard as a measurable quantity established in defined conditions. Organisations can set *ideal standards* or *attainable standards*. Ideal standards are based on the best possible working conditions, but attainable standards are more widely used. The main reason why attainable standards are more popular than ideal standards is because attainable standards are based on realistic efficient performance and allow for problems such as machine breakdown, material wastage, etc. Although ideal standards are useful for management decision-making, there is the risk that employees will be demotivated by the impossibility of achieving them.

19.3 **Variance Analysis**

Variance analysis is the investigation of the factors causing the differences between the standard and actual results. As in budgetary control, these differences are known as *variances*. Any variances are analysed to reveal their constituent parts, so that sufficient information is available to permit investigation by management. *Favourable variances* are those which improve the predetermined profit and *adverse variances* are those which reduce the predetermined profit.

Activity

In the stitching department of RWJ Ltd 100 pockets can be made in 1 standard hour. In an 8-hour day, 950 pockets are produced. Will this give rise to a favourable or adverse variance? Why is this?

The first step is to calculate how many pockets should be made in an 8-hour day:

100 units per standard hour × 8 actual hours

= 800 standard hours' production

Next you should have calculated the variance by subtracting the standard hours' production (800) from the actual production (950) to arrive at a figure of 150. This is a favourable variance because 150 more pockets are produced than the 800 planned. Now we are ready to make this part of the standard costing system, by expressing the variance in financial terms.

19.4 **Direct Materials Variances**

In a manufacturing organisation the direct product costs are normally *direct materials* and *direct labour*. The reasons for overspending or underspending on either of these costs is based on the following simple concept:

Total cost = Quantity used × Unit price

The difference between standard and actual total cost must be due to variations in the quantity used, the unit price or a combination of both. Predetermined standards are set both for the *usage level* of direct material for a given volume of production and the *price* allowed per unit of direct material. The price standards are based on the price per unit expected to be paid or budgeted for the level of purchases projected over the period for which the standard is to be applied.

In general, any price variance is regarded as the responsibility of the purchasing manager or buyer and variation in the volume or quantity of materials consumed is regarded as the responsibility of the production manager. However, due to the interdependence of price and usage, responsibilities may be difficult to assign.

The *direct materials variance* is based on the following formula:

Total direct materials cost = Quantity used × Price per unit

Standards are set for the *quantity* of materials to be used for a specific volume of production and the *price* to be paid per unit of direct material. The direct materials total variance is calculated by using the following formula:

(Standard quantity used × Standard price per unit) −

(Actual quantity used × Actual price per unit)

Activity

RWJ Ltd has decided to extend its range to include denim jackets. One jacket requires a standard usage of 3 metres of direct material which has been set at a standard price of £2.20 per metre. In the period, 80 jackets were made and 260 metres of material consumed at a cost of £1.95 per metre. Calculate the direct materials total variance.

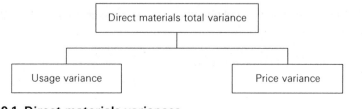

Fig. 19.1 **Direct materials variances**

To answer this question you need to put the figures into the above formula. However, the first stage is to calculate the standard quantity of materials for the actual level of production. As 80 jackets were made, and the company planned to use 3 metres of denim per jacket, the standard quantity for that level of production is 240 metres. Substituting the figures in the formula:

(240 metres × £2.20) − (260 metres × £1.95)

= £528 − £507

= £21 favourable variance

The difference of £21 between the planned cost and the actual cost is a favourable variance because the company has spent less on materials than planned for that level of production. Although this information is useful, it needs to be more precise to enable the management to take any action required. The reason why actual materials costs can differ from the planned materials costs for a given level of production is due to two factors. Either more or fewer materials have been used than planned and/or more or less has been paid per unit of materials than planned.

The direct materials total variance can be divided into a *usage variance* and a *price variance*, as shown in Figure 19.1.

The *direct materials usage variance* is the difference between the standard quantity specified for the actual production and the actual quantity used at standard price per unit. The formula is:

(Standard quantity × Standard price per unit) −

(Actual quantity × Standard price per unit)

Depending on the data you are given, you may find it more convenient to shorten this formula to the following:

(Standard quantity − Actual quantity) × Standard price per unit

Activity

Calculate the direct materials usage variance from the data for RWJ Ltd.

Once again, to answer this question you need to put the figures into the formula. The answer is:

(240 metres − 260 metres) × £2.20 = (£44.00) adverse variance

In this instance, there is an adverse variance because the company has used more materials than planned for that level of production.

The final stage is to find out the *direct materials price variance*. This is the difference between the standard and actual purchase price per unit for the actual quantity of materials purchased or used in production. The formula is:

(Standard price per unit × Actual quantity) −

(Actual price per unit × Actual quantity)

As with the usage variance, if the data is readily available, it may be more convenient to use the following shortened formula:

(Standard price per unit − Actual price per unit) × Actual quantity

Activity

Calculate the direct materials price variance from the data for RWJ Ltd.

The answer is:

(£2.20 − £1.95) × 260 metres = £65.00 favourable variance

The variance is favourable because the company has paid less for the materials than planned for that level of production. If you deduct the adverse usage variance of £44 from the favourable price variance of £65 you obtain the total direct material variance of £21 favourable. The first two variances therefore explain the last.

Of course, working out the figures is not the end of the task. Managers need to investigate the reasons for the variances and to determine whether any corrective action is required. There are a number of reasons for the adverse usage variance. Perhaps inferior materials were used and this led to higher wastage than planned, or the labour force was inexperienced and this led to high levels of wastage. Alternatively, some materials may have been lost or stolen.

One strong possibility for the price variance is that the company has used poorer quality, and therefore less expensive, materials. This would tie in with the possible reason for the adverse usage variance. Other reasons may be that the business is using a different supplier than originally intended, or has negotiated a bulk discount.

19.5 **Direct Labour Variances**

The same principles apply to the calculation of the *direct labour variances* as for the direct material variances. Standards are established for the rate of pay to be paid for the production of particular products and the labour time taken for their production. The standard time taken is expressed in *standard hours* or *minutes* and becomes the measure of output. By comparing the standard hours allowed and the actual time taken, *labour efficiency* can be assessed. In practice, standard times are established by work, time and method study techniques.

The direct labour variance is based on the following formula:

Total labour cost = Hours worked × Rate per hour

The *direct labour total variance* is calculated by using the following formula:

(Standard direct labour hours × Standard rate per hour) −

(Actual direct labour hours × Actual rate per hour)

Activity

The management of RWJ Ltd decides that it takes 6 standard hours to make 1 denim jacket and the standard rate paid to labour is £8 per hour. The actual production is 900 units and this took 5,100 hours at a rate of £8.30 per hour. Calculate the direct labour total variance.

With your knowledge of the calculation of material variances, this activity should have caused you few problems. The first stage is to calculate the standard direct labour hours for this level of production which is 900 jackets × 6 standard hours = 5,400 standard hours. The variance can then be calculated as follows:

(5,400 standard hours × £8.00) − (5,100 actual hours × £8.30)

= £43,200 − £42,330

= £870 favourable variance

The variance is favourable because the total labour cost is less than planned for that level of production. The direct labour total variance can be broken down into a *direct labour rate variance* and a *direct labour efficiency variance*, as shown in Figure 19.2.

The direct labour efficiency variance, sometimes referred to as the *labour productivity variance*, is the difference between the actual production achieved, measured in standard hours, and the actual hours worked, valued at the standard labour rate. The formula is:

(Standard hours × Standard rate per hour) −

(Actual hours × Standard rate per hour)

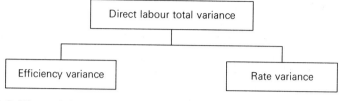

Fig. 19.2 Direct labour variances

Depending on the data you have available, it may be more convenient to shorten the formula to:

(Standard hours – Actual hours) × Standard rate per hour

Activity

Calculate the direct labour efficiency variance.

The answer is:

(5,400 standard hours – 5,100 actual hours) × £8.00

= £2,400 favourable variance

The *direct labour rate variance* is the difference between the standard and actual direct labour rate per hour for the actual hours worked. The formula is:

(Standard rate per hour × Actual hours) –

(Actual rate per hour × Actual hours)

Depending on the data you are given, you may find the following shortened formula more convenient:

(Standard rate per hour – Actual rate per hour) × Actual hours

Activity

Calculate the direct labour rate variance from the data for RWJ Ltd.

The answer is:

(£8.00 – £8.30) × 5,100 actual hours = (£1,530) adverse variance

The variance is adverse because we have paid the workforce more than we planned for that level of production.

If you deduct the adverse direct labour rate variance of £1,530 from the favourable efficiency variance of £2,400, you get the favourable total direct labour variance of £870. The most likely reason for the labour rate and efficiency variances is that the company has used more highly skilled labour than originally planned. Therefore, the rate paid was higher, but the output was greater than planned. There are other possible reasons – for example, the business may have given a pay rise, or overtime may have been worked. Further investigation would be required to identify the actual reasons and to determine whether any corrective action is required.

19.6 **Advantages and Disadvantages of Standard Costing**

As with budgetary control, many of the benefits of standard costing are associated with the processes of planning. Control is improved and it compels managers to make decisions, coordinate activities and communicate with one another.

Activity

What other advantages might there be, and what are the disadvantages of standard costing?

With your knowledge of budgetary control, you should not have had many problems with this activity. The main *advantages* of standard costing are as follows:

- Standard-setting establishes a benchmark against which actual costs can be compared.
- The technique permits a thorough examination of the organisation's production and operations activities.
- As the standards are based on future plans and expectations, the information provided to management is much more accurate than that based merely on past performance.
- By examining the reasons for any variances between standard and actual costs and income, management needs to concentrate only on the exceptions to the planned performance. This leads to greater managerial efficiency.
- Variance analysis may result in cost reductions, and control of costs is improved.

The main *disadvantages* are:

- It may be difficult to set standards, particularly in a new or dynamic organisation.
- The standard costing system may be expensive to maintain and the additional record-keeping may become a burden to busy managers.

- Standards will naturally become out of date and require revision. In a very dynamic organisation this may happen so quickly that managers lose confidence in the system.
- Information provided by the system is of value only if it is used by managers for control purposes. If the information has no credibility or is not understood, it has no value.

Self-check question

What are the main advantages and disadvantages of standard costing?

Practice questions

1 The following details have been extracted from a standard cost card of X plc:

PRODUCT X

Direct labour: 4 hours @ £5.40 per hour

During October 1997, the budgeted production was 5,000 units of product X and the actual production was 4,650 units of product X. Actual hours worked were 19,100 and the actual direct labour cost amounted to £98,350. The labour variances reported were:

	Rate £	Efficiency £
A	9,650 F	4,860 F
B	9,650 F	2,700 A
C	4,790 F	2,575 A
D	4,790 F	4,860 F
E	4,790 F	2,700 A

CIMA, Stage 2, November 1997

2 T plc uses a standard costing system, with its material stock account being maintained at standard costs. The following details have been extracted from the standard cost card in respect of direct materials:

8 kgs @ £0.80/kg = £6.40 per unit

Budgeted production in April 1995 was 850 units.

The following details relate to actual materials purchased and issued to production during April 1995 when actual production was 870 units:

Materials purchased   8,200 kg costing £6,888
Materials issued to production 7,150 kg

Which of the following correctly states the material price and usage variances to be reported?

	Price	Usage
A	£286 (A)	£152 (A)
B	£286 (A)	£280 (A)
C	£286 (A)	£294 (A)
D	£328 (A)	£152 (A)
E	£328 (A)	£280 (A)

CIMA, Stage 2, May 1995

3 The following information relates to R plc for October 1997:

Bought 7,800 kg of material R at a total cost of £16,380.
Stocks of material R increased by 440 kg.
Stocks of material R are valued using standard purchase price.
Material price variance was £1,170 Adverse.

The standard price per kg for material R is:

	Price **£/kg**
A	1.95
B	2.10
C	2.23
D	2.25
E	2.38

CIMA, Stage 2, November 1997

20 Standard Costing – Overhead Variances and Sales Variances

20.1 Introduction

When we examined absorption costing in Chapter 7, we saw that overheads could be charged to production in a variety of ways. The budgeted overhead for the period was divided by the appropriate units of base, a measure of time being the preferred method. One method of measuring output is in the form of *standard hours of production*. This is the method we will use in this chapter when considering *overhead variance analysis*.

It is possible to calculate variances for the total overheads – that is, fixed and variable overheads combined. Although this is slightly simpler, it is assumed in this chapter that the standard costing system uses total absorption costing principles and both fixed and variable overheads are absorbed into production costs. It is therefore more sensible to calculate fixed and variable overhead variances separately. When the standard costing system is based on *marginal costing* principles, only variable overheads are charged to production. It is therefore necessary to calculate only the variances for the variable overheads.

Sales variances are income variances and if the actual performance is greater than the standard, the difference is a favourable variance. The variances are derived from the sales margin because this assists management in their objective of controlling profit.

20.2 Fixed Overhead Variances

The *fixed overhead variance* is the difference between the standard cost of fixed overhead charged to production and the actual fixed overhead for the period. The most important point to remember when calculating fixed overhead variances is that fixed overheads do not change with changes in the level of production. Overheads are charged to production on the basis of the fixed *overhead absorption rate (FOAR)*, which must be calculated before production starts. The FOAR is therefore calculated from budgeted figures.

The *fixed overhead total variance* is calculated by using the following formula:

(Standard hours production × FOAR) – Actual fixed overheads

Activity

The following information is available from RWJ Ltd:

Budgeted fixed overheads for the period	£3,000
Budgeted standard hours of production	1,000
Actual fixed overheads for the period	£3,200
Actual standard hours produced	1,100

Calculate the fixed overhead total variance.

The first step is to work out the predetermined overhead absorption rate:

$$\text{FOAR} = \frac{\text{Budgeted fixed overheads}}{\text{Budgeted standard hours}}$$

$$= \frac{£3,000}{1,000 \text{ hours}}$$

$$= £3.00 \text{ per hour}$$

Now you need to put the figures into the formula:

$$(1,100 \times £3.00) - £3,200 = £100 \text{ favourable variance}$$

The variance is favourable because more overhead has been charged to production than has been incurred.

The fixed overhead total variance can be divided into an *expenditure variance* and a *volume variance*, as shown in Figure 20.1.

The *fixed overhead expenditure variance* is the difference between the budgeted fixed overhead and the actual overhead incurred:

Budgeted fixed overhead − Actual fixed overhead

Activity

Calculate the fixed overhead expenditure variance from the data for RWJ Ltd.

Fig. 20.1 Fixed overhead variances

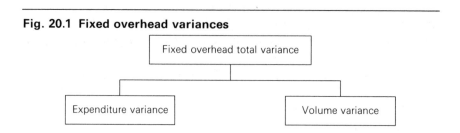

The answer can be found by putting the figures in the formula:

£3,000 – £3,200 = (£200) adverse variance

In this instance, there is an adverse variance because the actual fixed overheads were higher than planned.

The final stage is to find out the *fixed overhead volume variance*. This is the difference between the overhead absorbed in the production achieved and the budgeted fixed overhead for the period. It is calculated using the formula:

(Standard hours production × FOAR) – Budgeted fixed overhead

Activity

Calculate the fixed overhead volume variance from the data for RWJ Ltd.

Once again, the answer can be calculated by putting the figures in the formula:

(1,100 × £3.00) – £3,000 = £300 favourable variance

The fixed overhead volume variance is favourable because the actual volume of production was higher than the planned volume by 100 standard hours, thus a further £300 was absorbed into production than originally planned.

As you can see, the combined fixed overhead expenditure and volume variances agree with the fixed overhead total variance.

20.3 **Variable Overhead Variances**

The *variable overhead variance* is the difference between the actual variable overheads incurred and the actual variable overheads absorbed for the period. The most important point to remember when calculating variable overhead variances is that the variable overheads should fluctuate in relation to levels of production. This means that once the predetermined *variable overhead absorption rate (VOAR)* has been calculated, the original budgeted figures lose their relevance.

The formula for calculating the variable overhead total variance is:

(Standard hours production × VOAR) –
Actual variable overheads

Activity

The following information is available from WJM Ltd:

Budgeted variable overheads for the period	£3,000
Budgeted standard hours of production	1,000
Actual variable overheads for the period	£2,200
Actual standard hours produced	900
Actual hours worked	850

Calculate the variable overhead total variance.

The first step is to work out the predetermined overhead absorption rate:

$$\text{VOAR} = \frac{\text{Budgeted variable overheads}}{\text{Budgeted standard hours}}$$

$$= \frac{£2,000}{1,000 \text{ hours}} = £2.00 \text{ per hour}$$

For the purpose of calculating the variances we will not refer to the original budget figures again, but will use the **VOAR**.

Now we need to put the figures into the formula:

$$(900 \times £2.00) - £2,200 = £1,800 - £2,200 = (£400) \text{ adverse variance}$$

The variable overhead total variance is adverse because only £1,800 has been charged to production, but the actual variable overheads incurred were £2,200.

As you saw with the fixed overhead total variance, the variable overhead total variance can be divided into an *expenditure variance* and a *volume variance*, as shown in Figure 20.2.

The *variable overhead expenditure variance* is the difference between the variable overheads allowed for the actual hours worked and the actual overhead incurred. The formula is:

$$(\text{Actual hours worked} \times \text{VOAR}) - \text{Actual variable overheads}$$

Fig. 20.2 Variable overhead variances

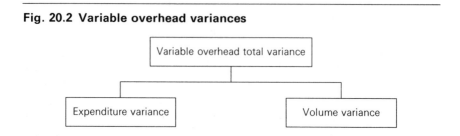

Activity

Calculate the variable overhead expenditure variance from the data for WJM Ltd.

The answer can be found by putting the figures in the formula:

$$(850 \times £2.00) - £2,200 = £1,700 - £2,200 = (£500) \text{ adverse variance}$$

The variance is adverse because the company should have incurred variable overheads of £1,700 on the basis of the actual hours of work, but the actual overheads were £2,200.

The *variable overhead efficiency variance* is the difference between the variable overheads allowed for the actual hours worked and the variable overhead absorbed in production. The formula is:

(Actual hours worked $\times$ VOAR) –

(Standard hours production $\times$ VOAR)

Activity

Calculate the variable overhead efficiency variance from the data for WJM Ltd.

Once again, the answer can be calculated by putting the figures in the formula:

$$(850 \times £2.00) - (900 \times £2.00) = £1,700 - £1,800$$
$$= £100 \text{ favourable variance}$$

This is a true efficiency variance. It is favourable because fewer hours were actually taken to produce a greater output as measured in standard hours.

As with the fixed overhead variances, the combined variable overhead expenditure and efficiency variances agree with the total variable overhead variance.

20.4 Fixed and Variable Overhead Variances Compared

It is essential to note that fixed overheads do not vary with production levels, but variable overheads do. When calculating overhead variances the comparison for fixed overheads must be with the original budget. With variable overheads there is normally a different level of production than the original budget. What becomes important is the amount the variable overheads should have been for the actual hours worked. This can be

Variance	Fixed overheads	Variable overheads
Total overhead variance	Actual overheads *less* overheads absorbed	Actual overheads *less* overheads absorbed
Expenditure variance	Actual overheads *less* budgeted overheads	Actual overheads *less* allowed overheads
Volume variance and efficiency variance	Budgeted overheads *less* overheads absorbed	Allowed overheads *less* overheads absorbed

Fig. 20.3 Comparison of overhead calculations

referred to as the *allowed variable overhead*. Figure 20.3 illustrates the differences.

The other key point is that the fixed and variable overhead absorption rates (FOAR and VOAR) must be calculated on the original budgeted figures. The absorption rate is a predetermined rate and the actual figures will not be available at the time of calculation.

Self-check question

What are the main differences between fixed and variable overhead variances?

20.5 Sales Margin Variances

Management is interested not only in controlling costs, but also in controlling income. The income from sales is controlled by concentrating on the profit or margin from sales. The *standard sales margin* is the difference between the standard selling price and the standard costs of production, including both fixed and variable costs. The *actual sales margin* is the difference between the actual selling price and the standard costs of production (not the actual costs of production).

The *sales margin total variance* is the difference between the budgeted margin and the actual margin, the cost of sales being at the standard cost of production. The formula is:

(Actual sales in units × Actual margin per unit of sales) −

(Standard sales in units × Standard margin per unit)

Activity

The following information is available from KJB Ltd

	Volume	Selling price per unit	Margin per unit
Budget	400	£10.00	£2.00
Actual	380	£11.00	£3.00

Calculate the sales margin total variance.

By now you should be familiar with putting the figures you have been given into the formula:

$(380 \times £3.00) - (400 \times £2.00)$

$= £1,140 - £800$

$= £340$ favourable variance

The sales margin total variance is favourable because although the sales volume was lower than anticipated, the selling price per unit was higher, thus resulting in a higher sales margin per unit.

The sales margin total variance can be divided into a *price variance* and a *quantity variance*, as shown in Figure 20.4.

The *sales margin price variance* is the difference between the actual margin per unit and the standard margin per unit multiplied by the actual sales volume. Both the actual and the standard margins are calculated on the basis of standard unit costs. The formula is:

(Actual margin – Standard margin) × Actual sales volume in units

Activity

Calculate the sales margin price variance from the data for KJB Ltd.

Fig. 20.4 Sales margin variances

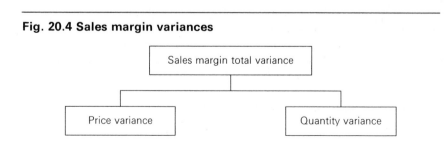

All you need to do is to put the figures into the formula:

$(£3.00 - £2.00) \times 380 = £380$ favourable variance

The sales margin price variance is favourable because a higher selling price per unit was charged.

The *sales margin volume variance* is the difference between the actual sales volume and the standard or budgeted sales volume, both measured in units, multiplied by the standard margin per unit of sales. The formula is:

(Actual sales in units – Standard sales in units) ×
Standard margin per unit of sales

Activity

Calculate the sales margin quantity variance from the data for KJB Ltd.

Putting the figures into the formula:

$(380 - 400) \times £2.00 = (£40)$ adverse variance

As you can see, the combined sales margin price and volume variances agree with the total sales margin variance. A favourable price variance may well be associated with an adverse volume variance, as the increase in price (and thus margin) may reduce demand.

Practice questions

1 The following details have been extracted from the standard cost card for product X:

	£/unit
Variable overhead	
4 machine hours @ £8.00/hour	32.00
2 labour hours @ £4.00/hour	8.00
Fixed overhead	20.00

During October 1997, 5,450 units of the product were made compared to a budgeted production target of 5,500 units. The actual overhead costs incurred were:

Machine-related variable overhead	£176,000
Labour-related variable overhead	£42,000
Fixed overhead	£109,000

The actual number of machine hours was 22,000 and the actual number of labour hours was 10,800.

REQUIREMENTS:

(a) Calculate the overhead cost variances in as much detail as possible from the data provided.

(12 marks)

(b) Explain the meaning of, and give possible causes for, the variable overhead variances which you have calculated.

(8 marks)

(c) Explain the benefits of using activity bases for variable overhead absorption.

(5 marks)

(Total marks = 25)

CIMA, Stage 2, November 1997

2 PQ Limited operates a standard costing system for its only product. The standard cost card is as follows:

Direct materials	(4 kg @ £2/kg)	£8.00
Direct labour	(4 hours @ £4/hour)	£16.00
Variable overhead	(4 hours @ £3/hour)	£12.00
Fixed overhead	(4 hours @ £5/hour)	£20.00

Fixed overheads are absorbed on the basis of labour hours. Fixed overhead costs are budgeted at £120,000 per annum arising at a constant rate during the year.

Activity in period 3 of 1995 is budgeted to be 10% of a total activity for the year. Actual production during period 3 was 500 units, with actual fixed overhead costs incurred being £9,800 and actual hours worked being 1,970.

The fixed overhead expenditure variance for period 3 of 1995 was:

A £2,200 (F). **B** £200 (F). **C** £50 (F). **D** £200 (A). **E** £2,200 (A).

CIMA, Stage 2, May 1995

3 P Limited has the following data relating to its budgeted sales for October 1997:

Budgeted sales	£100,000	
Budgeted selling price per unit		£8.00
Budgeted contribution per unit		£4.00
Budgeted profit per unit		£2.50

During October 1997, actual sales were 11,000 units for a sales revenue of £99,000.

P Limited uses an absorption costing system.

The sales variances reported for October 1997 were:

	Price £	*Volume* £
A	11,000 F	3,750 A
B	11,000 F	6,000 A
C	11,000 A	6,000 A
D	12,500 F	12,000 A
E	12,500 A	12,000 A

CIMA, Stage 2, November 1997

4 The following profit reconciliation statement summarises the performance of one of SEW's products for March 1997.

	£	
Budgeted profit	4,250	
Sales volume variance	850	A
Standard profit on actual sales	3,400	
Selling price variance	4,000	A
	(600)	

Cost variances:	Adverse £	Favourable £		
Direct material price		1,000		
Direct material usage	150			
Direct labour rate	200			
Direct labour effiency	150			
Variable overhead expenditure	600			
Variable overhead efficency	75			
Fixed overhead expenditure		2,500		
Fixed overhead volume		150		
	1,175	3,650	2,475	F
Actual profit			1,875	

The budget for the same period contained the following data:

Sales volume		1,500 units
Sales revenue	£20,000	
Production volume		1,500 units
Direct materials purchased		750 kgs
Direct materials used		750 kgs
Direct material lost	£4,500	
Direct labour hours		1,125
Direct labour cost	£4,500	
Variable overhead cost	£2,250	
Fixed overhead cost	£4,500	

Additional information:

• stocks of raw materials and finished goods are valued at standard cost;
• during the month the actual number of units produced was 1,550;
• the actual sales revenue was £12,000; and
• the direct materials purchased were 1,000kgs.

REQUIREMENTS:
(a) Calculate
    (i)   the actual sales volume;
    (ii) the actual quantity of materials used;
    (iii) the actual direct material cost;
    (iv) the actual direct labour hours;
    (v) the actual direct labour cost;
    (vi) the actual variable overhead cost;
    (vii) the actual fixed overhead cost.

(19 marks)

(b) Explain the possible causes of the direct materials usage variance, direct labour rate variance, and sales volume variance.

(6 marks)
(Total marks = 25)

CIMA, Stage 2, May 1997

21 Capital Investment Appraisal

21.1 Introduction

This chapter considers a number of techniques of *capital investment appraisal* which can be used to make a decision when investing in a long-term capital project. When a business wishes to invest in a new factory, computer facilities, production line or any other major project that requires capital investment, there are a number of decisions to be made. Some are organisational and personnel decisions, but it is crucial that the financial implications of any decisions are considered. At the very least, management will want to know that the business will get its money back.

We begin by looking at the purpose of capital investment appraisal. This is followed by a discussion of two particular methods of capital investment appraisal – the *payback period method* and the *accounting rate of return (ARR)*. We then go on to explain two methods which use *discounted cash flow (DCF)*, thereby taking into account the time value of money, known as the *net present value (NPV)* and the *internal rate of return (IRR)*.

21.2 Purpose of Capital Investment Appraisal

When a business is considering whether to invest a large amount of *capital* in a long-term project, it needs to be sure that the amount of money received during the life of the project will be higher than the amount originally invested. The annual profit and the distinction between fixed and variable costs is therefore of less importance than the timing and amount of the cash going in and out of the business. In some cases an investment is made, not to generate more cash, but to make a saving on costs. For example, a business may be deciding whether to replace a machine with a new model which is less expensive to run. The question that the business needs to answer is whether the savings in costs are sufficiently high to warrant the investment in the new machine. Once again, cash is the most important factor.

Activity

A business has a choice between three machines, each costing £100,000 to purchase. Each machine will last for 3 years and the company estimates that over that period the positive net cash flows, that is the difference between the cash coming in and going out each year, will be as follows:

Year	Machine 1 £	Machine 2 £	Machine 3 £
1	60,000	20,000	10,000
2	40,000	40,000	20,000
3	20,000	60,000	95,000

Which machine would you recommend the business purchases?

In order to make the comparison, you need to total the above cash flows:

Year	Machine 1 £	Machine 2 £	Machine 3 £
1	60,000	20,000	10,000
2	40,000	40,000	20,000
3	20,000	60,000	95,000
Total	120,000	120,000	125,000

Machines 1 and 2 both give the same total net cash inflow of £120,000 over the 3-year period and therefore either would be a worthwhile investment. However, you may decide that machine 1 is preferable because the cash comes in more quickly. Machine 3 looks better than the other two because the total net cash inflow is £125,000. However, you have to wait until year 3 before you get most of the cash, and this means that the risk is increased. With all three machines the company has estimated the cash flows and the further into the future the estimate is, the more unreliable it is likely to be. It is therefore difficult to decide which is the 'best' machine to buy and we need a specific technique to help us.

In this chapter we describe a number of different techniques of project appraisal. Each has advantages and disadvantages and may give different answers to the same problem. Therefore, management must decide which is the most appropriate technique to use in the circumstances.

21.3 Payback Period Method

The first technique we consider is known as the *payback period method*. It is a simple method and very popular with non-accountants. With this technique, it is necessary to find out the time it takes for the cash inflows to equal cash outflows. Normally the project with the shortest payback period, that is the one which pays back the investment fastest, is chosen.

To calculate the payback period the cash inflows and outflows are identified both in amount and timing, and the net cash flow is calculated.

Activity

Melrose Ltd has a choice of three projects, each requiring an investment of £20,000 to be paid at the beginning of the project, although one project has a different time span. The net cash flows and lengths of the projects are:

Year	Project A £	Project B £	Project C £
1	10,000	7,000	10,000
2	8,000	7,000	4,000
3	2,000	6,000	4,000
4	1,000	2,000	4,000
5	0	0	8,000

Using the payback period method, decide which project the company should choose.

The first step is to work out the cumulative net cash flows over the period:

Year	Project A		Project B		Project C	
	Net cash flows £	Cumulative cash flows £	Net cash flows £	Cumulative cash flows £	Net cash flows £	Cumulative cash flows £
0	(20,000)	(20,000)	(20,000)	(20,000)	(20,000)	(20,000)
1	10,000)	(10,000)	7,000	(13,000)	10,000	(10,000)
2	8,000	(2,000)	7,000	(6,000)	4,000	(6,000)
3	2,000	0	6,000	0	4,000	(2,000)
4	1,000	1,000	2,000	2,000	4,000	2,000
5	0		0		8,000	10,000

There are several things in this table which need explaining:

- Year 0 is a conventional way of saying start of year 1. Year 1, 2, 3, etc. means end of year 1, 2, 3, etc.
- It is customary to assume that cash flows during a year will be received at the end of that year. Of course, this is not true, but it simplifies the calculation and errs on the side of conservatism by giving a slightly pessimistic rather than an optimistic view if the cash flows are positive. It is possible to produce cash flows on a quarterly or monthly basis, but this is seldom done in payback calculations, because forecasting to this degree of refinement is rarely possible.
- Negative cash flows (cash going out) are shown in brackets, whereas positive cash flows (cash coming in) are not.

The cumulative cash flows for Projects *A* and *B* are shown as nil at the end of year 3. This means that at the end of year 3 the cash flowing in has reached the figure of £20,000, which is same as the initial cash outflow at the start of year 1. Therefore, we can say that although there is a significant difference in the timing of the net cash flows over the period, Projects *A* and *B* are ranked equal as the payback period for both is 3 years. Project *C* is ranked last as it takes 3½ years to repay the investment. The fact that Project *C* shows a greater total return of cash is not taken into account.

The main *advantages* of the payback period method are as follows:

- The technique is very simple to calculate and is understood by managers who are not very numerate.
- It produces results which are useful for risky projects, where the prediction of cash flows for more than the first few years is difficult, due to possible changes in the market. For example, changes in technology may make a product obsolete in a year or so, although the current market for the product seems assured.
- Some businesses may need to consider short-term cash flows as more important than long-term cash flows, perhaps due to lack of capital adequate to sustain long-term objectives. It is not much use aiming for long-term profitability if the business fails in 6 months' time from lack of cash.

The main *disadvantages* of the payback period method are:

- Net cash inflows in year 5 are given the same degree of importance as those for year 1. Cash now or soon is worth more than the same amount of cash in 5 years' time. This is known as the *time value of money*.
- The technique ignores cash flows after the payback period.

Activity

Returning to the example of machines 1–3 at the beginning of this chapter, which machine would you recommend purchasing on the basis of the payback period technique?

Your answer should be machine 1, because this has a payback period of only 2 years compared with longer periods for the other two machines. However, using the payback period would mean that we would not select machine 3, which gave the greatest return of cash. This is one of the disadvantages of the technique.

21.4 Accounting Rate of Return

The *accounting rate of return (ARR)* departs from the emphasis on cash as it is calculated by expressing average profit, after depreciation, as a percentage of the capital invested. The formula is:

$$\frac{\text{Average profit after depreciation}}{\text{Capital invested}} \times 100$$

There are variations on this definition, but the basic principles are the same.

Activity

Calculate the ARR for Projects *A*, *B* and *C* using the same data as in section 21.3. You can assume that the investment of £20,000 is charged in full as depreciation to arrive at the profit figures.

First, you need to calculate the total net cash flows for the three projects and deduct the depreciation to arrive at the figure of profit. Then you can calculate the average profit figure and put the figures into the formula to find the ARR. Check your answer against the following:

Year	Project A £	Project B £	Project C £
1	10,000	7,000	10,000
2	8,000	7,000	4,000
3	2,000	6,000	4,000
4	1,000	2,000	4,000
5	0	0	8,000
Total net cash flow	21,000	22,000	30,000
Less Depreciation	20,000	20,000	20,000
Profit	1,000	2,000	10,000
Average profit	$\frac{£1,000}{4 \text{ years}}$ $= £250$	$\frac{£2,000}{4 \text{ years}}$ $= £500$	$\frac{£10,000}{5 \text{ years}}$ $= £2,000$
ARR	$\frac{250}{20,000} \times 100$ $= 1.25\%$	$\frac{500}{20,000} \times 100$ $= 2.5\%$	$\frac{2,000}{20,000} \times 100$ $= 10\%$

On the criteria employed in this technique, Project *C* would be chosen, as it has the highest ARR (10%).

The main *advantages* of the accounting rate of return technique are as follows:

- Calculations are very simple.
- The entire life of the project is taken into account.

The main *disadvantages* of the accounting rate of return technique are:

- The timing of cash movements is completely ignored.
- There are a number of different definitions of profit and capital employed and therefore the calculation of the accounting rate of return can result in different figures.
- The crucial factor in investment decisions is cash flow and the accounting rate of return uses profits.
- The technique takes no account of the time value of money; a topic we discuss in Chapter 22.
- It takes no account of the incidence of profits.
- Averages can be misleading.

21.5 Discounted Cash Flow

Discounted cash flow (DCF) is the most sophisticated of the techniques, and is based on the concept that £1 in a year's time will not have the same value as £1 now. Ignoring the impact of inflation, the principle is that £1 that is available now can be invested immediately and by the end of the year its value will have grown by the amount of the interest gained. Because of this interest, paying £1 now in anticipation of receiving £1 in a year's time is unprofitable. With an interest rate of 100% only 50p would need to be invested in return for £1 in a year's time and only 25p £1 in two years' time.

The principle that £1 in a year's time is not worth £1 now can be likened to using different currencies; a conversion rate is needed to ensure that all the £1 have the same value. This is done by converting future cash flows from the project into equivalent values as at the present time, usually by using discount tables. The two main methods used are *net present value (NPV)* and the *internal rate of return (IRR)*.

Self-check question

What are the principles underlying the discounted cash flow technique?

Net present value

Net present value (NPV) converts the future net cash flows into present-day values and the project with the largest NPV is the one preferred. Many problems, both in real life and in exams, are concerned with choosing between alternatives, even if one alternative is to do nothing.

Activity

A company has to choose between two projects, both of which involve an investment of £20,000. The current cost of capital is 10%. The net cash flows of the projects are:

Year	Project A £	Project B £
1	1,000	14,000
2	2,000	4,000
3	2,000	4,000
4	7,000	2,000
5	20,000	8,000

Using the table of present value factors in Appendix A, calculate the NPV of these two projects.

You need to draw up a table in order to work out the NPV of each project:

Year	Discount factor 10%	Project A Net cash flows £	Present value £	Project B Net cash flows £	Present value £
0	1.000	(20,000)	(20,000)	(20,000)	(20,000)
1	0.909	1,000	909	14,000	12,726
2	0.826	2,000	1,652	4,000	3,304
3	0.751	2,000	1,502	4,000	3,004
4	0.683	7,000	4,781	2,000	1,366
5	0.621	20,000	12,420	8,000	4,968
Net present value			1,264		5,368

You can see from the table that whereas Project *A* has a NPV of £1,264, Project *B* gives the higher value of £5,368. Therefore Project *B* should be chosen. The present value is called *net* because the initial outlay has been deducted from the total of the discounted inflows.

The £5,368 from Project *B* is the present value of the ultimate benefit arising from the project if money is borrowed at 10%. The rate of 10% was selected for the discount factor because we were told that the cost of capital was that amount, but other criteria may be used to determine the discount factor. Since both projects have a positive NPV, the company would be getting a return on investment of more than 10%. If the NPV had been nil, the return would be 10%. If the projects had shown a negative NPV, the return would be less than 10%, and neither would be worth undertaking.

Internal rate of return

The *internal rate of return (IRR)* uses the same principles as NPV, but the aim is to find the discount rate which gives a net present value of 0 for the project. In other words, the aim of the technique is to show the percentage return you obtain on the investment.

The two projects in the activities in the previous subsection both gave a positive NPV using a discount rate of 10%. This means that their IRR must be higher than 10%. As the exact rate is not known, the figures must be recalculated using a higher discount rate to see whether that gives a zero NPV. The correct discount rate is unlikely to be selected by chance. We will start by taking a rate that we think will be in excess of the IRR, which should therefore give a negative NPV:

Year	Discount factor 20%	Project A Net cash flows	Present value	Project B Net cash flows	Present value
		£	£	£	£
0	1.000	(20,000)	(20,000)	(20,000)	(20,000)
1	0.833	1,000	833	14,000	11,662
2	0.694	2,000	1,388	4,000	2,776
3	0.579	2,000	1,158	4,000	2,316
4	0.482	7,000	3,374	2,000	964
5	0.402	20,000	8,040	8,000	3,216
Net present value			(5,207)		934

Project *B* still has a positive NPV so the IRR must be above 20%. With Project *A* the IRR must fall somewhere between 10% and 20%. The calculation is:

	£
NPV at 10%	1,264
NPV at 20%	(5,207)
Range of the present values	6,471

The difference between the two discount rates is 10%.

$$\text{IRR} = \frac{£1,264}{£6,471} \times 10\% = 1.95\%$$

Therefore the IRR is 1.95% along the range of present values. As the lowest discount factor used was 10%, the IRR is 10% + 1.95%, which equals approximately 12%.

As the IRR is relative, it is a measure of the intensity of capital use. If capital is limited it is better to invest in high-rate projects. The IRR also gives a return for risk. With Project *A*, if the cost of capital is 10% and the IRR is 12%, the return for risk is 2%.

21.6 Net Present Value and Internal Rate of Return Compared

The main advantages of the NPV and IRR are as follows:

- They use the concept of the time value of money.
- The entire life of the project is taken into account.
- They permit comparisons with other opportunities to be made.
- They enable the organisation to decide on its financing policy.

The main disadvantages of the two techniques are:

- The calculations are complex.
- It is difficult to decide what is the most appropriate discount rate to use.
- Managers may have difficulty in understanding the techniques.

The IRR is a slightly more difficult method to apply than NPV. In most cases both methods will give the same answer as to acceptance or rejection, but may vary on ranking, thus leading to different selections.

Care should be taken in basing a decision on the IRR. Although an IRR of 30% may appear enticing, if the return is on an investment of only £5.00 then an IRR of 20% on an investment of £5,000 is more sensible. The selection of a project with the highest IRR, particularly if of a short life, implies that at the end of the project other investment opportunities will present themselves with the same or higher returns.

Practice questions

1 What financial decisions will management take into account when making capital investment decisions?

2 What are the advantages and disadvantages of the payback period method?

3 A company has the choice of one of two projects each with a life span of 4 years and requiring an initial investment of £6,000. Select the best project by using NPV at a discount rate of 10%. The net cash flows for the two projects are as follows:

Year	Project A £	Project B £
1	2,000	4,000
2	3,000	3,000
3	3,000	3,000
4	4,000	1,000

22 Developments in Management Accounting

22.1 Introduction

Over the last 10 years or so there have been a number of developments in management accounting. In part, these changes have been brought about by dissatisfaction with the more traditional approaches to management accounting and the information which has been generated. Other influences have been related to changes in the nature of organisations and the activities they undertake, and the increasingly complex and competitive business environment.

As with all new systems and procedures, in the early days it is difficult to assess how successful they are and how long it will be before they are replaced by other novel approaches. In this chapter we examine two developments that have become firmly established and are widely accepted in principle, if not in practice. These are known as *activity-based costing (ABC)* and *throughput accounting (TA)*. We consider them in alphabetical order to avoid implying any ranking of importance.

22.2 Activity-based Costing

Activity-based costing (ABC) is a method of costing that recognises that costs are incurred by each activity that takes place within an organisation, and that products or customers should bear costs according to the activities they use. ABC first became prominent in the UK in the late 1980s and has been adopted in various forms by a number of organisations. It seeks to obtain a more realistic approach to ascertaining the total cost of a cost unit than is generated by traditional absorption costing. ABC is most closely associated with organisations which have some form of *advanced manufacturing technology (AMT)*, including such features as *computer-aided design (CAD)*, *computer-aided manufacturing (CAM)*, *flexible management systems (FMS)*, and *total quality management (TQM)*. The main reasons for the popularity of ABC are as follows:

- Organisations are operating in an increasingly complex and competitive environment, and managers need more sophisticated information systems.
- The diversity of product ranges have increased, requiring better data collection and recording procedures.
- The proportion of overheads have been increasing, making a rational and realistic basis for allocating and apportioning them even more critical.

A fundamental aspect of ABC is the assumption that most overhead costs can be analysed into two main groups:

- short-term variable costs that vary with the volume of production (such overheads can be charged to the cost unit by using recovery rates based on direct labour hours or machine hours, as we demonstrated with absorption costing in Chapter 15); and
- long-term variable costs that do not vary with volume of production, but with some other form of activity – for example, the costs of handling stock may be more dependent on the range of items manufactured and their technical complexity than the actual volume of production.

ABC seeks to recognise these differences by focusing on the activities in the organisation which incur costs. Any activity or series of activities that takes place within an organisation and causes costs to be incurred is known as a *cost driver*. Examples of cost drivers are the volume of raw materials handled in the organisation, the number of orders placed by customers or the number of machine hours. The cost drivers for short-term variable overheads are based on volume of activity as measured by direct labour hours or machine hours. The cost driver for long-term variable overheads could be the number of job runs for an activity such as machine set up costs.

A collection of costs charged to products by the use of a common cost driver is known as a *cost pool*. You should not confuse cost pools with departments. In one department there can be a range of activities which cause costs to be incurred. For example, in the production department the power used is related to the machine hours, but the costs incurred in the handling of raw materials may be related to the number of purchase orders made, and the costs incurred in setting up the various machines related to the number of different jobs undertaken.

Activity

In ABC, activities that cause costs to be incurred are known as:

a cost centres
b cost drivers
c cost pools
d cost units.

The answer is **b**. In ABC activities that takes place within an organisation and cause costs to be incurred are known as cost drivers.

We will now use an example to illustrate how ABC is used. Teddies Galore Ltd makes 3 products, the details of which for a financial period are as follows:

Product	Output (units)	Number of production runs	Material cost per unit	Direct labour hours per unit
Standard teddy	50	10	£10	2
Deluxe teddy	50	10	£30	6
Mini teddy	500	20	£5	1

The direct labour costs are £10 per hour and for the financial period the overhead costs are as follows:

	£
Short-term variable overheads	18,000
Machine set-up costs	10,000
Material handling cost	26,000
Total	54,000

First we need to calculate the cost per unit using absorption costing:

Teddies Galore Ltd

Cost per unit using absorption costing

	Standard teddy	Deluxe teddy	Mini teddy	Total
Number of units	50	50	500	600
	£	£	£	£
Direct materials	500	1,500	2,500	4,500
Direct labour	1,000	3,000	10,000	14,000
Direct costs	1,500	4,500	12,500	18,500
Overheads	6,000	18,000	30,000	54,000
Total cost	7,500	22,500	42,500	72,500
Cost per unit	£150	£450	£85	

Note:

Overhead absorption rate, based on a total of 900 direct labour hours:

$$\frac{£54,000}{900 \text{ hours}} = £60 \text{ per hour}$$

Now we need to repeat the procedure for ABC. The details are as before, but the cost drivers are as follows:

Short-term variable overheads:	Direct labour hours
Machine set-up costs:	Number of production runs
Material handling costs:	Number of production runs

Teddies Galore Ltd
Cost per unit using ABC

	Standard teddy	Deluxe teddy	Mini teddy	Total
Number of units	50	50	500	600
	£	£	£	£
Direct materials	500	1,500	2,500	4,500
Direct labour	1,000	3,000	10,000	14,000
Direct costs	1,500	4,500	12,500	18,500
Short-term overheads[1]	2,000	6,000	10,000	18,000
Machine set up[2]	2,500	2,500	5,000	10,000
Material handling[3]	6,500	6,500	13,000	26,000
Total costs	12,500	19,500	40,500	72,500
Cost per unit	£250	£390	£81	

Notes:

1 Short-run variable overheads:

$$\frac{£18,000}{900 \text{ hours}} = £20 \text{ per direct labour hour}$$

2 Machine set-up costs:

$$\frac{£10,000}{40} = £250 \text{ per production run}$$

3 Material handling costs:

$$\frac{£26,000}{40} = £650 \text{ per production run}$$

22.3 Advantages and Disadvantages of Activity-based Costing

At the beginning section 22.2 we explained the reasons for the introduction of ABC; the management of organisations that have implemented the method successfully would claim that it offers the following *advantages*:

• Costs are attributed to the activity that caused them to be incurred. In absorption costing, the costs are allocated and apportioned on an arbitrary basis to various parts of the organisation, and in marginal costing the fixed costs are ignored. ABC avoids these problems by associating costs with the actual activity and if the level of that activity changes one would expect to see a change in the level of costs incurred in the longer term.

- As costs are related to the activity that causes them to be incurred, the information produced is more useful for managers in planning and controlling the activities of the business. The products and services that caused the costs to be incurred are charged with these costs on a realistic basis.
- The increasing complexity of diverse product ranges and the potential impact on costs is recognised under this method of costing. For example, an order that requires a high level of technical input, or is for a low volume and therefore needs only a small production run, is charged with the costs that it incurs.

Although ABC appears to offer a number of advantages, there are critics of the method who argue that these are illusory or rarely enjoyed in practice. Some critics contend that ABC is no more than a more sophisticated version of absorption costing and that organisations have been using this sort of approach for a number of years; it is only consultants and academics inventing a new terminology that has given the method prominence. Other *disadvantages* of ABC are:

- The system is costly to implement and operate. Numerous cost drivers and cost pools have to be identified for the system to be fully effective. For many organisations this is neither practical nor possible.
- Although the information generated by the system may be more sophisticated, managers do not have the time or the knowledge to analyse it fully. ABC generates more information than is needed by the practising manager.
- ABC is only a method of collecting and recording costs, and claims too much for itself. An organisation is a complex, dynamic combination of many disciplines, including behavioural ones; ABC does not take account of the context in which businesses operate.

Self-check question

What are the advantages and disadvantages of activity-based costing?

22.4 Throughput Accounting

Throughput accounting (TA) is an approach to short-term decision-making in manufacturing in which all conversion costs are treated as if they were fixed costs and products are ranked if a particular *constraint* or *scarce resource* exists. It is an approach to management accounting that focuses on the fact that a number of organisations are constrained in the level of activity they can achieve by the presence of *bottlenecks* in the operations process. A bottleneck is a point at which the flow is constricted. For example, there may be a particular machine at the centre of the production activity which acts as a bottleneck to the entire process, or at peak times there may be such a queue of customers that service cannot be given fast enough to keep them moving through. It is the responsibility of managers to identify such bottlenecks and either attempt to remove them or ensure that they are always operating at full capacity.

Self-check question

What is a bottleneck?

If a bottleneck cannot be removed, the remainder of the operations process must be scheduled to ensure that it does not generate more than the bottleneck can absorb, as this leads to inefficiencies. In manufacturing, this will lead to stocks of work in progress being held before they can be cleared through the bottleneck. The process of identifying the bottlenecks and taking action to remove them is known by the somewhat elaborate title of the *theory of constraints*. The theory can be applied in organisations by using throughput accounting.

Self-check question

What is the theory of constraints?

Under TA, it is argued that managers can increase profitability by increasing throughput and, at the same time, reducing the costs of holding inventories and operational expenditure. However, in the short term, little action can be taken on operational expenditure, which is mostly fixed in nature so managers should concentrate on throughput followed by inventories. This implies that all operating expenses, including direct labour, is regarded as fixed. Only direct materials are regarded as a variable cost.

For decision-making, TA uses a similar approach to *marginal costing*, but the definition of variable costs is far stricter. The following formula is used to apply TA:

$$\text{TA ratio} = \frac{\text{Return per factory hour}}{\text{Costs per factory hour}}$$

where:

$$\text{Return per factory hour} = \frac{\text{Sales price} - \text{Material cost}}{\text{Time on key resource}}$$

$$\text{Cost per factory hour} = \frac{\text{Total factory cost}}{\text{Total time available on key resource}}$$

We will now use an example to show how the formula is used.

Blue Glass Ltd produces two types of drinking glasses for the export market. Both are finely engraved on two separate machines and the details are as follows:

	Goblets	**Schooners**
Estimated sales demand	1,500 glasses	1,500 glasses
Selling price per glass	£8.00	£7.50
Direct material costs	£2.00	£2.50
Engraving machine hours required per glass:		
Machine 1	1 hour	1 hour
Machine 2	4 hours	2 hours

The machine capacity in the financial period is limited to 4,000 hours for each machine and the total operating expenses are £12,000

The first step is to find out where the bottleneck is and we do this by calculating the machine hours required to meet the sales demand:

	Goblets	**Schooners**	**Total**
Machine 1	1,500 hours	1,500 hours	3,000 hours
Machine 2	6,000 hours	3,000 hours	9,000 hours

It is evident that the bottleneck is machine 2, which will have capacity in the financial period for only 4,000 hours, but the estimated sales demand is for 9,000 hours. Our calculation of the TA ratio will be based on machine 2.

	Goblets	**Schooners**
Return per factory hour	$\dfrac{£6}{4 \text{ hours}} = £1.50$	$\dfrac{£5}{2 \text{ hours}} = £2.50$
Cost per factory hour	$\dfrac{£12,000}{4,000 \text{ hours}} = £3.00$	$\dfrac{£12,000}{4,000 \text{ hours}} = £3.00$
TA ratio	$\dfrac{£1.50}{£3} = 0.50$	$\dfrac{£2.50}{£3} = 0.83$

On a ranking basis it is therefore more profitable to meet the demand for schooners fully before starting to manufacture goblets. This will mean that the production of 1,500 schooners will use 3,000 of the machine hours on machine 2 and the remaining 1,000 hours of machine capacity may be used for manufacturing 250 goblets. Of course, having identified the bottleneck, management should ascertain what scope it has to alleviate its impact.

Activity

Are the following statements true or false?

In throughput accounting, the return per factory hour is calculated by:

a deducting all direct costs from the selling price and dividing by the time of the key resource;

b deducting all direct material costs from the selling price and dividing by the time of the key resource;

c dividing direct material costs by the selling price;

d dividing the selling price by the direct material costs.

If you have remembered the TA formula you will know that only **b** is true; all the other answers are false.

For those who are familiar with marginal costing, TA offers no novel technical development and as such suffers the drawbacks of any technique which uses variable costs. Under marginal costing we could treat direct materials as the only variable cost and proceed to compute the contribution per unit of limiting factor – in this case, machine hours – to give the ranking to arrive at the same result as above. The value of TA is the emphasis on concentrating on bottlenecks and eradicating them. It may also help management to review what are the true variable costs in the short run.

Practice questions

1 A business has three products with the following TA ratios:

Product X = 0.63
Product Y = 0.82
Product Z = 0.75

The product(s) you would concentrate on if there is a bottleneck is/are:

a X and Z
b Y and Z
c X
d Y

2 In Activity Based Costing systems, costs are accumulated by activity using

A cost drivers.
B cost centres.
C cost pools.
D cost benefit analysis.

CIMA, Stage 1, May 1997

3 A cost driver is

    A   an item of production overhead.
    B   a common cost which is shared over cost centres.
    C   any cost relating to transport.
    D   an activity which generates costs.

CIMA, Stage 1, May 1995

Appendix A Present Value Tables

Present value of 1 at compound interest: $(1+r)^{-n}$

Years (n)	Interest rates (r)														
	1	2	3	4	5	6	7	8	9	10	11	12	13	14	15
1	0.9901	0.9804	0.9709	0.9615	0.9524	0.9434	0.9346	0.9259	0.9174	0.0901	0.9009	0.8929	0.8850	0.8772	0.8696
2	0.9803	0.9612	0.9426	0.9246	0.9070	0.8900	0.8734	0.8573	0.8417	0.8264	0.8116	0.7972	0.7831	0.7695	0.7561
3	0.9706	0.9423	0.9151	0.8890	0.8638	0.8396	0.8163	0.7938	0.7722	0.7513	0.7312	0.7118	0.6931	0.6750	0.6575
4	0.9610	0.9238	0.8885	0.8548	0.8227	0.7921	0.7629	0.7350	0.7084	0.6830	0.6587	0.6355	0.6133	0.5921	0.5718
5	0.9515	0.9057	0.8626	0.8219	0.7835	0.7473	0.7130	0.6806	0.6499	0.6209	0.5935	0.5674	0.5428	0.5194	0.4972
6	0.9420	0.8880	0.8375	0.7903	0.7462	0.7050	0.6663	0.6302	0.5963	0.5645	0.5346	0.5066	0.4803	0.4556	0.4323
7	0.9327	0.8706	0.8131	0.7599	0.7107	0.6651	0.6227	0.5835	0.5470	0.5132	0.4817	0.4523	0.4251	0.3996	0.3759
8	0.9235	0.8535	0.7894	0.7307	0.6768	0.6274	0.5820	0.5403	0.5019	0.4665	0.4339	0.4039	0.3762	0.3506	0.3269
9	0.9143	0.8368	0.7664	0.7026	0.6446	0.5919	0.5439	0.5002	0.4604	0.4241	0.3909	0.3606	0.3329	0.3075	0.2834
10	0.9053	0.8203	0.7441	0.6756	0.6139	0.5584	0.5083	0.4632	0.4224	0.3855	0.3522	0.3220	0.2946	0.2697	0.2472
11	0.8963	0.8043	0.7224	0.6496	0.5847	0.5268	0.4751	0.4289	0.3875	0.3505	0.3173	0.2875	0.2607	0.2366	0.2149
12	0.8874	0.7885	0.7014	0.6246	0.5568	0.4970	0.4440	0.3971	0.3555	0.3188	0.2858	0.2567	0.2307	0.2076	0.1869
13	0.8787	0.7730	0.6810	0.6006	0.5303	0.4688	0.4150	0.3677	0.3262	0.2862	0.2575	0.2292	0.2042	0.1821	0.1625
14	0.8700	0.7579	0.6611	0.5775	0.5051	0.4423	0.3878	0.3405	0.2992	0.2633	0.2320	0.2046	0.1807	0.5197	0.1413
15	0.8613	0.7430	0.6419	0.5553	0.4810	0.4173	0.3624	0.3152	0.2745	0.2394	0.2090	0.1827	0.1599	0.1401	0.1229
16	0.8528	0.7284	0.6232	0.5339	0.4581	0.3936	0.3387	0.2919	0.2519	0.2176	0.1883	0.1631	0.1415	0.1229	0.1069
17	0.8444	0.7142	0.6050	0.5134	0.4363	0.3714	0.3168	0.2703	0.2311	0.1978	0.1696	0.1456	0.1252	0.1078	0.0929
18	0.8360	0.7002	0.5874	0.4936	0.4155	0.3503	0.2959	0.2502	0.2120	0.1799	0.1528	0.1300	0.1108	0.0946	0.0808
19	0.8277	0.6864	0.5703	0.4746	0.3957	0.3305	0.2765	0.2317	0.1945	0.1635	0.1377	0.1161	0.0980	0.0829	0.0703
20	0.8195	0.6730	0.5537	0.4564	0.3769	0.3118	0.2584	0.2145	0.1784	0.1486	0.1240	0.1037	0.0868	0.0728	0.0611
25	0.7795	0.6095	0.4776	0.3751	0.2953	0.2330	0.1842	0.1460	0.1160	0.0923	0.0736	0.0588	0.0471	0.0378	0.0304
30	0.7419	0.5521	0.4120	0.3083	0.2314	0.1741	0.1314	0.0994	0.0754	0.0573	0.0437	0.0334	0.0256	0.0196	0.0151
35	0.7059	0.5000	0.3554	0.2534	0.1813	0.1301	0.0937	0.0676	0.0490	0.0356	0.0259	0.0189	0.0139	0.0102	0.0075
40	0.6717	0.4529	0.3066	0.2083	0.1420	0.0972	0.0668	0.0460	0.0318	0.0221	0.0154	0.0107	0.0075	0.0053	0.0037
45	0.6391	0.4102	0.2644	0.1712	0.1113	0.0727	0.0476	0.0313	0.0207	0.0137	0.0091	0.0061	0.0041	0.0027	0.0019
50	0.6080	0.3715	0.2281	0.1407	0.0872	0.0543	0.0339	0.0213	0.0134	0.0085	0.0054	0.0035	0.0022	0.0014	0.0009

	16	17	18	19	20	21	22	23	24	25	26	27	28	29	30
1	0.8621	0.8547	0.8475	0.8403	0.8333	0.8264	0.8197	0.8130	0.8065	0.8000	0.7937	0.7874	0.7812	0.7752	0.7692
2	0.7432	0.7305	0.7182	0.7062	0.6944	0.6830	0.6719	0.6610	0.6504	0.6400	0.6299	0.6200	0.6104	0.6009	0.5917
3	0.6407	0.6244	0.6086	0.5934	0.5787	0.5645	0.5507	0.5374	0.5245	0.5120	0.4999	0.4882	0.4768	0.4658	0.4552
4	0.5523	0.5337	0.5158	0.4987	0.4823	0.4665	0.4514	0.4369	0.4230	0.4069	0.3968	0.3844	0.3725	0.3611	0.3501
5	0.4761	0.4561	0.4371	0.4190	0.4019	0.3855	0.3700	0.3552	0.3411	0.3277	0.3149	0.3027	0.2910	0.2799	0.2693
6	0.4104	0.3898	0.3704	0.3521	0.3349	0.3186	0.3033	0.2888	0.2751	0.2621	0.2499	0.2338	0.2274	0.2170	0.2072
7	0.3538	0.3332	0.3139	0.2959	0.2791	0.2633	0.2486	0.2348	0.2218	0.2097	0.1983	0.1877	0.1776	0.1682	0.1594
8	0.3050	0.2848	0.2660	0.2487	0.2326	0.2176	0.2038	0.1909	0.1789	0.1678	0.1574	0.1478	0.1388	0.1304	0.1226
9	0.2630	0.2434	0.2255	0.2090	0.1938	0.1799	0.1670	0.1552	0.1443	0.1342	0.1249	0.1164	0.1084	0.1011	0.0943
10	0.2267	0.2080	0.1911	0.1756	0.1615	0.1486	0.1369	0.1262	0.1164	0.1074	0.0992	0.0916	0.0847	0.0784	0.0725
11	0.1954	0.1778	0.1619	0.1476	0.1346	0.1228	0.1122	0.1026	0.0938	0.0859	0.0787	0.0721	0.0662	0.0607	0.0558
12	0.1685	0.1520	0.1372	0.1240	0.1122	0.1015	0.0920	0.0834	0.0757	0.0687	0.0625	0.0568	0.0517	0.0471	0.0429
13	0.1452	0.1299	0.1163	0.1042	0.0935	0.0839	0.0754	0.0678	0.0610	0.0550	0.0496	0.0447	0.0404	0.0365	0.0330
14	0.1252	0.1110	0.0985	0.0876	0.0779	0.0693	0.0618	0.0551	0.0492	0.0440	0.0393	0.0352	0.0316	0.0283	0.0254
15	0.1079	0.0949	0.0835	0.0736	0.0649	0.0573	0.0507	0.0448	0.0397	0.0352	0.0312	0.0277	0.0247	0.0219	0.0195
16	0.0930	0.0811	0.0708	0.0618	0.0541	0.0474	0.0415	0.0364	0.0320	0.0281	0.0248	0.0218	0.0193	0.0170	0.0150
17	0.0802	0.0693	0.0600	0.0520	0.0451	0.0391	0.0340	0.0296	0.0258	0.0225	0.0197	0.0172	0.0150	0.0132	0.0116
18	0.0691	0.0592	0.0508	0.0437	0.0376	0.0323	0.0279	0.0241	0.0208	0.0180	0.0156	0.0135	0.0118	0.0102	0.0089
19	0.0596	0.0506	0.0431	0.0367	0.0313	0.0267	0.0229	0.0196	0.0168	0.0144	0.0124	0.0107	0.0092	0.0079	0.0068
20	0.0514	0.0433	0.0365	0.0308	0.0261	0.0221	0.0187	0.0159	0.0135	0.0115	0.0098	0.0084	0.0072	0.0061	0.0053
25	0.0245	0.0197	0.0160	0.0129	0.0105	0.0085	0.0069	0.0057	0.0046	0.0038	0.0031	0.0025	0.0021	0.0017	0.0014
30	0.0116	0.0090	0.0070	0.0054	0.0042	0.0033	0.0026	0.0020	0.0016	0.0012	0.0010	0.0008	0.0006	0.0005	0.0004
35	0.0055	0.0041	0.0030	0.0023	0.0017	0.0013	0.0009	0.0007	0.0005	0.0004	0.0003	0.0002	0.0002	0.0001	0.0001
40	0.0026	0.0019	0.0013	0.0010	0.0007	0.0005	0.0004	0.0003	0.0002	0.0001	0.0001	0.0001	0.0001	0.0000	0.0000
45	0.0013	0.0009	0.0006	0.0004	0.0003	0.0002	0.0001	0.0001	0.0001	0.0000	0.0000	0.0000	0.0000	0.0000	0.0000
50	0.0006	0.0004	0.0003	0.0002	0.0001	0.0001	0.0000	0.0000	0.0000	0.0000	0.0000	0.0000	0.0000	0.0000	0.0000

Glossary

ABSORPTION COSTING – a method of costing that, in addition to direct costs, assigns all, or a proportion of, production overhead costs to cost units by means of one or a number of overhead absorption rates.

ACTIVITY-BASED COSTING (ABC) – an approach to costing that recognises that costs are incurred by each activity, and that products or customers should bear the costs according to the activities they use.

AVERAGE COST METHOD – prices issues of materials by adding the total of the WIP valuation to the current period costs.

BATCH COSTING – a variation of job costing whereby a number of identical cost units are treated as one batch throughout one or more stages of production.

BOTTLENECK – a point at which the flow of an activity is constricted.

BREAK-EVEN ANALYSIS – an examination of the relationship between cost, volume and profit at different levels of activity.

BUDGETARY CONTROL – the establishment of budgets relating the responsibilities of executives to the requirements of a policy, and the continuous comparison of actual with budgeted results, either to secure by individual action the objectives of that policy or to provide a basis for its revision.

BY-PRODUCT – an output with a relatively small value that arises incidentally in the course of production of the main product(s).

CONTINUOUS-OPERATION COSTING – a method of costing used where the goods or services being costed are the result of continuous or repetitive operations or processes.

CONTINUOUS STOCKTAKING – a process whereby selected items of stock are physically counted at different times on a rotating basis.

CONTRACT COSTING – a form of job costing in which costs are attributed to individual contracts.

CONTRIBUTION – the difference between sales volume and the variable cost of sales.

CONTROLLABLE COST – a cost that can be influenced by its budget holder.

COST ACCOUNTING – the collection and collation of data to provide budgets, standard costs and actual costs of operations, processes, activities or products; and the analysis of variances, profitability or the social use of funds.

COST BEHAVIOUR – the way that costs vary at different levels of activity or volume.

COST CENTRE – a production or service location, function, activity or item of equipment for which costs are accumulated.

COST DRIVER – any factor which causes a change in the cost of an activity.

COST POOL – a collection of costs charged to products by the use of a common cost driver.

COST UNIT – a quantitative unit of product or service in relation to which costs are ascertained.

COST-VOLUME-PROFIT (CVP) ANALYSIS – the study of the effects on future profit of changes in fixed cost, variable cost, sales price, quantity and mix.

DIRECT COST – expenditure that can be economically identified with and specifically measured in respect to a relevant cost object.

DIRECT EXPENSES – such items as subcontract work or special tools or equipment bought for a particular job.

DIRECT LABOUR – converts the direct materials into the finished goods, and the time spent on cost units may be calculated from time sheets, job cards or computerised records.

DIRECT MATERIALS – part of the finished goods and can be charged direct to the cost unit.

DISCOUNTED CASH FLOW (DCF) – a technique which discounts projected net cash flows of a capital project to ascertain its present value.

DISTRIBUTION COSTS – the costs incurred from receipt of the finished goods from the production department to delivery to the customer.

DISTRIBUTION OVERHEADS – the indirect costs arising from the activity of getting the cost unit to the customer

FINANCIAL ACCOUNTING – concerned with classifying and recording actual transactions in monetary terms to provide a true and fair view of an organisation over a period of time or at the end of that time.

FIRST IN, FIRST OUT (FIFO) – a method of pricing issues of materials from stores which uses the price of the first delivery of materials to the company until that particular consignment is exhausted, then uses the price of the next delivery.

FIXED COSTS – costs which, in total, stay the same over a wide range of activity for a given period.

FLEXIBLE BUDGET – a budget that changes in accordance with levels of activity and reflects the different behaviours of fixed and variable costs.

GOODS RECEIVED NOTE (GRN) – an internal document raised when goods or services are received and compared with the purchase order.

INCREMENTAL COSTS – the additional costs arising from the production or sale of additional units.

INDIRECT COSTS – costs that cannot be identified with any one particular cost unit, but have to be shared over those units to which they are common or by which they are jointly incurred.

INTEGRATED ACCOUNTS – a set of accounting records which provides both financial and cost accounts using a common input of data for all accounting purposes.

INTERLOCKING ACCOUNTS – a system which maintains separate ledgers for the financial accounts and cost accounts with each ledger having a control account.

INTERNAL RATE OF RETURN (IRR) – the annual percentage return achieved by a project, at which the sum of the discounted cash inflows over the life of the project is equal to the sum of the discounted cash outflows.

JOB CARDS – refer to a single job or batch and show the times spent by all employees working on that particular job.

JOB COSTING – used where work is carried out to the specific requirements of customers and the job is of short duration.

JOINT PRODUCT COSTING – used when two or more products are produced from the same process, using the same commonly processed materials up to their point of separation.

JOINT PRODUCTS – two or more products, each with a significant value, which have been produced simultaneously in the course of production.

LAST IN, FIRST OUT (LIFO) – a method of pricing issues of materials from stores which uses the price of the last delivery of materials to tile company until that particular consignment is exhausted, then uses the price of the previous delivery.

LIMITING FACTOR – also known as key factor or principal budget factor, is that factor which prevents a company expanding indefinitely or constantly increasing its profits.

MANAGEMENT ACCOUNTING – concerned with providing information to managers so that policies can be formulated, activities planned and controlled, decisions or alternative courses of action taken, assets safeguarded and the activities of the enterprise reported to interested parties.

MARGINAL COST (VARIABLE COST) – the part of the cost of one unit of product or service that would be avoided if that unit were not produced or would increase if one extra unit were produced.

MARGINAL COSTING – also known as variable costing or direct costing, is where the variable costs only are charged to cost units and the fixed costs for a financial period are written off in total against the contribution for that period.

MARGIN OF SAFETY – the amount by which sales may decrease before the break-even point is reached and losses begin to arise.

MATERIALS REQUISITION – an internal document authorising the issue from stores of a specified quantity of materials.

MATERIALS RETURN NOTE – an internal document recording the return of unused materials to store.

NEGATIVE CASH FLOW – the cash and cheques being paid out by an organisation.

NET CASH FLOW – the difference between the positive and negative cash flows.

NET PRESENT VALUE (NPV) – the difference between the sum of the projected discounted cash inflows and outflows attributable to a capital investment or other long-term project.

NET REALISABLE VALUE – the actual or estimated selling price of stock net of any trade discounts, from which is deducted any cost incurred to put the stock into a saleable condition, and to which is added all costs incurred in the marketing, selling and distribution of such stock.

OPERATION COSTING – a costing method used where goods or services result from a sequence of continuous operations or processes producing normally identical units.

OPPORTUNITY COSTS – the value of the benefit sacrificed as a result of selecting one course of action in preference to an alternative.

OVERHEAD ABSORPTION – also known as overhead recovery, is the process by which overheads for a financial period are shared out amongst all the cost units produced in that period.

OVERHEAD ABSORPTION RATE – a means of attributing overheads to a product or service, based for example on direct labour hours, direct labour cost or machine hours.

OVERHEAD ANALYSIS – the charging of overheads to the appropriate cost centres by a process of allocation and apportionment.

OVERHEADS – indirect material, indirect labour and indirect expense costs.

PAYBACK PERIOD – the time required for the cash inflows from an investment project to equal the cash outflows.

PERIODIC STOCKTAKING – a process whereby the physical quantities of all stock items are physically counted and then valued.

PERPETUAL INVENTORY – the recording as they occur of receipts, issues, and the resulting balances of individual items of stock in either quantity or quantity of value.

PIECEWORK TICKETS – record employees time by each job having a number of piecework tickets attached to it referring to each stage of manufacture.

POSITIVE CASH FLOW – the cash and cheques coming into an organisation.

PROCESS COSTING – the costing method applicable where goods or services result from a sequence of continuous or repetitive operations or processes to which costs are charged before being averaged over the units produced during the period.

PRODUCTION COSTS – the costs incurred from receipt of the raw materials to completion of the finished product.

PRODUCTION OVERHEADS – the indirect costs arising from the provision of the production resources.

PURCHASE ORDER – a written order for goods or services specifying quantities, prices, delivery dates and contract terms.

PURCHASE REQUISITION – an internal request to the Purchase Department detailing requirements for specific materials, equipment or services.

RELEVANT COSTS – costs appropriate to aiding the making of a specific management decision.

REPLACEMENT PRICE METHOD – uses the replacement price on the day of issue to value materials issued from stores.

RETENTION MONIES – a proportion of the contract value withheld by the client for a certain period after the completion of the contract.

SALES OVERHEADS – the indirect costs arising from the selling of the cost unit.

SELLING COSTS – the costs incurred from receipt of the raw materials to completion of the finished product.

SEMI-VARIABLE COSTS – the costs which do not change in total in direct relationship to changes in the level of activity, neither do they remain fixed.

SERVICE COSTING – a method used when specific functions or services are costed.

SPECIFIC ORDER COSTING – the basic cost accounting method used where work consists of separately identifiable contracts, jobs or batches.

STANDARD COST – a cost which is a predetermined specified working condition.

STANDARD COSTING – a technique whereby actual costs incurred are compared predetermined standard and the variances analysed.

STANDARD PRICE METHOD – uses a predetermined price to value all issues and receipts of materials from and to stores.

STOCK RECORD CARD – a record giving not only the physical stock balance, but also outstanding orders and unfulfilled requirement and thus the pre-stock position.

SUNK COSTS – those costs which have been incurred by a past decision and will be unaffected by the present choice between different alternatives.

THROUGHPUT ACCOUNTING (TA) – an approach to short-term decision-making in manufacturing in which all conversion costs are treated as if they were fixed costs and products are ranked if a particular constraint or scare resource exists.

TIME SHEETS – forms completed by employees on a weekly or daily basis to record how time has been spent.

VARIABLE COST – costs that, in total, vary in direct proportion to the volume of activity.

VARIANCE ANALYSIS – the investigation of the differences arising between actual costs incurred and the predetermined standard costs.

Appendix C

Outline Answers to Practice Questions

Chapter 1

1 The main points to bring out in your answer are:

Detailed financial information will be provided on a regular basis which will help in the following ways:

- Control will be improved because the actual costs incurred for labour, materials and overheads in manufacturing the product will be known. This will help in cost reduction and monitoring.
- Planning will be improved because financial information on the past can be used as a basis for future activities and will also demonstrate which activities are financially the most beneficial
- Decision-making will be improved because information will be available on the financial implications of alternative courses of action.

2 This is covered in the chapter.
3 The essential point to bring out is that a financial accountant is preparing information according to a regulatory framework for external parties, whereas a management accountant is preparing information for internal use by managers.
4 The main points to bring out are that cost and management accounting helps managers to discharge their responsibilities for control, planning and decision-making.

Chapter 2

1 D
2 B
3 600 × £3.25 = £1,950
Material is in regular use. 500 kgs purchased to replace material used, 100 kgs purchased and used. Surplus material purchased will be stores and used on later jobs. Therefore answer is **D**.

Chapter 3

1 Replenishment level 2,800, therefore **B**
Maximum levels 4,900, therefore **C**
2 B
3 (a) (i) Continuous stocktaking refers to a system whereby stocktaking is carried out on an ongoing rota basis throughout the year, so that every stock item is checked at least once: items of greater value or importance may be counted several times during the year. As a result,

stocktaking effort can be directed so as to maximise control and minimise costs. In contrast to periodic stocktaking also avoids disruption to production.

(ii) Perpetual inventory is a system of entering details of all stock receipts and issues for each individual raw material/finished product onto a record card, thus enabling the stock quantity on hand to be known at any time. The stock quantity provides the necessary information for stock re-ordering and for verifying/reconciling physical stock counts.

(b) (i)

3,040 kgs × £0.765/kg	=	£2,325.60
1,400 kgs × 0.780/kg	=	1,092.00
4,440 kgs × 0.770/kg	=	3,417.60
(1,700) kgs × 0.770/kg	=	(1,309.00)
2,740 kgs × 0.770/kg	=	2,108.60
60 kgs × 0.770/kg	=	46.20
(220) kgs × 0.780/kg	=	(171.60)
1,630 kgs × 0.778/kg	=	1,268.14
4,2l0 kgs × 0.772/kg	=	3,251.34
(1,250) kgs × 0.772/kg	=	(965.00)
2,960 kgs × 0.772/kg	=	£2,286.34

(ii)

Material account

Day		£	Day		£
	Opening stock	2,325.60	2	Work in progress	1,309.00
1	Cost Ledger		4	Cost Ledger	
	Control	1,092.00		Control	171.60
3	Work in progress	42.60	5	Work in progress	965.00
4	Cost Ledger				
	Control	1,268.14		Closing stock	2,286.34
		£4,731.94			£4,731.94

Chapter 4

1. This is covered in the chapter.
2. 12 piecework hours @ £3 = £36.
3. This is covered in the chapter.

Chapter 5

1 A
2 E
3 D
4 (a) Answers may include:

    (i) *Choice*
        – Financial accounts are compulsory in order to establish profit/loss for a business and a balance sheet for reporting and tax purposes.

Cost and management accounts are prepared entirely at the discretion of each business.

(ii) *Regulations*
- Unifying concepts, standards, and rules are applied in financial accounting in order to provide consistency and thus understandable information from one business to another. In cost and management accounting the objective should always be to provide information that is relevant and useful for a particular purpose at a particular time. This provides much greater flexibility but at the same time a requirement to ensure that the recipient fully understands the information presented and the assumptions underlying it.

(iii) Internal/external
- Financial accounts are primarily for the benefit of the owners of a business, for example the shareholders of a limited company must be sent a copy of the financial accounts, and the Inland Revenue. They are essentially 'external' users. Cost and management accounts on the other hand are for 'internal' users all levels of management within a business who require information to help them manage the business.

(iv) *Past/future*
- Financial accounts provide a record of past financial transactions. The focus of cost and management accounting should be on the future; the purpose is to assist management in planning, control and decision-making.

(v) *Degree of detail*
- Financial accounts only need to record and group information in sufficient detail to meet periodic reporting requirements for the business as a whole. Cost and management accounting information will invariably be more detailed, focusing on different segments of a business, and with greater frequency.

(vi) *Monetary/non-monetary measures measures*
- Financial accounts consist of monetary measures. Cost and management accounting information will also include non-monetary measures, either on their own or in relation to cost/revenue, e.g. cost per unit, cost per employee.

(vii) *Degree of accuracy*
- Financial accounts must accurately record transactions which have occurred. Cost and management accounts, because they are more detailed and are concerned with the future, include many approximations/estimates in order to apportion costs and/or forecast the future.

(b) ──

Stores ledger control account

	£000		£000
Opening balance	176.0	Job ledger control A/c	206.4
Financial ledger control		Production o'head	
A/c	224.2	control A/c	24.3
		Closing balance	169.5
	400.2		400.2

Production wages control account

	£000		£000
Financial ledger control A/c	196.0	Job ledger control A/c	147.0
		Production o'head	
		control A/c	49.0
	196.0		
	196.0		196.0

Production overhead control account

	£000		£000
Financial ledger control A/c	119.3	Job ledger control A/c	191.1
Stores ledger control		Under-absorbed o'hd	
A/c	24.3	(P and L)	1.5
Production wages control			
A/c	49.0		
	192.6		192.6

Chapter 6

1 This is covered in the chapter.
2 Production department 1   £2,317
Production department 2   £2,023
3 B

Chapter 7

1 (a) (i)   Budgeted Professional Staff Hours (year to 31.3.96):

Actual overheads	£742,600
+ Overheads over-absorbed	4,760
Overheads absorbed	£747,360
÷ 7.50/hr	
= Actual professional staff hours worked	99,648
− Hours over budget	1,360
Budgeted professional staff hours	98,288

(ii) Budgeted Overhead Expenditure (year to 31.3.96):

Budgeted professional staff hours	98,288
× £7.50	
= Budget Overhead expenditure	£737,160

(b) Overhead Absorption Rates (year to 31.3.97):

21,600 × 1.4 =   30,240
79,300 × 1.0 =   79,300

109,540 adjusted hours

Split of overheads:

(i) Senior staff $= 784,000 \times \dfrac{30,240}{109,540} = $ £216,434

(ii) Junior staff $= 784,000 \times \dfrac{79,300}{109,540} = $ £567,566

$$\underline{\underline{£784,000}}$$

Absorption rates:

(i) Senior staff: $\dfrac{216,434}{21,600} = $ £10.020 per hour

(ii) Junior staff: $\dfrac{567,566}{79,300} = $ £7.157 per hour

(c) The previous blanket absorption rate did not differentiate between hours worked by different types of staff which is likely to be a key driver of overhead cost.

   The revised method does provide some differentiation (between senior and junior professional staff) and thus is likely to more accurately allocate overhead costs to client services. The cost of office space, for example, may be significantly affected by staff seniority. The premium applied to senior staff hours presumably rejects this and other differential overhead costs.

(d) Differences between overhead incurred and overhead absorbed using predetermined rates may be due to:
 – difference between budgeted and actual expenditure;
 – difference between the budgeted and actual activity level of the resource on which absorption rates are based.

2 (a)

TRI-D Ltd – Overhead analysis sheet for the period ending 31 December 1995

Cost allocated Indirect	Basis	Extrusion £000	Machining £000	Finishing £000	Production services £000	Total £000
wages	Allocated	15.00	21.00	8.00	58.00	102.00
Apportioned						
Depreciation	Fixed asset valuation	33.60	29.40	6.30	14.70	84.00
Rates	Floor area	4.00	6.00	5.00	7.00	22.00
Power	Machine hours	69.75	90.00	11.25	9.00	180.00
Personnel	Employees	10.00	14.00	23.50	12.50	60.00
Insurance	Fixed asset valuation	19.20	16.80	3.60	8.40	48.00
					109.60	
Production services	3:2:1	54.80	35.53	18.27	(109.60)	0.00
		206.35	213.73	75.92	0.00	496.00

(b) Overhead absorption rates:

Extrusion $\dfrac{£206,350}{15,500 \text{ machine hours}} = £13.31$ per machine hour

Machining $\dfrac{£213,730}{20,000 \text{ machine hours}} = £10.69$ per machine hour

Finishing $\dfrac{£75,920}{15,000 \text{ labour hours}} = £5.06$ per labour hour

(c) Recovery of overheads for the Extrusion Dept

		£
Overheads incurred		211,820
Overheads absorbed	£13.31 × 16,250	216,288
Over-recovery		4,468

3 (a) Predetermined departmental overhead absorption rates for period 3 (per production hr):

Casting	Dressing	Assembly
$\dfrac{225,000}{7,500} = £30$	$\dfrac{175,000}{7,000} = £25$	$\dfrac{93,000}{6,200} = £15$

(b) Over/(under) absorption of overheads for period 3:

	Casting £	Dressing £	Assembly £
Overheads absorbed:			
£30/hr × 7,950	238,500		
£25/hr × 7,280		182,000	
£15/hr × 6,696			100,440
Actual overheads	(229,317)	(182,875)	(94,395)
Over/(under) absorption	9,183	(875)	6,045

The Casting department had £9,183 of over-absorbed overheads in period 3. This could be due to:

- The fixed cost content of the absorption rate. As production hours increase beyond the amount used in setting the overhead absorption rate, overheads are likely to be over-absorbed; or
- The predetermined rate being based on estimated production overheads and estimated production hours for 110,000 units. Over-absorption could be due to an over-estimate of the production hours necessary to produce 110,000 units, or an over-estimate of the production overheads incurred for 110,000 units of production, or a combination of the two.

(c) Production has increased by approximately 7% in the Dressing department, overheads increased by 4.5% and production hours by 4%. This indicates an efficiency gain since for the production achieved, relatively fewer production hours were needed and thus an under-absorption of overheads ensued.

However, the position with the Assembly department is quite different. For the same level of increased production (7%), although overheads show only a 1.5% increase, production hours increased by 8%. This represents relative inefficiency and is indicated by an over-absorption of overheads.

Under/over absorption of overheads relates solely to the interaction of absorption hours and overheads and to the accuracy of forecasting. it is essentially a technical exercise used mainly for product costing. It cannot, nor is it intended to, guide management regarding operational issues or the control of expenditure.

Chapter 8

1 C

2 Overhead absorption rate $= \dfrac{258,750}{11,250} = £23$ per hour

Overheads absorbed $= 10,980 \times £23 = $ 252,540
Actual overheads $= $ 254,692

Therefore, overheads under-absorbed   2,152

Therefore answer is **A**

3 Use labour cost as overhead allocation basis:

Total labour cost $= £14,500 + £3,500 + £24,600 = £42,600$

Total overhead $= £126,000$ ∴ for every £1 of labour cost, following amount of overhead allocated:

$$\frac{126,000}{42,600} = £2.9577465$$

∴ For job CC2O, overhead to be added should be:

$$£24,600 \times £2.9577465 = £72.761$$

Therefore answer is **C**

Total cost of job BB15

	£
Opening WIP	42,790
Materials in period	0
Labour in period	3,500
Overheads in period:	
2.9577465 × £3,500 =	10,352
	56,642
Profit required (33⅓% on selling price)	28.321
∴ Selling price =	84.963

Therefore answer is **C**

Closing WIP = total cost of AA10 and CC2O

	Total £	AA10 £	CC20 £
Opening WIP		26,800	0
Materials in period		17,275	18,500
Labour in period		14,500	24,600
Overheads in period:			
2.9577465 × £14,500		42,887	
2.9577465 × £24,600			72,761
	217,323	101,462	115,861

Therefore answer is **D**

Chapter 9

1 (a)

HR Construction plc – Contract Accounts

tract	Contract A £000	Contract B £000		Contract A £000	Con- B £000
Stores	700	150	Stores returns	80	30
Plant	1,000	150	Transfers to *B*	40	–
Transfers from *A*	–	40	Materials c/fwd	75	15
Plant hire	200	30	Plant c/fwd	880	144
Labour	300	270	Cost to date:		
Overhead	75	18	Cost of work		
Direct expenses	25	4	certified c/fwd	1,065	453
			Cost of work not		
			certified c/fwd	160	20
	2,300	662		2,300	662
Cost of work			Contractee-value		
certified b/fwd	1,065	453	certified	1,500	500
Cost of work not			Cost of work not		
certified b/fwd	160	20	certified c/fwd	205	–
Profit taken	480	(33)			
Cost of work not					
certified c/fwd	–	60			
	1,705	500		1,705	500
Plant b/fwd	880	144	Cost of work not		
			certified b/fwd		60
Cost of work not					
certified b/fwd	205	–			
Materials b/fwd	75	15			

Profit Computation

	Contract A £000	Contract B £000
Contract price	2,000	550
Estimated total cost at completion (1,225 + 135)	1,360	583 (#)
Estimated total contract profit	640	(33)
Recognised (640 × 1,500/2,000)	480	(33)
Cost of sales	(i) 1,020	(ii) 533

    (i)   1,500 − 480
    (ii) 500 + 33
    (#)   453 + 20 + 110

(b) Balance Sheet extracts

	Contract A £000	Contract B £000
Fixed assets:		
Plant at cost	1,000	150
Depreciation	120	6
Written down value	880	144
Debtors:		
Value certified	1,500	500
Less: Cash received	1,440	460
	60	40
Work in progress:		
Costs to date	1,225	473
Less: Cost of sales	1,020	533
	205	(60)

Notes:
1 The above fixed asset and WIP balances are shown in the contract account.
2 In contract costing, the determination of profit and WIP valuation includes considerable judgement. Other approaches to the determination of these amounts may be acceptable.

(c) Job costing is used when each individual job consumes a significant amount of resources (material, labour or overhead) and is specified differently from other jobs, so that it is necessary to maintain records of the cost build-up of each job, in order to charge customers or to monitor cost/ margin levels. With job costing, each job has a separate identification number to which costs are charged. The cost unit is the job.

    Batch costing is similar to job costing, except that the cost unit is a batch of production. This is due to each individual product being identical to all others in the batch and probably, in itself, of insignificant importance as regards the usage of resources. Costs are therefore attached to a batch of perhaps 1,000 units, thereafter being either averaged over the units within the batch or simply being monitored at batch level.

Contract costing is the method used when the 'job' consumes significant resources, and may well extend over several accounting periods. With contract costing, the problem of how to spread the profit of the contract over the accounting periods of its construction has to be resolved (by independent valuation), and, particularly with large projects, the distinction between capital and revenue expenditure may become blurred.

2 (a) (i) Works order 488

This should be accounted for as a long-term contract since it spans two accounting years, and because the absolute sums of money involved in the contract are large.

Works order 517

This work also spans two accounting years with a significant sales value, so although the case for 'contract' status would not be as strong as for works order 488, this nevertheless would be appropriate.

Works orders 518 and 519

Both of these are of small value, and both have durations of approximately 2 months, although spanning a financial year-end. In neither case would the apportionment of profit over the 2 financial years be worthwhile, any profit taken being most likely to be taken at the end of the work. Should a loss be expected, however, this should be brought forward into the accounts of the first financial period covered. Long-term contract status would not be appropriate, however, so they should be accounted for using job costing.

(ii)

Works order number	488 £000	517 £000	518 £000	519 £000	P/L
Valuation	350	30	15	5	
Selling price	450	135	18	9	
Direct costs incurred to date	(191)	(17)	(9)	(4)	
Overhead at 40% on labour	(42)	(4)	(2)	(0.8)	
Total costs to date	**(233)**	**(21)**	**(11)**	**(4.8)**	
Costs to complete, inclusive of overheads	(66)	(99)	–	–	
Total costs to complete	**(299)**	**(120)**			
Estimated contract profit	151	15			
Recognised profit	118	nil	nil	nil	118
	(*)	(#)	(@)	(@)	

(*) £151 × 233/299 = £118
(#) No profit is recognised since the contract has just begun.
(@) As these works orders are not being treated as contracts, no profit is taken.

Work in progress valuations					
Works order number	488 £000	517 £000	518 £000	519 £000	B.S.
Total costs incurred to date	233	21	11	4.8	
Less: Cost of sales	232 (**)	–	–	–	
WIP	1	21	11	4.8	37.8

(**) Value of certificates less recognised profit (£350 – £118) = £232

(iii) The attribution of overhead to works orders on the basis of direct labour cost is potentially rather inaccurate, since it presupposes that not only are the overhead costs labour-related (rather than being related to the usage of equipment or to the undertaking of a variety of activities) but also that the overhead is related to labour cost rather than to hours worked. Thus, the higher the hourly rate of pay of an employee, the more overhead will be attracted to the work which that employee performs. The use of direct labour cost has the merit of simplicity, and therefore of economy in operation, but its sole use may lead to poor quality product costs and may result in impaired managerial understanding of the significance of reported costs, leading to poor decision-making.

(b) Process costing is used where the output of a production process tends to take the form of a large number of identical products, which may not have separate identities until they emerge from the process, and which may be produced, for stock, on a continuous basis. A distinguishing feature of process costing is that it is the process which is the focus of cost collection, product costs being determined by averaging the process costs over the output of the process.

The choice between process costing and specific order costing depends upon a number of factors, such as:

- the economic value of the product
- the nature of the production process
- the need to produce customer specific costs/prices
- the degree of homogeneity of the outputs.

In contrast to process costing, specific-order costing (job, batch and contract costing) is appropriate in situations in which the product is economically significant, may be customised and normally has a unique cost/price. Where specific-order costing is used, the product has a unique identification number which identifies it, and its components, as they move through the production areas, picking up costs as they progress to completion.

Chapter 10

1 B

Chapter 11

1 (a)

Main process account

	Kg	£		Kg	£
Materials	10,000	15,000	P Finished goods	4,800	16,390
Direct labour	–	10,000	Q Process 2	3,600	17,210
Variable overhead	–	4,000	By-product R	1,000	1,750
Fixed overhead	–	6,000	Normal toxic waste	500	–
Toxic waste disposal			Abnormal toxic		
(normal)	–	750	waste	100	400
	10,000	35,750		10,000	35,750

$$\text{Cost per kg of output} = \frac{(£35,750 - £1,750)}{(4,800 + 3,600 + 100)} = £4.00$$

Joint cost apportionment:

	P	Q	Total
Sales values	£24,000	£25,200	£49,200
Apportioned costs:			
$\frac{24}{49.2} \times £33,600$	£16,390	£17,210	£33,600

(b)

Normal toxic waste account

	£		£
Bank – disposal cost	900	Main process	750
		Abnormal toxic waste	150
	900		900

Abnormal toxic waste

	£	£	
Main process	400	Profit and loss account	550
Normal toxic waste	150		
	550		550

Process 2 account

	Kg	£		Kg	£
Main process Q	3,600	17,210	Finished goods Q	3,300	26,465
Fixed cost		6,000	Closing work in progress	300	1,920
Variable cost*		5,175			
	3,600	28,385		3,600	28,385

*$(3,300 + (300 \times 0.5) \times £1.50)$

Equivalent units

	Main process	Conversion
Finished goods	3,300	3,300
Closing work in progress	300	150
	3,600	3,450
Cost	£17,210	£11,175
Cost per equivalent unit	£4.78	£3.24

Valuation:

	£	£	Total £
Finished goods	15,776	10,689	26,465
Closing work in progress	1,434	486	1,920
			28,385

(c) Pre-separation costs are attributed to joint Costs on a sales value basis, which results in high-value products bearing a high share of the costs – a 'what the market will bear' approach to cost allocation which will result, other things being equal, in all products having similar percentage profit margins. The process whose costs are apportioned over output is being treated as a cost (rather than profit) centre, and therefore can do no more than break even.

In the above situation, since Q2 final sales value is determined after significant further processing in process 2, its use as a basis for apportioning pre-separation costs incurred in the main process is questionable. If this basis is to be maintained, the use of a notional market value at the point of separation should be considered.

(d)

	Per Kg £	
Sales value at separation point	4.30	
Final sales value	7.00	
Incremental revenue	2.70	Total
Incremental cost	1.50	£
Incremental benefit	1.20	4,320 (× 3,600)
Specific fixed costs avoidable		3,600
Net benefit		720

Therefore, product Q should continue to be processed into Q2 so long as the cost and revenue assumptions used above continue to hold.

2 (a) (i) Expected output (units):

Actual output	4,110	
+ Losses	190	
= input	4,300	
Expected output		
= 95% of input		
= 4,300 × 0.95	= 4,085	units

(ii) Abnormal loss/gain (units):

Normal loss		
= 5% of input		
= 4,300 × 0.05	= 215	
less Actual loss	190	
= Abnormal gain	25	units

(iii) Production cost per unit = $\dfrac{£14,012}{4,085}$ units

= £3.4301 per unit

Process 1 a/c

	£		£
Materials	6,335	Output:	
Labour and overhead	7,677	4110 units × £3.4301	14,098
Abnormal gain:			
25 units × £3.4301	86		
	14,098		14,098

(b)

	Materials	*Overhead*
Equivalent units:		
Output	4,210	4,210
+ Closing WIP	400	200
	4,610	4,410
− Opening WIP	500	250
= Production	4,110	4,160

Production cost per unit $\dfrac{£25,770}{4,110}$ = £6.27 per unit $\qquad \dfrac{£9,485}{4,160}$ = £2.28 per unit

Process 2 a/c

	£				£
Opening WIP	3,576	Output:			
Period costs:		Opening WIP	3,576		
Process 1 costs	14,098	+3,710 units × £6.27 =	23,262		
Materials	11,672	+3,960 units × £2.28 =	9,029	35,867	
Labour and		Closing WIP:			
overhead	9,485	400 units × £6.27 =	2,508		
		200 units × £2.28 =	456	2,964	
	38,831			38,831	

Chapter 12

1 (a) Joint products are two or more products of significant value which result from a process. The joint processing costs are apportioned to the joint products.

By-products are of significantly less value than other products emerging from a process. Joint process costs are not apportioned to by-products; instead the incidental revenue from by-products may be used to reduce the joint process costs to be apportioned to the joint products.

(b) Costs to apportion = joint process costs − revenue from Product C

$$= £272,926 − (2,770 \text{ kgs} × £0.80/\text{kg})$$
$$= £272,926 − £2,216$$
$$= £270,710$$

Market value of output:
Product A − 16,000 kgs × £6.10/kg = £97,600
Product B − 53,200 kgs × £7.50/kg = £399,000

£496,600

Apportionment of joint process costs:

$$\text{Product A} = 270{,}710 \times \frac{97{,}600}{496{,}600} = £53{,}204$$

$$\text{Product B} = 270{,}710 \times \frac{399{,}000}{496{,}600} = £217{,}506$$

Cost per kg:

$$\text{Product A} = \frac{53{,}204}{16{,}000} = £3.325/\text{kg}$$

$$\text{Product B} = \frac{217{,}506}{53{,}200} = £4.088/\text{kg}$$

(c) Production costs:

	£
Material P 0,000 kilosat £0.00/kilo =	00,000
Material P 3,220 kilos at £5.00/kilo =	16,100
Material T 6,440 kilos at £1.60/kilo =	10,304
9,660 kilos	26,404
Conversion costs	23,796
	50,200

Expected output:

Materials input	9,660 kilos
Normal loss (5%)	(483) kilos
Expected output	9,177 kilos

$$\text{Cost per unit} = \frac{50{,}200}{9{,}177} = £5.47 \text{ per kilo}$$

Abnormal loss = 9,177 − 9,130 = 47 kilos

Process account

	£		£
Raw materials	26,404	Output	49,943
Conversion costs	23,796	(9,130 kilos × £5.47)	
		Abnormal loss	257
		(47 kilos × £5.47)	
	50,200		50,200

2 (a)

Process 2 account, October 1997

	litres	£		litres	£
Opening WIP	5,000	60,000	Normal loss	3,250	6,500
Process 1	65,000	578,500	Paint X	30,000	402,180
Direct labour		101,400	Paint Y	25,000	369,820
Variable overhead		80,000	By-product Z	7,000	24,500
Fixed overhead		40,000	Closing WIP	6,000	74,400
Abnormal gain	1,250	17,500			
	71,250	877,400		71,250	877,400

Equivalent units: (FIFO)

	Process 1	Lab/Overhead
Opening WIP to complete	nil	3,000
X, Y	50,000	50,000
Closing WIP	6,000	3,600
Abnormal gain	(1,250)	(1,250)
Equivalent units	54,750	55,350

	£	£
	Process 1	Lab/Overhead
Process costs	576,500	221,400
Normal loss	(6,500)	–
By-product	(24,500)	–
Total	547,500	221,400

Cost/equivalent unit	£10.00	£4.00

Valuation:

	Process 1	Lab/Overhead	Total
	£	£	£
Opening WIP to complete	nil	12,000	12,000
X, Y	500,000	200,000	700,000
Closing WIP	60,000	14,400	74,400
Abnormal gain	12,500	5,000	17,500

Valuation of X and Y: £60,000 + £700,000 + £12,000 = £772,000

Apportionment of costs over X and Y:

Sales values at separation:	£435,000 + £400,000	= £835,000
Cost apportioned to X:	(435,000/835,000) × £772,000	= £402,180
Cost apportioned to Y:	(400,000/835,000) × £772,000	= £369,820

(b)

Abnormal gain account

	£		£
Normal loss	2,500	Process 2	17,500
Profit and loss	15.000		
	17,500		17,500

(c) Costs could also be apportioned on the basis of volume of output, if all outputs could be measured in the same units. Sometimes cost apportionments are necessary in order to obtain product costs, in situations where common or joint costs arise. It must always be remembered that any apportionment of common costs introduces an element of arbitrariness into resulting product costs and that any change in the basis of apportionment will result in changed product costs and therefore in changed product profitabilities. Such costs are therefore of very limited use in the measurement of product profitabilities.

Chapter 13

1 A Total variable costs

Option **B** will be constant, regardless of the level of output (within the relevant range). Option **C** will be unchanged at lower output levels, since unit variable cost is fixed. Unit fixed costs will rise if actual output is lower than budgeted output and therefore, Option **D** is unacceptable. Only Option **A** will fall in line with lower actual output.

2 (a) Direct cost per unit:

	Minor £		Major £
Direct materials	$\dfrac{2,700}{120 + (1.5 \times 70)} = 12$	£12 × 1.5 =	18
Direct labour	$\dfrac{1,560}{120 + (2 \times 70)} = 6$	£6 × 2 =	12
Variable overheads	$\dfrac{3,120}{1,560} \times 6 = 12$	£12 × 2 =	24
	30		54

XYZ Limited – Projected profit and loss account 1995

	Minor £000	Major £000	Total £000
Sales	7,200 @ £60	6,650 @ £95	13,850
Direct costs	3,600 @ £30	3,780 @ £54	7,380
Contribution	3,600	2,870	6,470
Fixed costs			4,200
Net profit			2,270

(b) Direct cost per unit:

	Major Plus £
Direct materials	24
Direct labour	17
Variable overheads	34
	75

XYZ Limited – Projected profit and loss account 1996

	Minor £000	Major £000	Major Plus £000	Total £000
Sales	7,200 @ £60	3,800 @ £95	5,000 @ £125	16,000
Direct costs	3,600 @ £30	2,160 @ £54	3,000 @ £75	8,760
Contribution	3,600	1,640	2,000	7,240
Fixed costs				4,800
Net profit				2,440

(c) Both 1995 and 1996 will produce a positive contribution and net profit. The additional product in 1996 increases both contribution and profit. The increased contribution obtained in 1996 is greater than the additional fixed costs incurred. The usefulness of the projected profit and loss accounts will depend on the accuracy of the estimates used.

Chapter 14

1 B

2 £10.50 + £10.00/2.
Therefore the answer is **E**

3

	M1	M2
Unit variable cost:	£4.60	£4.40
Specific fixed cost	–	£0.20*
Max price payable	£4.60	£4.60
* £2,500/12,500		

Therefore the answer is **B**

$$\frac{£12,000 + £10,000 + £50,000}{£5.40} = £13,333$$

Therefore the answer is **C**

4

	L	M	N
	£	£	£
Contribution/unit	30	42	38
Contribution/£mat	2	2.1	1.26
Ranking	2nd	1st	3rd

Therefore the answer is **E**

5

	Z1	Z2	Z3
Unit contribution	£8.00	£7.00	£4.30
Contribution/£ labour	£4.00	£1.75	£2.40
Ranking	1st	3rd	2nd

Therefore the answer is **D**

Chapter 15

1 (a) (i)

	1990	1994	Difference
Total cost (£)	70,000	81,880	
at 1990 cost levels (£)	70,000	71,200	+ 1,200
Activity index	100	106	+6

At 1990 cost levels the variable cost per unit of activity is £1,200/6 = £200
The fixed cost is, by substitution, £50,000

1995

Fixed costs	(£50,000 × 1.17)	£58,500
Variable cost	(£200 × 110 × 1.17)	£25,740
Total cost		£84,240

(ii)

Sales revenue   £100,000 × 1.2 × 1⁼1 £132,000

Contribution/Sales ratio $\dfrac{£106,260}{£132,000}$*   = 0.805

* Sales revenue – Variable costs

Break-even sales is £58,500/0.805 = £72,671

Break-even chart (not to scale)

(b) The high and low points method assumes that the fixed costs are static over the period, and that the variable costs are incurred at a constant rate per unit of output of service provided.

With constant fixed costs in total, and with linear variable cost movements, any difference in total costs can be ascribed to changes in variable costs and, therefore, cost levels can be identified. In the above example, the effect of inflation over the period had to be extracted before the underlying cost behaviour patterns could be detected.

In practice, costs are seldom purely fixed or variable and, in addition, the point of fixed cost incurrence may well differ for different types of fixed cost, complicating the problem of determining underlying cost behaviour. Should activity extend outside the 'relevant range', there may also be a shift between fixed and variable costs as the organisation attempts to adjust its resource consumption to a different scale of operations. This will also make the high and low points method difficult, if not impossible, to operate.

2 C
3 A

4 (a)

	August	*September*	*Change*
Sales	80,000	90,000	10,000
Cost of sales	50,000	55,000	5,000
Selling and distribution	8,000	9,000	1,000
Administration	15,000	15,000	nil

(i) Cost of sales:
    Fixed   £10,000   Variable   50p/£1 of sales (50% of sales)
(ii) Selling and distribution:
    Fixed   nil   Variable   10p/£1 of sales (10% of sales)
(iii) Administration
    Fixed   £15,000   Variable   nil

(b) Fixed costs   £25,000
    C/S ratio   0.4

Break-even sales value $\dfrac{£25,000}{0.4} = £62,500$

Contribution break-even chart (not to scale)

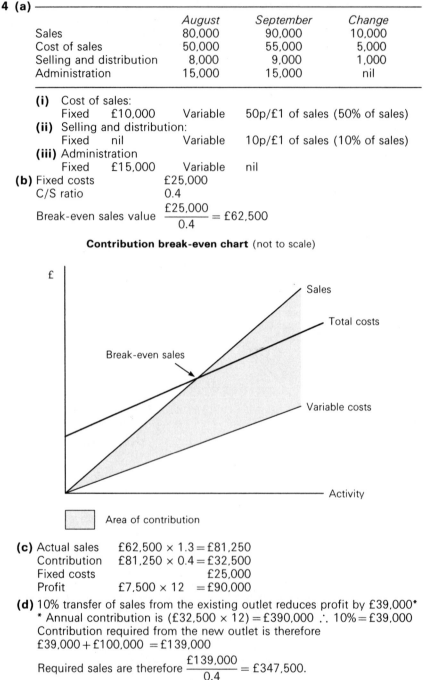

£

Sales

Total costs

Break-even sales

Variable costs

Activity

☐ Area of contribution

(c) Actual sales   £62,500 × 1.3 = £81,250
    Contribution   £81,250 × 0.4 = £32,500
    Fixed costs   £25,000
    Profit   £7,500 × 12 = £90,000

(d) 10% transfer of sales from the existing outlet reduces profit by £39,000*
    * Annual contribution is (£32,500 × 12) = £390,000 ∴ 10% = £39,000
    Contribution required from the new outlet is therefore
    £39,000 + £100,000 = £139,000

Required sales are therefore $\dfrac{£139,000}{0.4} = £347,500.$

(e) A divisionalised structure is required, with costs controllable by the outlet managers identified in the performance reports. Clear budgets, including both financial and non-financial information, would be useful, and participative budgeting should be implemented, as outlet managers will have the best idea of local trading conditions. Budgets can be used to set objectives for outlet management, and feedback on performance should be timely.

Chapter 16

1 B

Chapter 17

1 D
2 C

Chapter 18

1 (a) Demand, expressed in machine hours:

Product B (2,000 × 12 × 4)	96,000 machine hours
Product A (2,000 × 12 × 2)	48.000 machine hours
Total	144.000 machine hours

Capacity expressed in machine hours:

July	4,000
August	2,000
September–June (10 × 8,000)	80,000
Total	86,000

Therefore there is an annual shortage of 58,000 machine hours.

(b)

	A	B
July	2,000	nil
August	1,000	nil
September	2,400	800
October	1,000	1,500
November	1,000	1,500
December	1,000	1,500
	8,400	5,300

(c)

	A			B		
	Production	Stock	Sales	Production	Stock	Sales
July	667	–	667	667	–	667
August	333	–	333	333	–	333
September	1,333	–	1,333	1,333	–	1,333
October	1,333	333	1,000	1,333	333	1,333
November	1,333	667	1,000	1,333	667	1,333
December	1,333	1,000	1,000	1,333	1,000	1,333
			5,333			5,333

(d)

First six months	*Total*	*Contribution*	
		£	**£**
Sales of *A* as in **(b)** above	8,400	37,800	
Sales of *B* as in **(b)** above	5,300	2,120	
Total			39,920
Sales of *A* as in (c) above	5,333	23,999	
Sales of *B* as in (c) above	5,333	2,133	
Total			26,132
Reduction in profit (contribution)			13,788

2 A

Chapter 19

1

	£	
Actual cost	98,350	
Rate variance	4,790	(F)
Actual hours at standard	103,140	
Efficiency variance	2,700	(A)
Absorbed by output	100,440	

Therefore the answer is **E**

2 D

3 A

Chapter 20

1 (a)

	Variable overhead		Fixed overhead
	Machine hours	*Labour hours*	
	£	**£**	**£**
Actual cost	176,000	42,000	109,000
Actual machine hours at standard	176,000		
Actual labour hours at standard		43,200	
Budgeted cost			110,000
Absorbed by output	174,400	43,600	109,000

Variances:

Variable overhead:
Machine-related

	£	
Expenditure	nil	
Efficiency	1,600	(A)

Labour-related

Expenditure	1,200	(F)
Efficiency	400	(F)

Fixed overhead

Expenditure	1,000	(F)
Volume	1,000	(A)

(b)

Variance	Meaning	Cause
Machine-related:		
Expenditure	The variable overhead costs incurred are exactly in line with those which would have been budgeted for the machine hours worked.	Nil.
Efficiency	The output from the machines is lower than would have been budgeted based on the machine hours worked, therefore less variable overhead has been absorbed.	Necessary maintenance has been deferred, causing operational difficulties and reduced output.
Labour-related:		
Expenditure	The actual variable overhead cost incurred is lower than the standard cost allowance for the hours worked by the employees.	Some substitution of lower-paid employees for higher-paid employees has taken place.
Efficiency	The output produced was higher than would have been expected from the number of labour hours worked and therefore more variable overhead has been absorbed.	The employees were anxious to finish a large order on time to maximise the organisation's chances of receiving significant follow-up work. They therefore worked faster.

(c) The use of multiple activity bases for variable overhead absorption can have the following benefits:

- More realistic product costs may be produced, resulting in improved pricing and decision-making in general.
- Management will be more aware of the link between activity and cost behaviour, and will have more incentive to focus on the relationships between these two variables.

- Cost reduction activities within this area are more likely to be successful.
- It may become apparent that costs are not driven solely by output volumes, and therefore the focus of managerial attention may be significantly broadened. This may encourage managers to adopt a 'holistic' view of the organisation.

2 B

3
Budgeted volume	12,500		
Actual volume	11,000		
Volume variance	1,500	× £2.50 = 3,750	(A)
Actual revenue	£99,000		
Actual sales at budgeted unit selling price	£88,000		
Sales price variance	£11,000		(F)

Therefore the answer is **A**

4 (a) Budgeted information:

	£
Sales	20,000
Material: 750 kgs @ £6/kg	4,500
Labour: 1,125 hours @ £4/hour	4,500
Variable overhead	2,250
Fixed overhead	4,500
Profit	4,250

(i)
Budgeted volume		1,500 units	
Budgeted profit per unit:	£4,250/1,500 =	£2.833	
Sales volume variance:	£850/£2.833 =	300 units	(A)
Actual sales volume:	**1,500 − 300 =**	**1,200 units**	

(ii)
Flexed budget material usage:	1,550 × 0.5 kgs = 775 kgs		
Material usage variance	£150/£6 =	25 kgs	(A)
Actual quantity of materials used		800 kgs	

(iii)
1,000 kgs purchased at standard cost of	6,000	
Material price variance	1,000	(F)
Actual material cost	**5,000**	

(iv)
Standard hours per unit	1,125 hours/1,500 units = 0.75		
Flexed budget hours:	1,550 × 0.75	1,162.5	
Labour efficiency variance	£150/4	37.5	(A)
Actual direct labour hours		**1,200.0**	

(v)
		£	
Actual labour hours @ standard rate per hour	1,200 × £4	4,800	
Labour rate variance		200	(A)
Actual direct labour cost		**5,000**	

(vi) Actual labour hours × standard variable
  overhead rate per hour 2,400
  Variable overhead expenditure variance ... 600   (A)

  Actual variable overhead cost **3,000**

(vii)   **£**
  Budgeted fixed overhead cost 4,500
  Expenditure variance 2,500   (F)

  Actual fixed overhead cost **2,000**

(b)
- The direct materials usage variance may have been caused by the purchase of materials of an inappropriate specification, or by the use of machinery which is overdue for maintenance.
- The direct labour rate variance may have been caused by unanticipated additional payments to some employees for overtime working, or the movement of some trainees to a higher wage scale at the end of l training period.
- The sales volume variance may have been caused by a downturn in consumer spending in general, or by marketing activities of a competitor.

Chapter 21

1 (a) This is covered in the chapter.
2 This is covered in the chapter.
3 Project *A* NPV £3,281
  Project *B* NPV £3,050

Chapter 22

1 a
2 A
3 D

Index

A

abnormal loss   100
absorption cost statement   142
absorption costing   6, 51, 61, 141, 142
  and marginal costing compared   140
accounting rate of return (ARR)   184,
  188
Accounting Standards Board (ASB)   8
accounting system   35
activity-based costing (ABC)   6, 193,
  196
administration costs   13
administration overheads   69
algebraic method   58
allocation of overheads   50
allowed variable overhead   178
apportionment of overheads   50
architect's certificate   79
attainable standards   164
average cost method of valuing work in
  progress (WIP)   96
average cost per unit   87
average costing   87
average price method   23

B

bases of absorption   61
batch costing   5, 72, 74
bin card   19
bottleneck   197
break-even analysis   111, 129, 133, 134
break-even charts   129, 135
break-even point   129
budget   145
  committee   147
  period   145, 148
  phasing   154
budgetary control   6, 145, 146, 163
  process   147
  system   150, 154; advantages   151;
    disadvantages   152
budgets   3, 154
  cash   155
  fixed   159
  flexible   159
  interrelationship of   149
  production   157
by-product costing   104

C

capital investment appraisal   184
  accounting rate of return
    (ARR)   184, 188
  discounted cash flow (DCF)   184,
    189
  internal rate of return (IRR)   184,
    189, 191
  net present value (NPV)   184, 189
  payback period method   184, 185
cash budgets   154, 155
cash flow forecast   147
clock card   32
coding systems   15
Companies Act   1985   8
constraint   197, 198
continuous allotment method   57
contract costing   5, 79
  completed contracts   81
  incomplete contracts   82
  procedures   79
continuous-operation costing   6, 87
contract price   79
contribution   116, 122
  break-even chart   135
  ratio   117
control   4
cost   10
  accounting   3
  accounting ledger   41
  accounting system   35
  and management accounting   1, 3
  behaviour   114
  centre   10, 11, 53
  classification   10
  classification by function   13;
    administration costs   13;
    distribution costs   13;
    production costs   13; selling
    costs   13
  classification by nature   12;
    expenses   12; labour   12;
    materials   12
  driver   194
  elements of   10, 14
  ledger control account   41
  ledger, reconciliation with financial
    ledger   46

cost (*cont.*)
  plus pricing 72
  pool 194
  statement 87
  types of 11; direct costs 11; fixed
      costs 12; indirect costs 11;
      variable costs 12
  unit 10, 11, 88
  variances 154
cost–volume–profit (CVP)
  analysis 111
costing labour 29, 32
costing materials 17
costing methods 5
costing principles and techniques 6
  absorption costing 6
  activity-based costing (ABC) 6
  budgetary control 6
  marginal costing 7
  standard costing 7
  throughput accounting (TA)7
costs
  period costs 13
  product costs 13
  relevant costs 13
  sunk costs 13

D
day-rate schemes, 30
decision-making 4
developments in management
  accounting 193
  activity-based costing (ABC) 193,
    196
  throughput accounting (TA) 193,
    197
differential piecework 31
direct costs 11
direct labour efficiency variance 168
direct labour rate variance 168
direct labour total variance 168
direct labour variances 168
direct materials price variance 166
direct materials total variance 166
direct materials usage variance 166
direct materials variances 165
discounted cash flow (DCF) 184, 189
distribution costs 13

E
elimination method 56
  algebraic method 58
  continuous allotment method 57
  repeated distribution method 56

employee remuneration 29
  incentive schemes 30
  performance-based methods 29
  piecework schemes 31
  time-based methods 29
estimate 73
expenses 12

F
financial accounting 7
  ledger 41
  system 35
financial ledger
  control account 41
  reconciliation with cost ledger 46
first in, first out method (FIFO) 22, 96
fixed budgets 154, 159
fixed costs 89, 114
fixed overhead absorption rate
  (FOAR) 173
fixed overhead expenditure
  variance 174
fixed overhead total variance 173
fixed overhead variances 173
fixed overhead volume variance 174
fixed and variable overhead variances
  compared 177
flexible budgets 154, 159

G
gate keeping 32
general jobbing account 74
general ledger control account 41
goods received note (GRN) 19

I
ideal standards 164
incentive schemes 30
income variances 154
indirect costs 11
integrated accounts 35
inter-company comparison 88
interlocking accounts 35, 41
internal rate of return (IRR) 184, 189,
  191, 192

J
job account 74
job card 32, 33, 73, 74
job cost sheet 73, 74
job costing 5, 72, 74, 89
  procedures 73
job costs, collecting 73
joint product costing 104, 105
  apportioning common costs 106

L

labour 12
  requirement note 73
last in, first out method (LIFO) 23
limiting factor 120, 147

M

management accounting 1, 3
  activity-based costing (ABC) 193
  developments in 193
  throughput accounting (TA) 193
margin of safety 132
marginal cost statement 143
marginal costing 7, 129, 140, 173, 198
  accepting a special order 124
  arguments for using 142
  ceasing an activity 122
  decision-making 120
  making or buying a product 124
  purpose of 111
  statements 117, 122
  stock valuation 142
  terms 113
master budget 145, 149
materials 12, 17
  purchase and receipt 19
  storage 19
materials control system 17, 18
materials requisition note 73, 74
materials return note 19

N

net present value (NPV) 184, 189, 192
non-production overheads 69

O

output costing 87
overabsorption 67
overhead absorption 61
  bases of 61
  overabsorption 67
  rate 61; applying 64;
    predetermined 66
  underabsorption 67
overhead analysis 50
  statement 50, 52
overhead recovery 61
overhead variance analysis 173
overheads 50
  allocation 50, 52
  apportionment 50, 52
  classifying and collecting 51
  sharing 50

P

payback period method 184, 185
payroll 33
performance-based methods of
  employee remuneration 29
period costs 13
perpetual inventory system 20
phasing the budget 154
physical units basis of
  apportionment 106
piecework schemes 31
  differential piecework 31
  premium bonus schemes 31, 32
  straight piecework 31
piecework ticket 32, 33
planning 4
premium bonus schemes 31, 32
pricing issues of materials and stock 22
  average price method 23
  comparing methods 24
  first in, first out (FIFO) 22, 96
  last in, first out (LIFO) 23
  replacement price 23
  standard price 24
principal budget factor 120, 147
process costing 6, 87, 91
  cost elements 93
product costs 13
production budgets 154, 157
production cost centres 53
production costs 13
production schedule 73
profit chart 137
profit/volume (P/V) ratio 117, 122
purchase order 19
purchase requisition note 19, 73

R

ranking products 120, 121, 122
re-order level 21
re-order quantity 21
reciprocal services 56
reconciliation of the financial and cost
  ledgers 46
recording labour 32
relevant costs 13
relevant range 134
repeated distribution method 56
replacement price method, 23
retention monies 79

S

sales margin
  actual 178

sales margin (*cont.*)
  price variance   179
  quantity variance   179
  standard   178
  total variance   179
  variances   178
  volume variance   180
sales value basis of
      apportionment   106, 107
selling costs   13
selling overheads   69
semi-variable costs   115
service cost centres   53, 55
service costing   6, 87, 88
setting standards   163
specific-order costing   5, 72
split-off point   104, 105
standard costing   7
  advantages and disadvantages   170
  materials and labour   163
  overhead variances   173
  sales variances   173
standard costs   3, 163
standard hours of production   173
standard price method   24
*Statement of Standard Accounting
      Practice*   9, 22, 23, 24
stock record card   20
stocktaking   20
stores control   21
straight piecework   31

T
theory of constraints   198
throughput accounting (TA)   7, 193, 197

time sheet   32
time-based methods of employee
      remuneration   29
  day-rate schemes   30

U
underabsorption   67

V
valuation of work in progress
      (WIP)   96
variable and fixed overhead variances
      compared   177
variable costing   111
variable costs   89, 114
variable overhead absorption rate
      (VOAR)   175
variable overhead efficiency
      variance   177
variable overhead expenditure
      variance   176
variable overhead total variance   176
variable overhead variances   175
variable overhead volume
      variance   176
variance analysis   154, 163, 164

W
wages office procedure   33
waste   91, 98
work in process   91
work in progress   91, 96
works order   73